the power of
simple prayer

the power of
simple prayer

How to Talk with God About Everything

JOYCE MEYER

FaithWords

NEW YORK   BOSTON   NASHVILLE

Unless otherwise indicated, all Scripture quotations are taken from The Amplified® Bible (AMP). Copyright © 1954, 1962, 1965, 1987 by The Lockman Foundation. Used by permission.

Scriptures marked NKJV are taken from the New King James Version. Copyright © 1979, 1980, 1982 by Thomas Nelson, Inc.

Scriptures marked KJV are taken from the King James Version of the Bible.

Hachette Book Group
1290 Avenue of the Americas
New York, NY 10104
www.faithwords.com

The FaithWords name and logo are registered trademarks of the Hachette Book Group.

Printed in the United States of America

First Hachette Book Group printing: April 2007

10 9 8 7

The Hachette Speakers Bureau provides a wide range of authors for speaking events. To find out more, go to www.hachettespeakersbureau.com or call (866) 376-6591.

The publisher is not responsible for websites (or their content) that are not owned by the publisher.

Library of Congress Cataloging-in-Publication Data

Meyer, Joyce, 1943–
The power of simple prayer: how to talk with God about everything/ Joyce Meyer. — 1st ed.
p. cm.
ISBN-13: 978-0-446-53196-2 (regular edition)
ISBN-10: 0-446-53196-0 (regular edition)
ISBN-13: 978-0-446-57878-3 (large print ed.)
ISBN-10: 0-446-57878-9 (large print ed.)
1. Prayer—Christianity. I. Title.
BV210.3.M495 2007
248.3'2—dc22   2006027201

Contents

Introduction

If someone asked me, "Joyce, if you could make only one comment about prayer, what would it be?" I would have to respond by talking about its simplicity. I have been praying for many, many years and I can say a great deal about prayer, but if I could only emphasize one thing, I would tell people that it is *so much easier* than we think.

As God began to teach me to pray, I was surprised to learn that He has not made prayer complicated, but that it really is simple. Sometimes people make prayer dry and difficult; sometimes our religious mind-sets and "systems" present prayer in such a way that it seems out of reach for many of us. I tell you the truth when I say that God desires our prayer lives to be natural and enjoyable. He wants our prayers to be honest and heartfelt, and He wants our communication with Him unencumbered by rules, regulations, legalism, and obligation. He intends for prayer to be an integral part of our everyday lives—the easiest thing we do each day.

I suspect many people pray much more than they know and that they have more effective and successful prayer lives than they realize. They do not always recognize when they are praying because they have been taught that prayer requires a certain environment, a certain posture, a certain form, or that it must strictly adhere to certain principles. Prayer is simply talking to God. The truth is that we can pray anytime, anywhere—even just directing a thought toward God qualifies as silent prayer.

Whether you have been praying for years, are just learning to pray, have hit a "slump" in your spiritual life, or simply want your prayer life to improve, know this: God wants you to learn to pray more effectively and He wants your prayer life to be more fulfilling. Because you have opened this book, I am sure that something inside you wants to increase your intimacy with God through prayer. I believe you know that prayer is powerful, and that you long to see its tremendous power released in your life, the lives of those you love, and the situations that concern you.

Short, simple prayers can be mighty beyond description, but that does not take away from the fact that prayer is also a grand mystery. Watchman Nee, a Chinese Christian who wrote many profound books while imprisoned for his faith, writes, "Prayer is the most wonderful act in the spiritual realm, as well as a most mysterious affair."[1] I believe the greatest mystery of prayer is that it joins the hearts of people on earth with the heart of God in heaven. Prayer is spiritual and it goes into the unseen realm; it brings things out of that unseen realm into the realm we can see and into the world around us, right where we live. It ushers spiritual blessings into our natural, everyday lives and brings spiritual power to bear on our earthly circumstances. We human beings are the only creatures in our known universe who can stand in the natural realm and touch the spiritual realm. When we pray, we connect with that spiritual realm, which is where God is, and which affects our daily lives more than we often realize.

The fact that we want to pray—and that we believe that our prayer lives can be better—is evidence that we know the spiritual realm exists and that we believe what happens there affects what happens on earth. It proves that we know deep in our hearts that there is more to life than meets the eye and we value the things that are invisible more than the things we can see, just as Paul writes in 2 Corinthians 4:18: "We consider and look not to the things that are seen but to the things that are unseen; for the things that are visible are temporal (brief and fleeting), but the things that are invisible are deathless and everlasting." When we understand that there are invisible, everlasting spiritual realities that affect our earthly lives, we long to comprehend those things. We begin to perceive that God is inviting us to interact with Him, to perceive things spiritually and to partner with Him to accomplish them on earth—and that only happens through prayer.

I like to say that prayer opens the door for God to work. As we partner with God in the spiritual realm through prayer, we bring things out of that realm into our lives, into our world, into our society, and into the lives of other people. These things that come from heaven, these gifts of God, are already stored up for us, but we will never have them unless we pray and ask God for them. He has put together so much for us in the unseen realm; He is doing such wonderful things for us, things we cannot see with our natural eyes or perceive with our natural minds—and we receive and enjoy those things through the power and the privilege of prayer. The Bible says that "eye has not seen and ear has not heard and has not entered into the heart of man, [all that] God has prepared (made and keeps ready) for those who love Him [who hold Him in affectionate reverence, promptly obeying Him and gratefully recognizing the benefits He has bestowed]" (1 Corinthians 2:9).

Prayer is part of an obedient lifestyle. The Bible says that we do not have certain things because we do not ask God for them (see James 4:2), and part of the great mystery of prayer is that

He requires us to ask for what He already has in store for us. God—who is sovereign and can do anything He wants to do, anywhere, anytime, any way He wants to do it, and does not need anyone's permission—wants us to ask Him. He has set in motion a spiritual law, which He Himself abides by, that says He will not do anything on earth unless someone prays and asks.

God has always said to His people and is still saying to us: "You and I are partners. You are My body in the earth today." What does that mean? We are His body; we call ourselves "the body of Christ." Jesus Christ does not have an earthly body anymore. We are the representation of Who He is and what He does on earth. We are His mouth, His hands, His feet, His face. We are the ones who express His heart, demonstrate His love, and reveal His power to those around us. And so, we need to pray. We need to access the wisdom and the resources of heaven for ourselves and for others. We need to partner with God so that His purposes will come to pass in our lives and in the lives of those around us.

I believe you will find within these pages some extremely helpful encouragement for your prayer life. Everything in this book is related to prayer; not everything is necessarily specifically about prayer, but it pertains to developing and maintaining an easy, fulfilling, effective, never-ceasing lifestyle of communion with God.

I encourage you to begin this book by asking God to teach you to pray more effectively, and I pray that He will use these pages to help answer that request. As you go along, you will find out how to pray as an individual before God, free to express yourself to Him in ways that are natural and that suit the unique person He has called and created you to be. You will realize that prayer is not only an enormous privilege, but that it is indeed much simpler than many people think. You will discover how to uncomplicate your prayer life and understand how to be set free from any preconceived notions that prayer has to subscribe to any "rules" or that it must sound a certain way. In addition, I hope simple prayer will become so much a part of your daily life that you will be liberated from ever again feeling that praying is something you *have* to do, but something you can look forward to and enjoy.

I will also share with you that prayer is as easy as breathing and help you learn how to develop a lifestyle of prayer—praying all the time, everywhere you go, in the midst of your daily routine. As you read this book, you will be reminded of the awesome power of prayer, which is unlike anything else known to man, and you will be encouraged to experience its power in your everyday life, in your ordinary circumstances. As you read about the many aspects of prayer, you will learn that different seasons and situations of life call for different kinds of prayer—and you will learn about those various types of prayer so that your effectiveness in prayer will increase.

As a quick preview, here's an example: you will discover that simply saying "Thank You, God" is a type of prayer when you realize you could have been in a car accident, had you reached an intersection one minute sooner. Other types of prayer about which I will share include: consecrating your life to God, committing your problems to His care, asking God for what you need and want, persisting in prayer until an answer comes, interceding for others, agreeing with others in prayer, praying the Word of God and praying in the Holy Spirit. In addition, you will discover and begin to understand the keys to effective prayer—some of the heart attitudes that pave the way for your prayers to be answered. Finally, I will address fourteen hindrances to answered prayer so that you will know what to avoid if you want your prayers to be successful. All in all, I have endeavored to present you with not only a thorough look at prayer, but also with teaching that will really help you as you pray.

I believe you are reading this book because you really want to know your prayers make a difference, you want to see God's power at work in your life and the lives of those around you, you want to enjoy your communication with God and grow in your relationship with Him. I assure you, that's exactly what He wants too and He is eager to help you. Be blessed as you embark on this journey toward more intimate, more exciting, more effective prayer!

—Joyce Meyer

the power of
simple prayer

1

Lord, Teach Me

I want to ask you a question: do you believe your prayers are really making a difference? Think about it: deep in your heart, do you ever wonder if God is hearing you when you pray? When you finish praying, are you convinced that your prayers have accomplished something? Are you satisfied with your prayer life? Do you really know how to pray? Are you longing for a deeper, richer, more dynamic relationship with God through prayer?

If you are like thousands of others I have encountered in more than thirty years of ministry, you are saying, "Yes! Yes! Yes!" As I have traveled and interacted with people, I have discovered that people really want to pray; they want to know that God hears their prayers and that their prayers are being effective. People want to grow in their prayer lives and to see their prayers become more powerful as they pray for others and for themselves. In fact, a 2005 survey of more than eight hundred pastors in the United States revealed that only 16 percent say they are "very satisfied" with their prayer lives. That leaves an overwhelming 84 percent who feel their prayer lives could definitely be better. Like the pastors in the survey, there are countless others who are not satisfied with their prayer lives.[1] They are not sure God is really listening when they talk to Him; they do not understand why some prayers seem to go unanswered; they wonder if they are praying "right" or praying enough. They are generally frustrated in their prayer lives, eager to know what to do to feel more connected with God and to gain confidence that their prayers really do make a difference. *If ministers feel this way, what must their congregations say?*

One of the most important, most life-changing prayers a person can ever utter is: "Lord, teach me to pray." It is not just, "Lord, teach me to *pray*," but, "Lord, teach *me* to pray." You see, knowing about prayer is really not enough; we have to know how to pray as individuals who are in an intimate, dynamic personal relationship with the God to whom we pray. Although there are principles of prayer that apply to everyone, we are individuals and God will lead each of us individually. I attended many "prayer seminars," and then attempted to duplicate in my prayer experience what I heard others say about their own prayers. Eventually, though, I realized God had a personalized plan for me—a way for me to communicate most effectively with Him—and I needed to say, "Lord teach *me* to pray."

I believe many people today are asking the same questions Jesus' disciples asked almost 2000 years ago: "Lord, teach us to pray" (Luke 11:1). Even though they spent a great deal of up-close and personal time with Him, listening to Him, learning from Him, and watching Him work miracles, they still felt the need for His instruction on prayer. The disciples went to Jesus as a group asking Him to teach them to pray, but as I made that same request as an individual, God answered me in a powerful way and brought wonderful improvements to my prayer life.

For example:

- I have moved from praying panic-based, carnal, soulish prayers (prayers that come from a person's mind, will, or emotions) to praying Spirit-filled, Spirit-led, faith-based prayers.
- I no longer focus primarily on prayers for my "outer life" (my circumstances, the activities I am involved in, the things that happen around me). I now pray for my inner life (the condition of my heart, my spiritual growth, my attitudes, and my motives). As God has taught me to pray, I have learned that my job is to pray to be strengthened internally and to ask Him to help me live out of a pure heart from the right motives; and His job is to take care of the externals.
- I have gone from laboring and striving to pray for five minutes every few days to enjoying—and actually personally needing and wanting—beginning my day with prayer, then to praying throughout the day as things come to my heart, and finally ending my day communicating with the Lord as I fall asleep.
- I have moved from a sporadic, irregular prayer life to regular times of prayer that are disciplined without being legalistic.
- Where I once thought I was fulfilling an obligation to God by praying, I now realize that I absolutely cannot survive a day and be satisfied and content if I do not pray. I realize that prayer is a great privilege, not a duty.
- I no longer approach God in fear, wondering if He will really hear me and send an answer to my prayers. I now approach Him boldly, as His Word teaches me to do, and with great expectation.

I believe if you will ask God to teach you to pray too, that you will also experience great changes in the way you pray, increased effectiveness in your prayers, tremendous satisfaction in your relationship with God, and a refreshing freedom and enjoyment in prayer.

In this book, I will provide you with a substantial amount of teaching on prayer. I hope you will learn from these insights, but I know that God is the only one who can take this information and cause it to spring to life so that prayer becomes

> God is the only one who can take this information and cause it to spring to life so that prayer becomes exhilarating, exciting, and effective for you.
>
> ⇒ • ⇐

exhilarating, exciting, and effective for you. I am praying and believing that He will do that for you in an incredible, life-changing way.

God will take the biblical information I will be sharing and help you apply it in ways that will be just right for you, your personality, and the particular season you are in at this time in your life. For example, a mother with four very young children may not be able to spend the first hour of each day praying. She has many duties to attend to and some of them won't wait. She is in a season of her life that won't last forever and God will lead her to pray in ways that work for her during that time. She can begin her day with prayer and pray throughout the day, but not necessarily in the same manner as a woman who no longer has children at home and can make her own time schedule.

I remember attending a prayer seminar and listening to an elderly woman speak about how she prayed every morning from five to nine. She had been doing that for many years and had the grace from God to do so. I did not yet understand the special abilities that God gives each of us, so I went home determined to do the same thing she did. All I did was get bored and sleepy after about the first fifteen minutes! Through that experience and others like it, I learned that we cannot compare our prayer lives with those of other people. We are all unique and God has a unique plan for each of us. The Bible teaches us that He gives each of us grace to do something and we should do whatever that is with our whole heart. The woman at the prayer conference had the grace from God to pray for hours each day. Similarly, I have grace to study for a very long time because I am called as a teacher in God's kingdom. I encourage you to be all you can be, but don't try to be what only someone else can be. God will never help you be anyone but you!

IT'S PERSONAL

Everything about our spiritual lives depends on our personal faith in God and our personal relationship with Him. We can enjoy that relationship because Jesus' death on the cross gives us free, unhindered access to our heavenly Father and our faith makes it possible for us to have an intimate, dynamic relationship with Him.

I recently read Ephesians 3:12, which says: "In Whom, because of our faith in Him, we dare to have the boldness (courage and confidence) of free access (an unreserved approach to God with freedom and without fear)." As I meditated upon this Scripture, I became quite excited to realize that as ordinary human beings we have *free access* to God at *any time* through prayer. We can approach Him boldly without reserve, without fear, and with complete freedom. How awesome is that! Personal faith in God opens the door to unlimited help from Him.

Early in my prayer journey, I came across a wonderful little book that has helped millions of believers over the years learn how to pray. In this classic volume, titled *With Christ in the School of Prayer,* Andrew Murray addresses this matter of asking God to teach us to pray, and writes: "None can teach like Jesus, none but Jesus; therefore we call on Him, 'Lord, teach us to pray.' A pupil needs a teacher, who knows his work, who has the gift of teaching, who in patience and love will descend to the pupil's needs. Blessed be God! Jesus is all this and much more. . . . Jesus loves to teach us how to pray."[2] Don't just *try* to pray, ask Jesus to teach you!

Jesus not only loves to teach *us*—corporately—how to pray, He also loves to work with us as individuals. He wants to take us just the way we are and help each of us discover our own rhythm of prayer and develop a style of prayer that maximizes our personal relationship with Him. He wants prayer to be an easy, natural, life-giving way of communicating with Him as we share our hearts with Him and allow Him to share His heart with us. Prayer is so simple; it is nothing more than talking to God. It also includes listening to what He has to say. God speaks to us in many ways. If you desire to learn more about *how* He speaks, I encourage you to read my book entitled *How to Hear from God.*

God is far too creative to teach every person on earth to interact with Him through prayer in exactly the same way. He is the one who designed us all differently and delights in our distinctiveness. As I stated previously, there are "prayer principles" that apply to all believers, but God leads each of us as individuals. We are all in different places in our walk with Him, we are all at different levels of spiritual maturity, and we all have had different types of experiences in prayer. When we learn principles of prayer, we need to move beyond intellectual knowledge about how to pray and take those principles to the Lord and say, "Teach *me* to apply this in *my* life, in *my* situation, to *my* heart. Show me how this idea is supposed to work for *me*. God, I'm depending on You to teach me how to pray, to make me effective in prayer, to make my relationship with You through prayer the richest, most rewarding aspect of my life."

EMBRACE YOUR UNIQUENESS

Because we relate to God as individuals—and that's the way He wants it—we pray as individuals. Even when we pray corporately with others, we are all still individuals; we simply join our hearts with others as one voice. During these corporate prayer times, I believe that God wants our hearts to be in unity much more than He wants our methods to be the same. When we say, "Lord, teach me to pray," we are asking Him to teach us to pray in a distinctly personal way and to enable our prayers to be easy, natural expressions of who we are. We are not supposed to check our individuality at the door of the prayer closet.

We need to go before God just the way we are and give Him the pleasure of enjoying the company of the "original" He has made each one of us to be. We need to approach God with our own strengths, weaknesses, uniqueness, and everything

> Because God has fashioned our hearts individually, our prayers need to flow naturally out of our hearts and be consistent with the way He has designed us.
>
> ➤➤ • ◄◄

else that so wonderfully distinguishes us from everyone else in the world. God enjoys meeting us where we are, developing a personal relationship with us and helping us grow to become everything He wants us to be.

Psalm 33:15 says, "He fashions their hearts individually; He considers all their works"(NKJV). Because God has fashioned our hearts individually, our prayers need to flow naturally out of our hearts and be consistent with the way He has designed us. As we develop our individual styles of communication with God, we can learn from people who may be more experienced than we are, but we need to be careful not to make them our standard. I hope to be an example to many, but I want Jesus to be their standard. There is nothing at all wrong with incorporating something someone else is doing into your own prayer life if you truly feel led by God's Spirit to do so. But, it is wrong to force yourself to do what others do if you are not comfortable with that in your spirit. Do not try to keep up with others or copy their prayer styles—and do not feel compelled to work every prayer principle you have ever learned every time you pray.

Most people are afraid not to be like everyone else. Many people are more comfortable following specified rules than daring to follow the leading of God's Spirit. When we follow man-made rules, we please people, but when we step out in faith and follow God's Spirit, we please Him. We do not need to feel pressured to pray a certain way or for a certain length of time or to focus on specific things because other people are doing so. Instead, we need to be free to express our uniqueness as we pray the way God is teaching us as individuals.

Somehow we feel safe when we are doing what everyone else is doing, but the sad thing is that we will feel unfulfilled until we learn to "untie the boat from the dock," so to speak, and let the ocean of God's Spirit take us wherever He wills. When we are in control, we know what will happen next, but when we let God's Spirit take the lead, we are in for a lot of surprises in life. We need to be determined to be ourselves and refuse to spend our lives feeling guilty because we are not like someone else.

My husband, Dave, has a passion to pray for the United States of America and he does so on a regular basis. I have a passion to see God's children mature. I also have a great passion for the poor and oppressed, so I spend much of my prayer time praying about these situations. I know some people who focus intensely on the abortion issue when they pray and others who focus on missions with the same type of fervor. My point is that God places different things on each of our hearts and, in that way, everything is covered. No one can pray about everything that needs to be prayed about every day, but God's Spirit leads each of us if we allow Him.

I suffered for a long time before I learned what I am sharing with you and I don't want you to suffer as I did. Let my pain be your gain! Start right now asking Jesus to teach you as an individual how to apply to your life all of the principles of prayer you have ever been taught in His own unique way for you. I believe variety is the key to enjoying everything, including prayer, so let God's Spirit lead you to use various principles as they are needed in your personal situations.

THE KEY TO PRAYER

If I had to identify the most important key to effective prayer, I would say that it is approaching God as His friend. When we go to God believing that He sees us as His friends, new wonders are opened to us. We experience freedom and boldness, which are both necessary to effective prayer.

If we do not know God as a friend, and if we are not confident that He thinks of us as His friends, we will be reluctant to tell Him what we need or to ask Him for anything. If we have stiff, distant relationships with God, our prayers can be legalistic. But if we go to Him as our friend, without losing our awe of Him, our prayers will stay fresh, exciting, and intimate.

A natural friendship involves loving and being loved. It means knowing that someone is on your side, wanting to help you, cheering you on, and always keeping your best interest in mind. A friend is someone you value, a comrade, a partner, someone who is dear to you, someone you want to spend time with, and someone you enjoy. You become someone's friend by investing time in them and with them, and by sharing your life with that person.

Developing your friendship with God is similar to developing a friendship with someone on earth. It takes time. The truth is that you can be as close to God as you want to be; it all depends on the time you are willing to invest in the relationship. I encourage you to get to know Him by spending time in prayer and in the Word. Your friendship with God will also deepen and grow as you walk with Him over time on a regular basis and as you experience His faithfulness. The difference between developing a relationship with God as a friend and building relationships with people is that with God, you end up with

> You can be as close to God as you want to be; it all depends on the time you are willing to invest in the relationship.
>
> ⇢ • ⇠

a friend who is perfect! One who will never leave you nor forsake you. One who is faithful, dependable, loving, and forgiving.

Make a priority of developing a great friendship with God and inviting Him to be a vital part of everything you do, every day. That starts with simple prayer—just talking to Him and sharing your life with Him as you go about the things you have to do. Include Him in your thoughts, in your conversation, and in all your everyday activities. Don't just run to Him when you are desperate; talk to Him in the grocery store, while you are driving your car, combing your hair, walking the dog, or cooking dinner. Approach Him as your partner and your friend and simply refuse to do anything without Him. He really wants to be involved in your life! Let God out of the Sunday-morning box that many people keep Him in and let Him invade your Monday, Tuesday, Wednesday, Thursday, Friday, Saturday, and all day Sunday as well. Don't try to keep Him in a religious compartment, because He wants to have free access to every area of your life. He wants to be your friend.

Abraham

Perhaps no one mentioned in the Bible is more often referred to as "God's friend" than Abraham. In Isaiah 41:8, God calls Abraham "My friend," and James 2:23 says, "...he was called God's friend." In the Old Testament, King Jehoshaphat, while he was talking to God one day, said that Abraham is "Your friend" (2 Chronicles 20:7). While the Bible refers to David as "a man after God's own heart" and to John as "the disciple Jesus loved," Abraham has the distinct honor of being called the *friend* of God in more than one place in Scripture.

When God decided to execute judgment on the wickedness of the people of Sodom and Gomorrah, He told Abraham what

He planned to do. We read about this in Genesis 18:17, which says: "Shall I hide from Abraham [My friend and servant] what I am going to do?" Why? Because they were friends.

In a friendship, people talk to each other about what they are going to do. How many times has a friend said to you, "What are you doing today?" and you reply with something like, "I'm going to the grocery store this morning and to a ball game tonight." Or how often have you asked someone, "What's your schedule next week?" and he or she responds, "I have a doctor's appointment on Tuesday and a meeting on Thursday. But would you like to have lunch on Wednesday?"

Because God considered Abraham His friend, He told him what He was going to do—just like you would tell your friend. The Bible tells us in Proverbs 3:6 to acknowledge God in all of our ways and that He will direct our steps. To *acknowledge* means to care about what someone thinks. We should care about what God thinks of our plans, just as we would care about what a close friend thinks. We should discuss everything with Him in a conversational manner, just as we would with a spouse or close friend.

When Abraham heard about the devastation God planned to release against Sodom and Gomorrah, he "came near and said, 'Would You also destroy the righteous with the wicked?'" (Genesis 18:23, NKJV). Just as God had shared His intentions with Abraham because they were friends, Abraham "came near" to God and questioned His intentions—because they were friends. They had a relationship in which they could communicate freely; they could talk openly. Abraham was so confident in God's friendship with him that he questioned God Almighty! That's intimacy; that's security in a relationship.

The story is recorded in Genesis 18:17–33, but you may already know how it ends: Abraham and God continued their dialog.

Abraham prayed and interceded for Sodom and Gomorrah, asking God to withhold judgment against the sinful cities so the righteous people who lived there would not suffer the punishment due the wicked. He started by asking God not to destroy the cities if He could find fifty righteous people in them, but then Abraham realized that might not be possible. After quite a bit of going back and forth, Abraham finally asked God to spare them for the sake of only ten righteous people—and God agreed. Why was Abraham able to intercede with such boldness? Because he knew God was his friend and he appealed to Him on the basis of that relationship.

You

Just as God shared His plans with Abraham, He will share things with you—His heart, His desires, His purposes and intentions—when you are His friend. He will give you understanding and insight into what is happening in your life and tell you what to do about it. He will lead you and help you be prepared for the future. If you are God's friend, you do not have to be caught off guard or ambushed by your circumstances. You can be informed and ready—because you are a friend of God. He may not reveal everything you would like to know exactly when you would like to know it, but He will give you understanding as you patiently trust Him.

You may be asking, "How do I get to be God's friend?" According to John 15:15, you already are. In this verse, Jesus said to His disciples, "I have called you My friends...."

> One of the best ways to ensure a deepening friendship with God is to have a heart that wants to obey Him.
>
> ⇥ • ⇤

If you are a follower of Jesus, you are a modern-day disciple and you are His friend. As is the case with any friendship, you can be a casual friend or you can be a close, intimate personal friend. Your friendship with God grows and develops just as your friendships with other people grow and develop. Just as a natural friendship requires time and energy to develop, so does your relationship with God.

One of the best ways to ensure a deepening friendship with God is to have a heart that wants to obey Him. When our hearts are pure, tender toward His leading and eager to respond obediently, we are in a terrific position to experience God's friendship. I do not mean that we must be doing everything right or that we try to be perfect all the time; I simply mean that we are not purposefully disobedient, rebellious, hard-hearted, or always trying to see what God will let us get away with. I mean that we willingly put His desires before our own desires because we love Him and we trust Him as our friend—and we know that what He wants is always best for us anyway.

As you grow in your friendship with God, never forget that your relationship is based on who He is and not on what He can do for you. Keep seeking His presence, not His presents; keep seeking His face, and not His hand. You must know that one of the hindrances to a vibrant, maturing friendship with God is allowing ourselves to focus on the benefits of friendship with God instead of focusing on *Him* as our friend. As human beings, we do not appreciate finding out that certain people want to be our friends because we have an ability to get them something they want; we feel valued when we know people want to be friends with us simply because of who we are and just because they actually like us—the same principle applies with God.

Friendship Breeds Boldness

When we begin to understand our friendship with God and see ourselves as His friends, our prayers become more Spirit-led, more faith-filled, and much bolder. Jesus told a story in Luke 11, immediately after He taught His disciples to pray using what we call the Lord's Prayer. We can surmise that He was using the story to illustrate His lesson on prayer. He said: "Which of you who has a friend will go to him at midnight and will say to him, Friend, lend me three loaves [of bread], for a friend of mine who is on a journey has just come, and I have nothing to put before him; and he from within will answer, Do not disturb me; the door is now closed, and my children are with me in bed; I cannot get up and supply you [with anything]? I tell you, although he will not get up and supply him anything because he is his friend, yet because of his shameless persistence and insistence he will get up and give him as much as he needs" (Luke 11:5--8).

Notice that the man who needs bread only gets it "because of his shameless persistence and insistence." We will only "shamelessly persist" with our friends—because friendship makes us bold, and the more we grow and progress in our friendships, the bolder we can be. Through the writer to the Hebrews, God invites us to "come boldly to the throne of grace, that we may obtain mercy and find grace to help in time of need" (Hebrews 4:16, NKJV).

We are not bold with people we barely know. For example, let's say that Dave and I go to a restaurant for dinner and have a server named John. When John approaches our table for the first time, he introduces himself to us. Dave does not say, "Nice to meet you, John. This is my wife, Joyce, and she needs a ride to work next Thursday morning. Would you mind taking her?" We are friendly to our server, but we are not in the kind of friendship with him that would give us the boldness to ask him for a favor of that nature.

Because John's job is to wait on us, I would not hesitate to ask him for extra lemon or salad dressing on the side. But because we are not friends, I would never dream of asking him to give me a ride to work next Thursday while my car is being serviced. On the other hand, I would ask a true friend to take me to work. Even if I had to be there at five o'clock in the morning, I know I have certain friends who would be glad to take me simply because they are my friends—and I would be bold enough to ask them because of our relationship.

Similarly, friendship with God brings boldness in prayer. Writing about this matter, Charles Spurgeon notes that "love knocks at [God's] door until He opens."[3] We will press on and be persistent when we know that God has what we need and wants to share with us because we are His friends. On the other hand, if we are not secure in our relationship with Him, we may be hesitant or tentative when we approach Him.

I believe God is looking for men and women who will pray bold prayers. One of the prayers I hear people pray often, and have prayed many times myself, is what I call a "just" prayer. We do it so many times and are usually unaware of it. A "just" prayer sounds something like this: "Now, Lord, we *just* thank You for this food"; "God, we *just* ask You to protect us"; "Father, we *just* come to You tonight…"; "Oh, God, if You would *just* help us in this situation, we would be so thankful…." Do you see what I mean? We sound as if we are afraid to ask God for very much. That's not the way we talk to good friends!

The word "just" can mean *righteous* or *fair*, but it can also mean *barely enough to get by* or *by a narrow margin*. God wants to give us exceedingly, abundantly, above and beyond all that we can dare to hope, ask, or think (see Ephesians 3:20). Why should we approach Him asking for barely enough to get by on? Why should we approach God, our friend, as if we are afraid to ask for too much? When we approach Him that way, it seems as if we do not believe He is generous and good. We must realize that He is not a God who gives "just" enough to barely get by, but He desires to bless us abundantly, to open the windows of heaven and pour out blessings so great that we cannot contain them (see Malachi 3:10).

> He wants to hear bold, confident, faith-filled prayers prayed by truly just and righteous people who are secure in their friendship with Him.
>
> ➤➤ • ◄◄

Sometimes punctuating our prayers with "justs" is simply a habit, and if so, we need to break it. God does not want to hear sheepish, insecure "just" prayers. He wants to hear bold, confident, faith-filled prayers prayed by truly just and righteous people who are secure in their friendship with Him. Always be respectful toward God as you approach Him, but do not be afraid! The Bible instructs us to have reverential fear and awe, but it never tells us to draw back in fear. As a matter of fact, Hebrews 10:38 tells us that if we draw back in fear, God's soul has no delight or pleasure in us.

Friendship Benefits Others

When we are friends with God, that friendship not only benefits us, it also benefits those around us. When people come to us with needs or concerns, we may be able to offer some help, but we may not be able to meet their needs at all. Even if we do not have what people really need, God does. When we are friends with God, we can say to people, "I don't have what you need, but I know Someone who does. I'll ask my friend! I will intercede before God for you." When we are friends of God, we know that He has the power to intervene in people's circumstances, to help their children stop using drugs, to bring financial breakthroughs, to work medical miracles, or to reconcile marriages. The more intimately we know God, the more confident we are in His willingness and ability to help people. When they come to us, we can go to Him and know He will come through for them. We can actually ask God to do us a favor and help someone we love even when we know that they don't deserve it. We can pray with compassion out of a heart of love—and God hears and answers.

I can remember being very sad about my father's spiritual condition. He abused me when I was a child and for many years I truly hated and resented him for it. Praying for him was the last thing I would have done or wanted to do. However, as I grew closer to God and learned His ways, I realized I not only needed to completely forgive my father, but that I also needed to pray for his salvation. God gave me the grace to forgive my dad and a heart of compassion toward him.

For many years, I prayed at various times for my father to come to know Jesus, but I never saw even the slightest change in him. He had always been a very hard-hearted man and I saw no signs that his heart was softening at all. I was discouraged and thought it was useless to keep praying.

Then God asked me to do one of the most difficult things He has ever asked of me. He asked me to move my parents close to where we lived, buy them a house, and take care of them until they died. At the time, they were in their early seventies. Since we have longevity in our family bloodline, I knew that moving them nearby might well mean years and years of taking care of someone who had never done anything but hurt me. I was less than enthusiastic about the situation and God dealt with me for quite a while until I finally knew I had to obey.

Three more years went by and I still did not see much change in my dad. Sometimes I did not pray for him for several months, and then God would put him on my heart again. I distinctly remember driving to work one morning and saying something like this to God, "Father, I think it would be a shame if You used me to lead people all over the world into a personal relationship with You through faith in Jesus and for my own father to die and go to hell. I have done what you have asked me to do and now I am asking You as a personal favor to me: save my father. Forgive his sins and draw him into a relationship with You." I prayed similar prayers in the past, but not with the intensity I felt that day.

A few weeks later, my mother called and said that my dad had been crying for three days and wanted to see me. Dave and I went to their house, and my dad apologized for abusing me when I was a child. He kept crying and saying how sorry he was. I asked him if he was ready to make Jesus the Lord of his life and he said yes. We led him in prayer that day and baptized him two weeks later. My dad recently passed away, and we rejoice in knowing that he will live for eternity with Jesus. Don't ever doubt that prayer is powerful. Your friendship with God can make an eternal difference in the life of someone you love.

We cannot control other people with our prayers, but I do believe that approaching God boldly on behalf of others opens the door for God to work in their lives in strong and powerful ways.

My father still had to make a choice, but I know that God dealt with him aggressively because I prayed boldly and persevered in prayer.

> Through Jesus Christ, we have a right to be comfortable with God and to go boldly to the throne of grace.
>
> ➤➤ • ⤙⤙

Truly, our friendships with God benefit other people. Of course, they benefit us greatly as well. I cannot think of anything more awesome than being a friend of God. There is nothing I would rather hear God say than, "That Joyce Meyer, she's My friend." I do not want Him to say, "You know, Joyce Meyer—she knows all the prayer principles, she uses perfect prayer posture, she has the right tone of voice; she sounds very eloquent when she prays and she even has all her *thee's, thy's,* and *thou's* all straightened out!" No! I want to know that God thinks of me as His friend, and I believe you long for Him to think of you that way, too. Through Jesus Christ, we have a right to be comfortable with God and to go boldly to the throne of grace to get the help we need in plenty of time to meet our needs and the needs of others (see Hebrews 4:16).

One of the best things you can ever do is develop your friendship with God. Jesus has made you righteous through the blood He shed on the cross, so there is no reason you cannot approach God as boldly and as naturally as you would your best friend on earth. Remember, friendship with God takes an investment of time and energy to develop. But also remember that as your friendship deepens, your prayer life progresses. A growing, vibrant, increasingly intimate friendship with God will naturally lead to a growing, vibrant, increasingly effective prayer life.

SUMMARY

When our hearts cry out, "Lord, teach me to pray," God answers. We do not learn how to pray simply by becoming a Christian or by going to church—even if we have been attending for years and years. We learn to pray more and more effectively over time as we develop a personal relationship with God. He has made each of us uniquely and He teaches us to pray in ways that celebrate and express who He has created us to be. He wants us *as individuals* to relate to Him through prayer in uniquely personal ways.

Our personal faith in God and our personal relationship with Him directly affect the quality and the effectiveness of our prayers. In fact, being God's friend is the most important key to a vibrant, dynamic prayer life. He wants us to draw near to Him, to trust Him, to love Him, to share our hearts with Him, and to listen as He shares His heart with us. In the context of friendship with God, we will continue to learn how to pray.

Prayer Points

➤ If you are frustrated in your prayer life and wondering whether your prayers are really effective, then cry out from your heart, "Lord, teach me to pray!"

➤ The depth and strength of our prayer lives relate directly to the depth and strength of our personal relationship with God.

➤ Prayer is simple. It is nothing more than talking and listening to God.

⤏ In teaching us to pray, God deals with us as individuals with unique personalities, diverse temperaments, and different ways of communicating. We need to be careful not to compare ourselves with others and to just be ourselves and let Him teach us to pray.

⤏ Being a friend of God—and all that entails—is the key to effective prayer.

⤏ Developing a great friendship with God takes time and energy, but it is the best investment of time and energy we can possibly make.

⤏ Approaching God on the basis of friendship enables us to pray bold prayers. As the friendship becomes more intimate, our boldness increases.

2

The Simple Privilege

I believe prayer is the greatest privilege of our lives. It's not something we *have* to do; it's something we *get* to do. Andrew Murray observed that "...prayer is so simple that even the feeblest child can pray, yet it is at the same time the highest and holiest work to which man can rise. It is fellowship with the Unseen and Most Holy One. The powers of the eternal world have been placed at its disposal."[1]

Prayer is the way we partner with God to see His plans and purposes come to pass in our lives and in the lives of those we love. It is the means by which we human beings on earth can actually enter into the awesome presence of God. It allows us to share our hearts with Him, to listen for His voice, and to know how to discover and enjoy all the great things He has for us. Communicating with God is indeed the greatest privilege I can imagine, but this high and holy work is also the simplest privilege I know.

I do not think prayer was ever meant to be complicated and that, from the very beginning, God intended it to be an easy, natural way of life by which we stay connected with Him all day, every day. Madame Jeanne Guyon, who was imprisoned for her Christian faith in France during the 1700s, wrote in *Experiencing the Depths of*

Jesus Christ that " ... God demands nothing extraordinary. On the contrary, He is very pleased by a simple, childlike conduct. I would even put it this way: The highest spiritual attainments are really the ones that are the most easily reached. The things that are most important are the things that are the least difficult!"[2]

God really wants prayer to be simple, but the devil has twisted our thinking about prayer because he not only knows how powerful it is, he also knows how easy it should be for us. Just ask yourself, *Why would God create us for communication and fellowship with Him and then complicate it?* God has not complicated anything, He has made a simple and enjoyable way for us to pray and enjoy spending time with Him. Satan tells us that prayer always has to take a long time and that we must assume a certain posture or pray a certain way. He surrounds prayer with rules and regulations and steals the creativity and freedom that God desires us to enjoy as we pray. He tries to keep us from having faith and to convince us that we really are not worthy enough to be talking to God anyway. He tries to make prayer legalistic and obligatory and to condemn us by telling us that we do not pray enough or that we are not praying effectively. He tries to distract us, steal our time, tell us that our prayers do not make a difference, and cause us to doubt that God hears short, simple prayers.

For these reasons, as I noted in chapter 1, I have observed people often pray and then feel they did not do it right, did not accomplish anything, did not pray long enough, or did not really get through to God.

> When I say that prayer can be short and still be effective, I do not mean to imply that extended seasons of prayer are not also necessary and valuable.
>
> ⤖ • ⤚

In general, many people seem to be dissatisfied with their prayer lives; they try to pray and then feel guilty and condemned—which is exactly what the enemy wants. *Believing* prayer is the type of prayer that God answers. Therefore, we can easily understand why Satan tries to fill us with doubt and unbelief concerning the power, effectiveness, and value of our prayers.

When I say that prayer can be short and still be effective, I do not mean to imply that extended seasons of prayer are not also necessary and valuable. They certainly are. In fact, in addition to daily prayer, I recommend setting aside entire days or even several days in succession a few times a year dedicated specifically to seeking God in prayer, fasting, and studying His Word. Even though prayer is simple and should never be viewed as complicated, there are also times when prayer is work. Sometimes we must labor in prayer until a specific matter that God has placed on our hearts is lifted. But, at the same time, we should not allow Satan to make us believe that prayer must be hard and complicated.

Satan is working overtime trying to rob us of the honor of communicating with God. In this chapter, I want to dispel some of the enemy's most often used lies about prayer and to help you rediscover the simple privilege of a rich, fulfilling, rewarding prayer life.

IT'S EASY!

Prayer is so much easier than many people think. In fact, Charles Spurgeon, who had a very sophisticated theological mind, said succinctly: "When we pray, the simpler our prayers are, the better."[3] God hears the simplest, faintest cry and receives the most childlike requests. I have raised four children and, as of this writing, I have eight grandchildren—and I can tell you that one thing children are *not* is complicated. Children have no trouble letting you know what they want, running into your arms when they are afraid, or giving you a big generous kiss, sometimes for no apparent reason. They need to be encouraged to do things that are hard, but they will gladly do almost anything that is easy. They are not sophisticated enough to hide their hearts or feelings very well, and as a result, communicating with them can be easy and refreshing.

That's the way God wants us to be when we talk to Him. We need to approach God with childlike simplicity and faith. Just as children are naturally inclined to trust their parents completely, we also need to be guileless, pure, and free from doubt as we trust God. When we pray with simple, childlike faith, we can experience God's miracle-working power and see things change.

We do not want to be child*ish* in our faith or in our praying; we want to be child*like*. The Lord is not looking for complicated relationships. He is looking for sincere hearts, because He is a God of hearts. He is also looking for faith, which is not an emotion, but a spiritual force that impacts the unseen realm. Furthermore, God is a God of order, but not a God of rules and regulations and laws; and He does not want us to wear ourselves out trying to pray long, drawn-out prayers that are not Spirit-led or that follow a formula and require a certain posture. That would be legalistic, and *the Spirit makes alive, but the law kills* (see 2 Corinthians 3:6).

When we follow the leading of the Holy Spirit, our prayers will be filled with life. We will have no need to watch the clock, determined to fulfill the specified amount of time we have committed to prayer. When we approach prayer as an obligation and a work of our own flesh, five minutes can seem like an hour, but when our prayer is energized by the Holy Spirit, an hour can seem like five minutes.

I recall one time during my journey with God when He challenged me to make an effort to ask Him for what I wanted and needed in as few words as possible. I had a bad habit of talking too much in prayer. I would go on and on because I had the mistaken idea that short prayers were not good prayers.

We must learn to begin with the Holy Spirit's help and to finish when He finishes, not to continue praying in the energy of our flesh long after the Holy Spirit finishes, because that makes the prayer time seem laborious rather than enjoyable. Approach God in simple childlike faith and pray as long as you feel led by God's Spirit to pray. It is not the length of our prayers that makes them effective, but the sincerity and faith behind them.

It Doesn't Have to Be Long

Perhaps the biggest lie Satan tells people about prayer is that it needs to take a long time. He will make you think you have to pray for hours before you have really prayed, but I am telling you that prayer does not have to be long in order to be powerful. They don't have to be short to be powerful, either. The length of our prayers really makes no difference to God. All that matters is that we pray the way He is teaching us to pray and that our prayers are Spirit-led, heartfelt, and accompanied by true faith. I have learned to pray until I feel full and satisfied in my spirit—and that takes longer on some days than it does on others.

I believe we can get so tangled up in the *words* of our prayers that we begin to lose the *power* of our prayers. I want to stress again that there is certainly nothing wrong with praying for an extended period of time. As previously stated, I do believe we should all set aside times for prolonged prayer and that our willingness or lack of willingness to spend time with God determines our level of intimacy with Him. But, I do not believe we need to labor to put in a certain number of hours in prayer apart from the leading of the Holy Spirit, out of a sense of obligation or as a work of the flesh.

If issues in our lives really require us to pray at great length, then we need to do that, but we do not have to pray prolonged prayers just for the sake of logging time.

> Just a few words will connect us with heaven as we call upon the Lord to act on our behalf.
>
> ⇢ • ⇠

When God challenged me to make my requests of Him in as few words as possible, He simply asked me to be concise and to-the-point and then to be quiet. When I did, I could not believe the increased power that came to my prayer life. To this day, when I pray that way, I sense more of the Holy Spirit's power and presence than I do if I go on and on and on and on. I have learned that some of the most powerful, effective prayers I can pray are things like, "Thank You, Lord," "Oh, God, I need Your wisdom," "Give me strength to keep going, Lord," or "I love You, Jesus." And perhaps the most powerful of all: "Help!!!!!!!" See? Just a few words will connect us with heaven as we call upon the Lord to act on our behalf.

Let me give you an example of a quick, effective prayer. Dave and I once went to our lake house for me to have some quiet, uninterrupted time to finish writing a book. While I was there, our neighbors arrived with several teenagers who played very loud music. Instead of falling to my knees telling the Lord how important my book was and how it could help millions of people and how hard

I was trying to finish it and how disruptive the music was, I simply said, "Lord, those people have the same right to enjoy their lake house as we have to enjoy ours, but could You arrange for me to have some peace and quiet so I can concentrate on the work I am doing for You?"

Within less than a minute after I breathed that simple prayer, the music went silent. I did not have to beg or build a case for my need; I did not have to bind demons or "war in the Spirit"; all I had to do was ask. A short, simple prayer opened the door for God to work. I prayed for about five seconds and God answered immediately.

Jesus knew the power of a short, simple prayer. When He taught about prayer during the Sermon on the Mount, He said, "And when you pray, do not heap up phrases (multiply words, repeating the same ones over and over) as the Gentiles do, for they think they will be heard for their much speaking" (Matthew 6:7). In fact, all the way through the Bible are some incredibly brief, but awesomely powerful, prayers, just a few of which are listed below:

- Moses prayed: "Now therefore, I pray, if I have found grace in Your sight, show me now Your way" (Exodus 33:13a, NKJV).
- Moses also cried out for his sister: "Please heal her, O God, I pray!" (Numbers 12:13b, NKJV).
- The Psalmist pleaded: "Have mercy and be gracious unto me, O Lord, for I am in trouble" (Psalm 31:9a).
- Elijah prayed: "O Lord my God, I pray, let this child's soul come back to him" (1 Kings 17:21b, NKJV).
- Jabez called on the Lord: "Oh, that You would bless me indeed, and enlarge my territory, that Your hand would be with me, and that You would keep *me* from evil, that I may not cause pain!" (1 Chronicles 4:10, NKJV).

- Jesus said: "Father, forgive them, for they do not know what they do" (Luke 23:34a, NKJV).
- The Apostle John prayed for his friend: "Beloved, I pray that you may prosper and be in health, just as your soul prospers" (3 John 1:2, NKJV).

If God always wanted our prayers to be long and drawn out, I really believe He would have put only long, drawn-out prayers throughout the Bible. He always gives us examples, and so many of the examples of prayer in Scripture are short and concise. The enemy is the one who tells us we need to pray for hours, and then makes us feel guilty when we don't. It is fine with God for us to pray using only a few words and for it not to take any longer than absolutely necessary. Remember what Jesus said: "...do not heap up phrases (multiplying words, repeating the same ones over and over)..." (Matthew 6:7).

If you have thought your prayers had to be long in order to be effective, I hope you have now been relieved of that burden. The power of our prayers is in no way dependent on how long we pray. There is no correlation between how many minutes or hours we pray and whether God hears us. Just one word spoken to Him in faith from a sincere heart can reach His heart and move His hand.

It Doesn't Have to Be Complicated

Another lie the enemy tells people is that prayer is complicated— that it is difficult, that it has to follow a certain method or take place in a certain order, that we can only pray about certain things, that we better not overload God by asking for too much, that we have to be careful what we ask for, and that we have to fully understand the will of God before we pray so that we won't pray outside His will. We do need to pray according to God's will, but we should not allow the enemy to ensnare us in so much fear that we are afraid to ask God for the things that are on our hearts. The worst that can happen if we pray outside God's will is that we won't get what we ask for—and that will be for our ultimate good! God knows our hearts and He will not become angry if we make a mistake and ask for something that is not His will. We don't need to approach Him with the fear that we might make a mistake or that He will not be pleased if we ask for too much. We need to go to Him in faith, boldly, confidently, and freely.

> God knows our hearts and He will not become angry if we make a mistake and ask for something that is not His will.
>
> ->>- • -<<-

If we believe all of the lies I have just enumerated, prayer *will* be complicated. But if we refuse to think the thoughts with which the enemy tries to hook us and if we reject the ideas that complicate prayer for us, then we will be able to embrace its simplicity. We will find that it is not complicated at all and that, in fact, it is the easiest thing in the world. Remember, prayer should be as natural as breathing.

Another mistaken idea that further complicates prayer for some people and prevents them from praying is that prayer is only prayer when a person's eyes are closed, his hands are folded, and his head is bowed. That could not be further from the truth! You may have seen the famous picture that I believe is called "Praying Hands." It shows an elderly man seated with head bowed, eyes closed, and hands folded while he prays. It is a beautiful picture, and though it depicts one posture we may assume while praying, it does not depict the *only* posture that is acceptable.

I have a tendency to pray with my eyes closed, simply because I can concentrate better that way—not because I think I am break-ing a "prayer rule" if my eyes are open. Dave, on the other hand, usually prays with his eyes open. A long time ago, I was so rule-oriented that I followed rigid rules and formulas for everything, including my prayers. I thought my prayers had to be loud and sound authoritative, so I would talk loudly or even shout as I prayed. I also walked while I prayed, but I still believed the "eyes closed" rule, so there were times when I actually walked smack into a wall or tripped over a piece of furniture while praying at the top of my lungs. Sometimes I wonder if God Himself even gave a loving chuckle at how immature and legalistic I was!

At the same time, Dave would sit in a chair with his eyes open, looking out the window, calmly and genuinely communing with the Lord. His lips hardly moved and he certainly did not shout or even talk loudly. When I opened my eyes long enough to catch a glimpse of him, I thought, *You aren't praying! You aren't even clos-ing your eyes!* But, of course, Dave was praying; I was merely being judgmental. I was the one who was deceived into believing I was not really praying if I did not obey the "rules."

My wrong beliefs about prayer had complicated it for me and stole the joy God intended me to have as I prayed. The Bible says to "ask and you will receive, so that your joy may be full" (John 16:24). That does not sound very complicated to me!

Then there are people who may or may not subscribe to the "closed eyes" idea, but do not think prayer is really prayer unless it is offered on bended knees. That would really complicate prayer for me because my knees really hurt when I kneel on them for more than a few minutes at a time. If I prayed in that position, I would end up thinking about how much my knees hurt and I would not focus on talking to God. I have a friend who kneels for hours, and when I see her pray, she seems so spiritual, but I have learned that my prayers are spiritual too, even though I cannot kneel while praying.

I love to lie facedown on the floor and pray. It helps me shut everything else out and feel as if I am alone with God. I prayed that way until it started hurting my back and I had to quit! I am glad I did not have to feel unspiritual because I had to change my posture in prayer. All I can tell you is that there is no certain posture you have to struggle to maintain in order to pray. If your knees hurt, lie on the floor. If your back hurts or you fall asleep on the floor, get up and walk around. If you are like Dave and you can pray while sitting and looking out the window, then pull up a chair. Just find a place and a way in which to pray that makes you comfortable and allows you to focus on the Lord.

Be free from everything you have heard about the formulas of prayer or the positions of prayer—and just pray! I challenge you to uncomplicate your prayers. Reject any idea that prayer needs to be complicated and begin to enjoy it as the simple privilege God intends for it to be.

It Doesn't Have to Be Eloquent

Another one of the enemy's lies about prayer is that a person must use the "right words" and speak eloquently. I have literally heard people shift their entire vocabulary and way of speaking when they begin to pray. I don't know why, but some people actually speak in King James English when they pray, using words they would never use in everyday life, such as: "Oh most magnificent Heavenly Father, Thou Most Holy God Omnipotent, we thank Thee for Thy bounteous care and we beseech Thee for Thine abundance of blessings evermore," and so on.

> If you are approaching God, trying to sound eloquent, then *stop it* and be yourself.
>
> ⤜ • ⤛

Unless you lived in the days of King James, such words would be out of character for you; they would be unnatural and uncomfortable. I can assure you that God wants you to be comfortable with Him so that you will talk to Him just like you talk to your friends. If you use poetic language when you are on the telephone with your best friend, then go ahead and use poetic language with the Lord. But if you are approaching God, trying to sound eloquent, then *stop it* and be yourself. If you have a particular accent because of the place you were born or the place where you live, there is no need to try to sound different when you pray. If you use funny expressions in your everyday conversation, it is not necessary to abandon them when you talk to God. He has a sense of humor too, you know! The point I want to make is that prayer should be a natural extension and expression of your unique communication style. Prayer needs to be comfortable and enjoyable for you, and it needs to come from the heart.

I do not think I speak with much eloquence, and you may not think your way of communicating is very sophisticated, either. I no longer worry about the way I sound when I pray; I simply tell the Lord what is on my heart—and I tell it the way it is—plain, simple, and straightforward. That is the way I talk to my husband; that's the way I talk to my children; that is the way I talk to people I work with; so that is the way I talk to God and that's the way He talks to me. I am not trying to impress Him; I am trying to share my heart with Him—and I can do that best when I am simply being myself. God made us the way we are, so we need to approach Him without pretense and without thinking we have to sound a certain way for Him to hear us. As long as we are sincere, He will hear. Even if what is on our hearts cannot be articulated, He still hears and understands what it is. A heart lifted up to Him is precious in His sight and He hears even words that cannot be uttered. Sometimes we hurt too bad to pray and all we can do is sigh or groan—and God understands even that.

You Don't Have to Be Perfect

James 5:16b declares that "the earnest (heartfelt, continued) prayer of a righteous man makes tremendous power available [dynamic in its working]." Another version renders these words: "The effective, fervent prayer of a righteous man avails much"(NKJV). When people struggle in their prayer lives, they sometimes say, "Well, there you have it. My prayers aren't working because I am not righteous. Maybe if I start being more holy and doing everything right, I will be more righteous and my prayers will be more effective."

E. M. Bounds writes, "Happy are those who have no righteousness of their own to plead...."[4] That's all of us! But, if we are born again, we are righteous. We may not *do* everything right; but we *are* 100 percent righteous all the time. Second Corinthians 5:21 tells us, "For He made Him who knew no sin *to be* sin for us, that we might become the righteousness of God in Him"(NKJV). Now, there is a difference between righteousness and "right" behavior. Righteousness describes our standing—our position or condition before God—*because of the blood of Jesus.* We cannot make ourselves righteous; only the blood of Jesus makes us righteous, as if we had never sinned at all. God views us as righteous even though we still make mistakes. Because He sees us as righteous, we have a God-given right to pray and expect our prayers to be heard.

Immediately after we see that "the effective, fervent prayer of a righteous man avails much," we read, "Elijah was a human being with a nature such as we have [with feelings, affections and a constitution like ours]; and he prayed earnestly for it not to rain, and no rain fell on the earth for three years and six months. And [then] he prayed again and the heavens supplied rain and the land produced its crops [as usual]" (James 5:17–18). Those comments about Elijah do not seem to fit between James's teaching on prayer and his writings about bringing people back from error into truth, do they? Actually, I believe they are well-placed because God knew people would stumble over that word "righteous." He knew that Satan would tell people they had no right to pray and expect their prayers to be answered because of their imperfection. Elijah's story is included to remind us that we all struggle, we are not perfect, and we all have victories and defeats, even the great prophet. If he could mess up once in a while and still have his prayers answered, we can, too. God used Elijah mightily and often, yet there was also a time when Elijah showed fear, discouragement, and depression. Elijah was a man of God, but he also made mistakes and displayed weaknesses. If he could pray effective prayers, we can, too. We are just as righteous as Elijah was—and even more so because Christ lives in us and has made our righteousness a done deal.

Look at Isaiah 41:10–14, which says, "Fear not, for I *am* with you; be not dismayed, for I *am* your God. I will strengthen you, yes, I will help you, I will uphold you with My righteous right hand.... Those who war against you shall be as nothing, as a nonexistent thing. For I, the Lord your God, will hold your right hand, saying to you, 'Fear not, I will help you. Fear not, you worm Jacob, you men of Israel! I will help you,' says the Lord and your Redeemer, the Holy One of Israel" (NKJV).

This passage really encourages me and I hope it will encourage you, too. When we start reading verse 10, we think, *Wow. God must be talking to people who really have their act together. He's talking to some superrighteous people who really "get it."* But He is not. No, God is saying, "You do not have to live in fear. I'm with you. I'm holding your hand. My Spirit is upon you. I'm going to help you. I'll crush every enemy that comes against you." We read those words and tend to think, *Oh, I wish I could live in such a way that God would help me like that!* And then He speaks again and reveals what kind of people He is really addressing. The great Lord and Redeemer, the Holy One of Israel, says: "Fear not, *you worm* Jacob, you men of Israel! I will help you" (emphasis mine).

God called Jacob a worm! There are not many life-forms lower than a worm and a person has to be pretty messed up to be called a worm! But isn't it good to know that God gives the kind of help described in Isaiah 41:10–14 to the worms of the world? I love that because there are days when I feel and act like a worm. But I do not have to worry, and neither do you, because even when we act like worms and don't do everything right, God is still eager to help us in the most astounding ways. His mercy is amazing!

THE SIMPLEST, MOST EFFECTIVE WAY TO DEAL WITH ANY SITUATION

Charles Spurgeon writes that: "The desire to commune with God is intensified by the failure of all other sources of consolation."[5] How true! Sometimes I marvel at how long Christians can struggle in a situation before they think to pray about it. We complain about our problems; we grumble; we murmur; we tell our friends; we talk about how God should do something about it. We struggle with situations in our minds and in our emotions, while we often fail to take advantage of the simplest solution there is: prayer. But worse than that, we then make perhaps the most stupid statement known to man: "Well, I guess all I can do is pray." I am sure you have heard that before and maybe you have even said it. We all have. We're all guilty of having treated prayer as a last-ditch effort and saying things like, "Well, nothing else is working, so maybe we should pray." Do you know what that tells me? It tells me that we really do not believe in the power of prayer as we should. We carry burdens we do not need to bear—and life is much harder than it has to be—because we do not realize how powerful prayer is. If we did, we would pray about everything, not as a last resort, but as a first response.

James 5:13–14 says: "Is anyone among you afflicted (ill-treated, suffering evil)? He should pray. Is anyone glad at heart? He should sing praise [to God]. Is anyone among you sick? He should call in the church elders (the

> We carry burdens we do not need to bear—and life is much harder than it has to be—because we do not realize how powerful prayer is.
>
> ⟶ • ⟵

spiritual guides). And they should pray over him...." Based on this verse, how should an afflicted person respond to these problems? He should pray. A very simple, three-word solution: he should pray. The Bible does not give us twenty-five paragraphs about what we need to do, it merely says, "He should pray." So:

- When you have a problem, pray.
- When you have a need, pray.
- When somebody hurts your feelings, pray.
- When you are offended, pray.
- When you are sick, pray.
- When you feel like giving up, pray.
- When someone you love is suffering, pray.
- When you are discouraged, pray.
- When you don't know what to do, pray.

Whatever situation you find yourself in, you should pray—and pray before you do anything else.

One time, a member of my extended family did something that really hurt me, and I felt rejected as a result. After it happened, I was sitting in the car and I felt so much pain in my soul that I simply said: "God, You've got to comfort me. I need You to comfort me. I don't want to feel like this. I don't want to get bitter. I don't want to develop resentment. I've experienced this same kind of pain from this person before and I don't even want to let it bother me. But I'm having trouble handling it and I have to have Your help."

Do you know what happened? As though God reached down from heaven and touched me, all my bad feelings went away! But how many times, instead of turning to Him in prayer, do we turn to other people and say, "Well, you will not believe what they said, and you just won't believe what they did, and now I'm hurt, and I'm so sick and tired of the way they treat me, and it's just not right." We tend to do everything we can think of, and nothing ever changes the situation. We would be so much better off if our first response to every emergency and every kind of emotional pain was to pray. If we will pray before we do anything else, we will experience major breakthroughs in our lives.

God promises that we will overcome in life, but many Christians do not seem to have much victory in their lives. There must be a reason so many of us are living beneath the level of victory that is available to us. The Bible says that God causes us to triumph in every situation through Christ (see 2 Corinthians 2:14), so we need to be walking triumphantly, genuinely displaying a victorious lifestyle to the world and causing people to be hungry for what we have. I believe they will want what we have if we will be the believers God intends for us to be.

> If our first response is to pray, we will see the power of God come into our lives in ways that will leave our mouths hanging open in awe.
>
> ->> • <-<-

I really think the missing ingredient in our personal lives and in our witness to others is the power of prayer on a large scale. Yes, people do pray; there are neighborhood prayer groups and there are prayer meetings in our churches and there are spontaneous moments of prayer that take place in coffee shops and on athletic soccer fields and over the telephone. But right now I am talking about our personal prayer lives. I am not including all the things that present themselves as prayer needs: national crises, current events, natural disasters, wars, or the many very serious prayer requests we receive by e-mail. I am focusing on the issues that go on in our lives and the things that happen to us. Are we praying about every situation that comes our way? Are we praying especially for the ones we know we cannot do anything about? If our first response is to pray, we will see the power of God come into our lives in ways that will leave our mouths hanging open in awe.

As we close this chapter, let me give you just one example of a family who did not pray as their first response. One of our little granddaughters used to wake up in the middle of the night—every night—screaming at the top of her lungs. She was a picky eater, so I suppose she must have gotten hungry after she went to sleep. For two-and-a-half years, she awakened, screamed, and woke up the rest of the family. For all that time, no one in the house had a good night's sleep. All of us knew what was happening, and we responded with, "Well, boy, that is such a shame. Well, I wonder what's wrong with her? Well, maybe we ought to do this, or maybe we should do that." Then we proceeded to look at each other and say, "What do you think we ought to do?"

You would not think it would take a preacher two-and-a-half years to think about praying for a situation, would you? But we kept on reasoning and talking about the situation until somebody finally received the revelation that we needed to pray. For two-and-a-half years, all we needed to do was to get four or five of us together and just say: "Now we agree, in Jesus' name, God, show us what's wrong here. Show us what we need to do. We ask You to heal this little girl and cause her to sleep well at night." When we prayed, she started sleeping peacefully every night. We prayed a simple, sincere prayer—and God answered us. We should have thought of prayer first!

SUMMARY

Prayer really is an awesome privilege, but at the same time, it is so simple. Prayer does not need to be long or drawn out, and one word or a quick phrase can bring miraculous results. Prayer is not difficult or complex, and when we pray we don't need to follow all sorts of rules and regulations or to make sure we get the words "right." We only need to approach God in the righteousness that is ours through the blood of Jesus and believe that He hears us when we pray from a sincere heart. Prayer is a tremendous privilege, not an obligation.

Prayer is not only the greatest power available to us, it is also the simplest and best way to handle everything that comes our way. Prayer should always be our first response to every situation. No matter what happens, we need to run to God before we do anything else. James gave us terrific advice—advice we should follow—when he wrote, "Is anyone among you suffering? Let him pray." And whatever situations we find ourselves in, let us pray.

Prayer Points

→→ Prayer is the greatest, simplest privilege of our lives as believers.

→→ The enemy has told us all kinds of lies about prayer, but the truth is that prayer is as easy and natural as breathing.

→→ Prayer does not have to be long in order to be powerful. In fact, some of the most powerful prayers we can pray are concise and to-the-point.

→→ Prayer does not have to be complicated. It only needs to come from the heart and it does not require us to assume a certain position or adhere to certain "rules."

→→ Prayer does not have to be eloquent. We can communicate with God the same way we talk to other people.

→→ We do not have to be perfect to pray or for God to hear our prayers.

→→ Prayer is the easiest and best way to deal with any situation. We need to pray before we do anything else in response to the things that happen in our lives.

3

Just Like Breathing

Ephesians 6:18 says that we are to "pray at all times (on every occasion, in every season) in the Spirit, with all [manner of] prayer and entreaty." In other words, Paul is saying that we are to pray in every circumstance, following the Holy Spirit's direction, using different types of prayer in different situations. To pray at all times is to "pray without ceasing" (1 Thessalonians 5:17, NKJV), but how do we do that? We do it by keeping an attitude of thanksgiving and total dependence upon God as we go about our everyday lives, turning our thoughts toward Him in the midst of doing all the things we have to do. I believe that God really wants us to live a lifestyle of prayer and that He wants to help us stop thinking about prayer as an event and begin to see it as a way of life, as an internal activity that undergirds everything else we do. He wants us to talk to Him and listen to Him continually—to pray our way through every day with our hearts connected to His.

ANYTIME, ANYWHERE

We can pray anytime, anywhere. Our instructions are to "pray at all times, on every occasion, in every season" and to "pray without ceasing," but we know that we cannot spend all day long in a corner communing with God. If we did, we could not live our lives. Prayer needs to be like breathing—regular, easy, second-nature—and we need to just pray our way through life as part of the way we live. In fact, just as our physical lives are sustained by breathing, our spiritual lives should be maintained by praying. We can pray out loud or we can pray silently. We can pray sitting down, standing up, or lying on the floor. We can pray while we are moving or while we are being still. We can pray while we are shopping, waiting for an appointment, participating in a business meeting, doing household chores, driving, or taking a shower. We can pray things like, "Thank You, Lord, for everything You're doing," or, "Praise God, I need You to help me," or "Oh, Jesus, help that lady over there who looks so sad." Actually, this approach to prayer is God's will. The devil's will, which can lead to the sin of prayerlessness, is for us to think we have to follow a certain model or prescribed method.

We often hear about a prayer need or think about a situation and say to ourselves, *I need to pray about that later when I pray.* That thought is a stall tactic of the enemy. Why not pray right that minute? We do not pray right away because of the wrong mind-sets we have about prayer. It would be easy if we just followed our hearts, but Satan wants to complicate prayer. He wants us to procrastinate in the hope that we will forget the matter entirely. Praying as we sense the desire or need to pray is simple, and it is the way we can pray continually and stay connected to God in every situation throughout the day.

I once listened to a tape, "The Half Hour," by Pastor Tommy Barnett. In that message, he encourages us to use our time wisely—to be productive with the time we have instead of murmuring about

not having enough time. He
said that he has written all
of his books in one-hour
increments, usually sitting
in airports waiting to board
flights.

> When we start honoring God
> with the little time we do have,
> He will multiply it.
>
> ➤➤ • ⫷⫷

That should be a great
encouragement to people who feel they are too busy to pray.
Sometimes people say, "Well, I just don't have thirty minutes to
pray." That's all right, because when we pray without ceasing, we
can accomplish a lot in thirty seconds. When we start honoring
God with the little time we do have, He will multiply it.

We really do live in a time-crunched world and just about
everything we do seems to be urgent. The enemy has been
extremely successful in his scheme to keep people from praying
and spending time in the Word by keeping us so terribly busy.
We live under incredible pressure and we run from one thing to
the next to the next to the next—to the point that we neglect the
things that are really important in life: family, our health, God,
and building up our spiritual lives. Then we get more and more
stressed out—and the only way to deal with that and get life back
in order is to get with God. It's true; we really cannot handle life
apart from Him. We cannot handle the pressure, the confusion
and the stress without Him. Our marriages will suffer, our children will suffer, our finances will get messed up, our relationships
won't thrive—if we do not spend time in the Word and in prayer.
God will strengthen us and enable us to handle life peacefully and
wisely if we start praying about things instead of merely *trying* to
get through the day. The Bible says that when we take time with
God, He renews our strength and enables us to handle life and not

be weary (see Isaiah 40:31). But we have to start by using the time we have.

Whether you are a busy mother, a schoolteacher, a pastor, a computer technician, an executive, a mechanic, or a brain surgeon, you are busy! You not only have the requirements of your job to fulfill, you may also have caretaking responsibilities with family or extended family. You have social obligations or church activities; you have shopping and cleaning to do and bills to pay. And somewhere, in the midst of everything else, you would like a few minutes to breathe!

So, practically, how do you pray amid so many demands and so much to do?

For example, if you are an exhausted stay-at-home mom who cleans house and changes diapers all day, then just take one minute to be still and say, "Oh, Jesus, I love You. Strengthen me right now. God, I need some energy and some patience. I am worn out. Give me grace, God. Help me walk in the fruit of the Spirit with my children because they are on my last nerve. Help me receive my husband properly when he comes home from work. Thank You, Jesus. Somebody's crying now, Lord, so I've got to go!"

It is okay to talk to God that way! It really is. That kind of prayer may not sound like what you are accustomed to hearing at church, but it's just as effective if your heart is sincere. It's continual prayer; it's the kind of prayer that is woven through the fabric of your day like a bright thread in a beautiful tapestry.

Men, if you have a day when you cannot find time to pray in the midst of trying to provide for your family and withstand the pressures at work, then pray in the midst of whatever you are doing. You might get under your car to change the oil and take an extra ten minutes to say, "Oh, hallelujah. Lord, I worship You. Thank

You, God, for Your goodness to me. Make me a godly man and a godly husband and a godly father. Make me a real man of God. Help me lead my family well. Help me manage my time. Help me walk in love. Forgive me for my sins. Thank You, Jesus. Dinner's ready. She's calling me, so I'd better go. Thanks, Lord!"

If you are a single person with a high-powered career and days when you have more work to do than hours in the day, then use your time in the car to thank God for blessing your work and to ask Him to give you great ideas that will help you and benefit your company. As you walk to the restroom or ride the elevator, whisper, "Jesus, I'm so glad You're my Savior. Thank You for being there for me. Help me be a good witness in this office and to be kind and encouraging to all the stressed-out people around me! Lord, help me keep my peace when the pressure gets high. Thank You, God, for Your grace!" Take advantage of the time you do have instead of complaining about the time you don't have.

People who pray at all times lay their heads on their pillows at night saying, "Thank You, Lord, for this day. Thank You for all You've done. I praise you, God. You're wonderful. Watch over me tonight. Give me good dreams. Teach me, God, even as I sleep. Thank You for watching over me. I bless Your name." Those people, when they wake up in the middle of the night, *mumble,* "(Yawn), I love You, Jesus" before curling up to go back to sleep. Then they wake up in the morning with a prayer on their lips, saying, "Thank You, Lord, for a new day. I can't make it through this day without You, God. Oh, Jesus, I'm so thankful! I praise You, Lord, for helping me walk in Your will. Please give me wisdom today. I magnify Your name. You're awesome, God."

What I have just described to you, I practice continually. I believe God wants all of us to pray that way—to just offer up little acknowledgments of Him, make brief requests, and offer short thanksgivings. Just think about how you would feel if your children said, "I love you, Mom!" or "I love you, Dad!" every time they walked by you. If one of my children stops by my office and says, "Hey, Mom, you're awesome! See you later!" it makes my day. Just letting people know you think they're great is the kind of communication that develops relationships.

When we treat the Lord that way, our relationship with Him goes deeper and grows stronger, and we stay connected to Him through "anytime, anywhere" prayer. And He loves it.

> I believe God wants all of us to pray that way—to just offer up little acknowledgments of Him, make brief requests, and offer short thanksgivings.
>
> ⤜ • ⤛

I am not suggesting that we do all of our praying while we are busy doing other things. We do need to honor God by being willing to set apart time just for Him, but praying our way through the day is equally as important as devoting set-apart time to prayer. Do both if at all possible, but when you cannot do everything you want to do, then "do something, lest you do nothing!" Don't just feel guilty if you miss your set-apart time; go ahead and pray your way through the day!

"IN THE SPIRIT"

In addition to praying at all times, Ephesians 6:18 also instructs us to "pray in the Spirit." Simply put, "praying in the Spirit" means letting the Holy Spirit lead us as we pray instead of just praying anything we want. Different groups of people throughout the body of Christ interpret "praying in the Spirit" differently, and I will address that later in this book, but in its broadest definition, it means to follow the Holy Spirit in prayer, praying the things He leads us to pray. It means focusing on what He wants us to pray instead of what we feel like praying or think we should pray. This may require waiting quietly in God's Presence until He places something on our hearts.

Many times we are so wrapped up in our busy lives and so conscious of our problems that we do not think to do anything other than tell God all "our stuff" when we talk to Him. We often invest so much time and energy praying "our" prayers and treating God like a supernatural dumping ground where we unload all our junk. We tend to pray "our" prayers—prayers for what we think would make us feel better, what we think we should pray for, or what seems to be appropriate, instead of praying what God leads us to pray.

I think one of the reasons we sometimes feel unfulfilled in prayer or sense that we are not "finished" praying about a matter is that we spend so much time just praying *our* prayers. But I tell you: there is a better, higher, more effective way: praying *God's* prayers. To be honest with you, if I am praying my prayer, I can pray about something for fifteen minutes and still feel unfinished; but if I am being led by the Holy Spirit and praying God's prayer, I can pray two sentences and feel completely satisfied.

> If we will pray about our inner lives—about our thoughts and motives and about our relationship with God—then He will take care of the externals.
>
> ⤛ • ⤜

When I write about not praying "our" prayers, what I mean is that we can move beyond praying carnal, soulish prayers to praying Spirit-filled, Spirit-led prayers. We can pray God's prayers instead of our own if we are willing to make some adjustments in the way we think about prayer and how we approach God. For example, when we pray our prayers, we focus on praying for ourselves—our health and well-being, our financial needs, the challenges we face, our families, and other things that concern us. But I believe if we will pray about our inner lives—about our thoughts and motives and about our relationship with God—He will take care of the externals. If we will pray to build ourselves up on the inside, God will take care of the outside.

I began to sense tremendous fulfillment in my prayer life when I stopped praying so many *carnal, selfish* prayers and prayed more like I thought Jesus would have prayed. I want to reiterate that there is nothing wrong with asking God to meet our needs. I believe we can freely ask Him for anything without fear of reproach, but I have also come to understand that the things we pray about reveal our level of spiritual maturity.

Asking God for what we need and desire in the natural realm is definitely not wrong, but we should not major on those things. God's Word says that He knows what we need before we ask Him, so all we need to do is simply ask and let Him know that we are trusting Him to take care of everything that concerns us while we focus the majority of our prayer time on talking to Him about the needs of others (both natural and spiritual), the growth of His kingdom, and our spiritual needs. For example, I need to endure everything that comes my way with good temper much more than I need a new dress for a party. I need to abound in love and show kindness to people at all times much more than I need a larger house. I need to use wisdom with my spoken words much more than I need a promotion at work.

Here is another example of how to pray a Spirit-led prayer. Let's say you have two rowdy, rebellious teenage children in your house. And let's say, when you pray, you start by telling God how those two are on your last nerve and you just want to scream. Then you move on to complaining about them and telling Him how miserable you are. After you pray, you yell at your teenagers, tell them how awful they are, and inform them that their lives will never amount to anything. If this is the case, then your home is probably filled with strife; your family is never at peace, and your spouse is as angry and unhappy as you are. It is quite easy for our prayer time to become "complaining sessions" rather than true prayer. These types of prayers never bring God's help into a situation.

If you will begin to pray God's prayers for the situation, instead of running to Him with all your complaints, you will begin to see change. A "God prayer" would go something like this: "God, I am so frustrated with these teenagers today, but Your Word says my children are a heritage from the Lord, the fruit of the womb is a reward and they are like arrows in the hand of a warrior. Your Word also says great shall be their peace. So, God, I come before You with thanksgiving and I ask for wisdom as I deal with my teenagers. Lord, give me understanding about the things they go through and help me have the ability to help them. I ask that You would pour out Your love in my heart for them. I pray Your love would abound in me, Your grace would flow through me, and my heart would be right before You and toward my family. Let the peace of Christ rule and reign in my heart—and let it reign in our home."

When you pray according to the example above, your anger will begin to dissipate. You will begin to be able to love your teenagers with the love of God and you will be able to begin to establish peace in your home. God will begin to do things in your circumstances because you have stopped praying soulish prayers that are focused on your circumstances, you are no longer murmuring and complaining about the children you asked Him to give you and you have begun to pray about what is more important to Him—the condition of your heart.

Let the Holy Spirit Lead

Part of the way God teaches us to pray is to help us learn to follow the Holy Spirit as we pray. Without a doubt, the most effective way to pray God's prayers is to let the Holy Spirit lead us, and we do that by staying before the Lord and asking Him to put on our hearts what He wants us to pray about—things that originate in God's heart, not in our minds. As I have already written, we really must move beyond praying our own prayers for what *we* want. Prayer is a more serious business than that—and the Holy Spirit will lead us into the most amazing exploits in prayer if we will simply ask Him what to pray, wait for Him to answer, and then obey.

We are extremely unwise when we say we do not have time to wait on God and allow Him to lead us as we pray. We find ourselves waiting forty-five minutes for a table at a restaurant, but say we do not have time to wait on God. We can save all kinds of time and energy later if we will wait on God now. You see, trying to figure out what to pray and striving to drum up prayers can be tiring. That kind of drudgery in the flesh simply is not fruitful; it is not grace-filled. Our spirits know—even when our minds try to convince us otherwise—when we are not accomplishing anything in the spiritual realm and when our prayers are not effective.

I have learned that in order to pray effective prayers—whether I am praying for my children, myself, the ministry, a neighbor, or a crisis on the other side of the world—I have to wait on God and let Him lead me. I just take a few minutes and say, "Okay, God, such-and-such is on my heart. What is it You're trying to say here? Show me what You want me to pray for that person or that situation." Most of the time, within a few seconds, impressions will start to come to my heart: I will understand how I need to pray; I will pray more specifically than I normally would; I will quickly feel satisfied.

> Letting the Holy Spirit lead our prayers will bring great freedom to our lives and make prayer so much easier and so much more fun.
>
> ⇢ • ⇠

If we will begin our prayers by asking the Holy Spirit to lead us, we will not find ourselves becoming bored when we pray because we will not pray about the same situations or for the same people all the time. Prayer can become boring if it is not kept fresh, but the Holy Spirit is full of creativity. Furthermore, when He leads, our wandering minds will not be in control of our prayers; we will not be praying out of a sense of obligation and our prayers will not be ritualistic. We will simply know what is on God's heart, pray about those things, and allow the Holy Spirit to help us pray in ways that keep our communication with Him fresh and life-giving.

Letting the Holy Spirit lead our prayers will bring great freedom to our lives and make prayer so much easier and so much more fun. It completely relieves us of the feeling that we are responsible for praying for everything we read about or hear about. This is because we understand that we are only responsible for praying about what God puts on our hearts and for the people and situations that fall into our realm of responsibility. Personally, I do not ever feel guilty when I am not praying what other people are praying for, because I know that God uses different people to pray for different situations. If each person will pray for the things God calls him or her to pray for and allow the Holy Spirit to lead, the entire world will be covered!

Also, we need to be free from legalism and obligation as we pray. God does not want us to pray because we think we have to or we think we should. We need to follow the Holy Spirit and pray about whatever He leads us to address in prayer, for however long He leads us to pray. When our spiritual ears are tuned in to His voice, we will be able to hear His instruction and His encouragement. We will know what matters to Him and be able to pray exactly the way He wants us to pray—which always yields tremendous results.

PRAYING WITH THE MIND

In his book *The Spiritual Man*, Watchman Nee wrote about allowing the mind to aid the spirit when the spirit seems to be silent. I am sure he was not advocating praying soulish prayers, but he meant when we see a need or think of something we feel should be prayed about, then we should simply begin praying based on what we know in our minds and wait to see if our spirits affirm the direction in which we are praying. Paul said in 1 Corinthians 14:15, "I will pray with my spirit [by the Holy Spirit that is within me], but I will also pray [intelligently] with my mind and understanding."

In prayer, we need not always wait for God's burden to fall upon us before we begin to pray. We may begin in the mind and search for what the Spirit cooperates with. We don't always understand the ebb and flow of the Spirit. Sometimes the power of the Holy Spirit is abundant and we feel strongly led in one direction or another, but at other times we must confess that He is totally silent and still. During those times, we must begin to pray according to the knowledge we have in our minds. As we do, we will either sense strength and enthusiasm coming from the Spirit or continue to experience silence and no help from Him. In that case, we should go on to something else and continue doing so until we discover what is on God's heart for us to pray about.

When we see needs around us, we are not to wait until a wonderful feeling overtakes us and energizes us to pray. We begin in faith, praying about a need we are aware of, and we find out soon enough whether or not we are praying according to God's will. We will either feel a wonderful flow in prayer, in which we do not have to struggle for words, or we will sense that we are struggling, merely trying to come up with something spiritual to say because we feel we "should" be praying about that situation. Praying in the Spirit can simply mean that we are committed not to pray without Him. Even though we may begin on our own, we will not persist unless the Holy Spirit hooks up with us and gives His approval and divine energy.

OPPOSITION IN PRAYER

We do encounter resistance as we seek to follow the Holy Spirit in prayer, and many times that opposition comes in the form of fear—not just major fears, such as fear of a natural disaster or a terrible disease or some other catastrophe—but a nagging sense of anxiety and unrest about common, ordinary things. The devil even tries to make us afraid of praying boldly. He wants us to approach God in fear rather than in faith. He reminds us of our sins and shortcomings and makes us feel as if we have no right to ask God for much of anything. The Bible teaches us repeatedly to "come boldly" to the throne (see Ephesians 3:12; Hebrews 4:16).

Some people live their everyday lives with a constant undercurrent of little fears, making comments like, "I'm afraid I won't get to work on time with all this traffic," or "I'm afraid I'll burn the roast," or "I'm afraid it's going to rain out the ball game on Saturday." These everyday fears really are minor ones, but they are still fears and they still hinder a lifestyle of prayer by keeping people focused on their worries and anxieties. Instead of allowing the enemy to pick at us with little things and infect our lives with these low-level, ongoing fears, we need to pray and trust God.

We need to replace the little fear-filled thoughts and conversations in our everyday lives with short, simple prayers. My motto is "pray about everything and fear nothing." When we are developing a lifestyle of prayer, we will need to eliminate the habits and thought patterns that do not promote or support prayer. The Holy Spirit wants to help us do that, so we need to ask Him to lead us out of negative habits and into the kind of prayer that keeps us regularly connected to God in faith throughout the day. As we continue to allow the Holy Spirit to lead us in this way, our prayers will become as easy and habitual as breathing.

WE GROW AS WE GO

Just as breathing helps us grow naturally, a lifestyle of prayer will help us grow spiritually. Then, as we mature spiritually, our prayer lives will keep developing and our prayers will become increasingly effective. One of the best things about prayer is that it is progressive. It is not a skill we master; it is an unfolding relationship we enjoy. As it unfolds, we learn to pray more often and more effectively; we learn to follow the Holy Spirit more closely; we learn to pray with more confidence; we learn to commune with God on a deeper level and to hear His voice more clearly.

> One of the best things about prayer is that it is progressive. It is not a skill we master; it is an unfolding relationship we enjoy.
>
> ✈ • ✈

Have you ever been happy in your prayer life, feeling that it was going well for a while and then, for no apparent reason, you start to feel restless, bored, distracted, or weary? Have you ever felt a nagging that something just was not right about your prayers or a stirring to do something differently, but you did not know exactly what it is? Has it ever seemed that you were striving to pray, even though you did not really want to, or that prayer had become overly laborious? Most of the time, when you have such impressions, the Holy Spirit is trying to tell you something.

Your inner man (your spirit, the part of you that communes with God) knows when something is not right in your prayer life, because the Holy Spirit lives in your spirit and will let you know when your prayers are not as they should be or when something needs to change. The good news is that many times when we feel that way, God knows we are ready for more and is urging us on to the next level. Sometimes when we become uncomfortable in our prayer lives, God is trying to teach us something to help us grow in our relationship with Him. He will always *love* us where we are, but He will not *leave* us where we are, and that is true in prayer just as it is in other areas of our lives.

Even though God wants us to live joyful, contented lives, He sometimes causes a discontent or a feeling that something is not right because He does not want us to continue doing the same old things anymore. He wants to prod us to seek Him to find out what's wrong because He wants to take us to new levels. He may be wanting us to pray in a new way or even to dedicate more time to prayer. He might be leading a person who already prays a short while in the morning to set aside the lunch hour at work for prayer and fellowship with Him. He might be leading a person to study more in the area of prayer so he or she can learn what to do next. He might be leading an individual who often prays alone to join a group that meets regularly for prayer.

God always wants us to grow stronger, to go deeper, and to increase in intimacy with Him through prayer. Most of the time, He leads us into that process of maturity by leading us out of places where we have been comfortable in the past. In this process, though, it is important to realize this: As God is teaching us to pray and moving us along in the process of prayer, we do not need to let ourselves feel condemned or stay frustrated and aggravated;

we need to find out whether God is calling us into a new place or whether the devil is harassing us. This is because discomfort, dissatisfaction, or the absence of peace in our prayer lives can also be the work of the enemy; sometimes he opposes believers when we try to pray.

The devil is a liar and he delights in trying to make us feel as if our prayers are useless and of no value. When we reach the point that we feel something is "just not right" in our prayer lives, we simply need to ask God what is happening and take time to wait on Him to answer. He will show us if He is calling us to a new level in prayer or if the devil is trying to steal the prayer life we have already developed. We must always remember that the devil hates prayer on any level and will try to stop it. If God wants us to pray (and He does), He wants us to enjoy it. He always accepts us just the way we are and He never condemns us. He will hear and answer even the puniest, most pitiful prayer when it comes from the heart, and He always honors sincerity and faith. At the same time, He will not let us stay in those places of immaturity, but He will call us to move on to greater levels of faith, power, and effectiveness.

Every person's prayer life is different, so feel free to pursue prayer the way God leads. Prayer is not about laboring or striving or trying to perform; it's simply about talking to God. As I wrote in chapter 2, we do not need to try to be where someone else is or pray with the proficiency someone else has because that person may be enjoying a prayer life that has taken years of practice and we may not be as far along in our walk with God as that person is. It's all right for us to be "younger" than others in prayer; God still hears and answers us, no matter the extent of our experience. Comparing ourselves with others only makes us miserable. God is happy simply because we are learning and growing.

Some people can pray more effective prayers than others; some have more faith than others; some understand the ways of God better than others; some obey God more quickly than others; some spend more time in the Word than others. Sometimes, a people may be ready to move to a new level in prayer, but cannot because another issue needs to be addressed. For example, they may need to forgive someone before their relationship with God can improve. Or, a person may need a deeper revelation of God's love before undertaking a challenging personal or ministry opportunity. Regardless, we all start somewhere and go somewhere. God allows us to begin wherever we are and then helps us grow.

> We never become certified experts in prayer and we never stop learning to communicate with God; our experiences just keep getting richer and better.
>
> ⤙⤜ • ⤙⤜

Prayer is progressive and we all move from one level to another. No one ever "masters" prayer because there is no limit to the depth of relationship we can have with God; it just keeps growing, keeps going deeper, keeps getting stronger. Our ability to pray develops and improves over time. We never become certified experts in prayer and we never stop learning to communicate with God; our experiences just keep getting richer and better.

You may not have arrived at your final destination, but you can thank God you are on the pathway that will take you there. As long as you are making progress, it really does not matter if you are crawling, walking, or running. Just keep pressing on!

SUMMARY

God does want us to enjoy set-apart times of prayer, but He has so much more for us! He longs for us to pray simple prayers to Him on a continual basis. He wants us to live a life of prayer and to pray our way through every day. His desire is for our hearts to be sensitive to the many things He does for us and to remember to offer a quick "Thank You, Lord!" He is eager for us to ask Him for everything we need in every situation and to keep a running dialog with Him as we go about the activities of our lives. God loves us; He wants us to be aware of His presence at all times; and He wants to be in constant communion with us as we make prayer a way of life.

We never stop learning to pray more effectively and we never stop discovering the riches of communicating with God. As we allow the Holy Spirit to lead us, our prayer lives become richer, deeper, more exciting, and more effective. Prayer is a progressive experience and we keep growing in it as we keep going in it. If we will stay sensitive to the Holy Spirit, pray God's prayers, and be willing to make adjustments in the way we pray as He directs, He will keep leading us to new places of maturity in our spiritual lives and to new levels of intimacy in prayer.

Prayer Points

➤➤ We are to pray "at all times, on every occasion, in every season." We can pray anytime, anywhere, and prayer should be as easy and as natural as breathing.

➤ Thinking *I should pray about such-and-such when I pray* is a stall tactic of the enemy. God hears sincere, short, immediate prayers just as much as He hears all other prayers.

➤ Most of us live busy lives, but we can pray in the midst of doing other things. We need to make the most of the time we have.

➤ We are also to pray "in the Spirit," which means praying God's prayers instead of our own and letting the Holy Spirit lead us as we pray.

➤ Remember that prayer is progressive. When something seems to be missing in our prayer lives, God may be wanting to take us to a new level of maturity, faith, or effectiveness of expression in prayer.

➤ God wants us to pray, and He wants us to enjoy praying.

4

The Power of Prayer

I believe that prayer is one of the greatest powers available in the entire universe. That's a bold statement, I know, given the other kinds of power that are available today, but I am convinced beyond the slightest doubt that it is true. When we think of atomic power, we think of forces greater than we can imagine. When we think of something as basic as fuel power in a motorcycle on the highway, we think of something extremely noisy, intense, and potentially dangerous.

But every kind of power we encounter on earth means nothing in heaven. Atomic power could wipe out an entire city of people, but it cannot give them eternal life. This power once commanded the attention of every nation on earth, but it never healed a broken heart. Fuel power takes us where we want to go in the world, but it does not help us make any spiritual progress in our lives or move forward in God. The power we know of in the physical world is natural, but prayer power is spiritual. As I mentioned earlier, prayer opens the door for God to work. It is the activity that you and I can engage in on earth when we need the power of heaven to come into our lives and bring wisdom, direction, encouragement, or a miraculous breakthrough. Prayer releases the power of God Almighty into our daily lives and the power of prayer is that it connects us to the power of God—and that is why it is a greater force than anything else we can ever imagine.

Only the power of prayer can move the hand of God. And only the power of God can change an individual heart, free a person from bondage and torment, overturn disappointments and devastations, break the power of an addiction, or heal a person's emotions. Only God's power can bring peace, instill joy, grant wisdom, impart a sense of value and purpose to a person who doesn't know what to do in life, and work every kind of miracle. Only God's power can restore trust and intimacy to a marriage in which both people are so angry and hurt that divorce seems to be the only option. In fact, did you know that the current divorce rate in the United States is 50 percent, but that when couples pray together in their home, the divorce rate is only .3 percent?[1] Now *that* is a testimony to God's power and to the power of prayer.

The awesome, tremendous power of God—the greatest release of power in the universe—is released in our lives through simple, faith-filled prayer. Because we can pray, we are ordinary people with extraordinary power; we are natural people who can live supernatural lives. We can overcome problems we thought we could never overcome; we can do things people do not believe we can do; we can make brilliant decisions; we can walk in victory over the big challenges in our lives and over the everyday

> Because we can pray, we are ordinary people with extraordinary power; we are natural people who can live supernatural lives.
>
> ->> • <<-

hassles—as long as we are connected to the power of God, which is only possible through prayer.

PRAYER RELEASES GOD'S POWER

We all need God's power in our lives, and prayer is the dynamic that releases His power, sometimes in dramatic ways. One of the best biblical examples of this is the story of Jehoshaphat, king of Judah, in 2 Chronicles 20. Many "ites"—the Moabites, the Ammonites, and the Meunites—came to fight Jehoshaphat and his troops. The Bible says that these nations composed "a great multitude" against Judah and that Jehoshaphat was afraid of them. But he began to pray and fast, and he called all the people of Judah to do the same. We read that "Judah gathered together to ask help from the Lord; even out of all the cities of Judah they came to seek the Lord [yearning for Him with all their desire]" (2 Chronicles 20:4). As the people prayed together, the Spirit of God came upon a man named Jahaziel and he began to prophesy: "The Lord says this to you: Be not afraid or dismayed at this great multitude; for the battle is not yours, but God's.... You shall not need to fight in this battle. Take your positions, stand still, and see the deliverance of the Lord" (2 Chronicles 20:15–17).

After prayers, fasting, seeking God corporately, and hearing the prophetic word that God would give them victory, Jehoshaphat began to implement the strategy for victory. He "appointed singers to sing to the Lord and praise Him in their holy [priestly] garments as they went out before the army, saying, Give thanks to the Lord, for His mercy and loving-kindness endure forever" (2 Chronicles 20:21). Before we go further, I want you to realize that praise and thanksgiving are types of prayer. I will write about this in greater detail in chapter 5, but for now I want you to pay particular attention to the results of these prayers: "And when they began to sing and praise, the Lord set ambushments against the men of Ammon, Moab, and Mount Seir who had come against Judah, and they were [self]-slaughtered" (2 Chronicles 20:22).

When we pray, God acts. I will remind you once more: prayer opens the door for God to work. In Jehoshaphat's case, the enemies ended up in total confusion and destroyed each other, while the people of Judah did indeed see God's deliverance. They had been faithful in fervent prayer, and as a result, God did fight and win their battle for them. The power of prayer caused them to prevail!

Modern-Day Miracle

Judah's victory is an awesome story about the power of prayer to bring victory in our lives. God's power released through prayer is just as real and valid today as it was in Old Testament times. I recently came across an awesome testimony of the power of prayer.

Most people in the United States and many around the world remember the terrible, tragic shooting rampage that took place at Columbine High School in Littleton, Colorado, in April 1999. One of the victims injured that day was a young man named Mark Taylor, whose story was covered in the *Rocky Mountain News*.

Mark was one of the first students shot that day. He was outside waiting to go into the cafeteria when the shooting started. He remembers feeling the unbearable pain of the first shot and seeing blood gushing from his body as he screamed, "Oh, my God, help me!" By the time it was over, he had been shot twice in his back and five times in his chest, piercing his spleen and tearing through the area directly behind his aorta. "I was in so much pain I could hardly breathe," Mark recalled. He remembers that several students climbed over his bleeding body as they ran away from the shooters. They thought he was dead. "No one was helping me," Mark said. "God helped me."

Mark was afraid he was dying as he rode in the ambulance to a nearby hospital. "I called to God to save me, and he answered my plea. I knew right then, I was certain that God was going to save my life."

Mark's family physician remembered talking to the surgeon operating on Mark and being told, "I'm looking at a dead man." But that was not the case. God heard Mark's prayers that day, and after surgery and hospital treatment, Mark recovered from his injuries.[2]

PRAYER POWER TODAY

Not only do I often read stories such as Mark's and hear people talk about the power of prayer, I have also seen it in action in my own life, in my family, and in the lives of more people than I can even count. Many times, during our conferences and on our television broadcast, I pray for various needs I sense in the audience. I do not need to know the details of every person's situation; I simply pray in faith that God knows and will do what is best for them. We also receive prayer requests by telephone and through our web site, and our prayer teams are diligent to pray over them. Over the years, we have heard many other miraculous reports and I would like to share some recent testimonies with you as even more evidence of the power of prayer:

- Susie went to the doctor before attending one of our recent women's conferences. He diagnosed her with gallstones. During the conference, I prayed and asked God to touch people with His healing power. When Susie returned home and had the same tests rerun, her gallstones were gone.

- Over the phone, our prayer representative prayed with a woman who desperately needed income. She had been working in a job she loved for years as a volunteer, but soon after we prayed, she was offered that same position for pay.

- A woman who had been smoking for twenty-five years was finally able to quit after she received prayer at one of our conferences.

- Denise had been on disability for four years. She was unable to stand up straight and was in tremendous pain. After hearing me pray for healing on a television broadcast, Denise fell asleep. When she awakened, she was pain-free and able to stand up straight.

- Mary called the prayer line extremely upset because she and her husband did not have any money. He had recently gotten a job, but had to drive more than one hundred miles each way. Soon after he started his job, his car engine blew up and they could not pay to get it fixed. Within one hour of praying with our prayer representatives, she received a phone call from their mortgage company, informing her that some sort of accounting error had been made and that a check for $1,200 was in the mail.

- Victoria called our prayer line after being told that her grandson was going to die as a result of a serious car accident. She was standing in his hospital room watching the doctors prepare to remove her grandson's life support as she was on the phone praying with us. She later called back to report that her grandson had experienced a miraculous recovery and had been completely restored.

- An inmate wrote to us requesting prayer for her teenage son, who had been diagnosed with Cushing's disease and had been undergoing treatment for six years. After this mother prayed, and after our prayer teams prayed, we received another letter informing us that the doctors said her son had no more signs of disease in his body.

I also want to share with you one of the most remarkable testimonies we received at Joyce Meyer Ministries, one I believe will strengthen your faith and serve as a great encouragement to you as you grow in your prayer life.

My mother was diagnosed with ovarian/uterine cancer. When we met the doctor, she signed consent forms for the hysterectomy and also for a colostomy (in case the cancer had invaded her bowel). Basically, we were told to prepare for the worst. I wrote and asked you to pray for her. You responded with a nice letter informing me that you had teams of intercessors who would pray for her. I enlisted the help of all of my friends from New York to Miami, as well as those at work. My husband and sister asked all their friends to pray too. I know in my heart that God hears my own simple prayer, but I wanted lots of voices calling up to heaven just to be sure He would hear.

When the day of the surgery came, I asked the hospital staff if I could pray over her before they took her to surgery. They agreed. In the presence of my father and mother, I asked God to give the team "skill to their hands, compassion to their hearts, and knowledge to their minds." I also asked God to have them treat my mom as they would treat their own loved ones. I had been quite stoic up to that point, but then I cried. She was then taken to surgery.

Exactly two hours after the surgery, the doctor came out. He asked my father and me to come to a conference room. At that moment, fear had the upper hand.

We sat down and the doctor ran his hand through his hair. He looked us straight in the eye and said something I will never forget as long as I live: "I couldn't find any cancer. I looked everywhere. I opened up areas where it could be hiding; I made the pathologist do multiple frozen sections. I couldn't even find the place where the tumor was on the x-ray."[3]

The letter went on to say that woman had very little pain from a normally painful surgery and was released from the hospital in three days. This is truly a miraculous testimony of the power of prayer!

The people who call our ministry, send in prayer requests, attend our conferences, and watch our broadcasts are all regular, every-day people, just like you and me. They are real people with real life situations, just like yours and mine. The power of prayer has made a difference in their lives, even and especially in the midst of seemingly insurmountable obstacles. The power of prayer can make a difference in your life, too. Prayer brings the power of God to bear on the situations of our lives, and when God's power touches a situation it cannot stay the same; it *has* to change.

> Prayer brings the power of God to bear on the situations of our lives.
>
> ➤➤ • ◄◄

POWER IN PERSPECTIVE

Many times, when we think of "power," we think of something that happens quickly, with almost miraculous speed and force. But the power of prayer is not determined by whether or not results come instantly or dramatically. In fact, James 5:16, which I mention often in this book, teaches us that one way tremendous power becomes available as we pray is through the "earnest (heartfelt, *continued*) prayer" (emphasis mine). Prayers that require diligence and faithfulness over time are equally powerful, and we know that anytime God responds to prayer by doing something that seems totally impossible is a testimony to its power.

> The power of prayer is not determined by whether or not results come instantly or dramatically.
>
> ->>- • -<+-

Years ago, when Dave and I were first married, he simply could not understand all the problems I had with my personality due to the abuse I had suffered as a child and young adult. Because I was difficult to be in a relationship with, Dave often spent time alone praying for God to change me and give him strength to stay in our marriage. Dave shares that he was rarely sure what to do, but that after he prayed, he would begin to see small changes in me. Over time, he could see the powerful impact of his prayers. You see, I did start to change as God began to heal me emotionally and I can honestly say today that God has transformed my personality.

I'm sure there were times when Dave felt discouraged and wanted to give up. Even though continually praying for me was difficult for him, the point is that he did keep praying, even when progress was hard to see. He understood the power of persevering prayers, and his prayers certainly made a difference in my life! I am not sure I would have the ministry I have today if Dave had not stayed strong in this area and continued to pray for me and our situation.

I want to encourage you right now not to give up on the situations for which you are praying—even if you have been praying for someone or some circumstance for days, months, or years. Rest assured that God is working on your behalf even if you do not see results right away. Prayer *is* powerful. Even when the answers seem slow in coming, prayer can open the door for God to change the situations that appear most desperate in your life.

In another family situation years ago, I had to pray and pray for my oldest son, David, before I began to see the breakthrough I needed with him. David was my "hard-to-handle" child for many years. Our personalities grated on each other and I felt he was always opposing me, no matter what I did. He had a quick temper, was hard to please, and was extremely insecure. He constantly seemed to want Dave and me to prove that we loved him.

As he grew into a man, he was very difficult to get along with. He had a good heart, but stubborn flesh! He worked with us, which only increased our challenges because we were together all the time. I had prayed for many years about various things I saw that really needed to change in him. At times, I did see some results, but he always seemed to go back to being the way he had always been. On various occasions, Dave and I would sit him down and correct him sternly. When we did, he would change for a while, but as I said, it never lasted long. To be honest, he was a lot like I once was, but God had been working in my life and changing me, so I struggled terribly as I tried to be patient with him.

I remember one day when I was extremely frustrated and decided that our trying to work together simply could not continue. I thought we might be better off if we tried to have a mother-son relationship without also having to deal with each other on a daily basis at work. I was tired of praying and basically made the decision to wash my hands of the whole mess. I was going to fire him, and that was that! Basically, I had given up hope that he would ever change and I simply did not want to deal with the situation any longer. I forgot that prayer is powerful, even (and especially) in situations that seem most hopeless.

I was on my way to work to talk to him when I distinctly heard God speak to my heart, "Joyce, don't give up on David." His message to my heart was undeniable, and I knew that I needed to keep praying and waiting.

Eventually, David did change. Not overnight, but little by little, just as all the rest of us do. We now enjoy a good relationship and work together in ministry. David is CEO of our world missions program and is doing a fantastic job. We travel together and are sometimes with each other almost constantly for as much as two or three weeks at a time, and we rarely ever have even a tense moment.

God is able to do anything. All things are possible with Him, but we must not quit praying. Some prayers are answered very quickly and others require more time. If you have a child that frustrates you or some other situation you are tired of praying about, I encourage you not to faint and give up. I am really glad now that

> God is able to do anything. All things are possible with Him, but we must not quit praying.
>
> ⤜ • ⤛

I didn't. You will see the day when the seeds you have sown in tears will be reaped with joy. Just keep trusting God, keep believing for a breakthrough, keep remembering that prayer really is powerful— and you will see change.

WHEN GOD'S PEOPLE PRAY

I trust your faith is being strengthened as you read about the power of prayer in people's lives, and I hope you realize that God does not play favorites. He is willing and able to act just as powerfully in response to your prayers as to the prayers of people I mention in this book. The power of prayer is nothing new and we find many great stories about it throughout the Bible. The prophet Jeremiah certainly was right when he prayed to God saying, "There is nothing too hard for You" (Jeremiah 32:17, NKJV). In both the Old and New Testaments, people prayed to the God for Whom nothing is impossible and He answered them in mighty ways. Just take a look at a few of them.

Hannah

A woman who is unable to conceive a child is in a desperate situation. Today, advancements in medical technology have helped to make this more of a possibility, but in Old Testament times, there were no medical interventions available. A barren woman truly had no hope. For years, Hannah wanted a child more than anything else in the world. The day came when she prayed to God and asked Him to do the impossible. What happened? Against all odds, Samuel was born and grew up to be a great prophet and priest in Israel.

Elisha

Only the power of God can bring life to something or someone that is dead. Second Kings 4:8–36 tells us about a woman known only as "the Shunammite Woman," who showed kindness to Elisha the prophet during his travels. Elisha prophesied that she and her husband would have a son at a certain time, and they did. But, several years later, the boy died and she sent for Elisha. When Elisha arrived, he knew the boy was dead, but he went in to the boy's room, shut the door, "and prayed to the Lord" (2 Kings 4:33). At first, the boy's flesh became warm, and then he sneezed seven times and opened his eyes.

Hezekiah

The Old Testament king Hezekiah was so sick that he was almost dead when the prophet Isaiah visited him with a message from God. "Thus says the Lord: Set your house in order, for you shall die; you shall not recover" (2 Kings 20:1). But Hezekiah desperately wanted to live, so he immediately began to weep bitterly and pray fervently, saying, "I beseech You, O Lord, [earnestly] remember now how I have walked before You in faithfulness and truth and with a whole heart [entirely devoted to You] and have done what is good in Your sight." Before Isaiah had even had time to leave the palace courts, God spoke to him again, telling him to go back to Hezekiah and say: "Thus says the Lord . . . : I have heard your prayer, I have seen your tears; behold, I will heal you" (2 Kings 20:5). Hezekiah's prayer had power. God not only healed him, but added fifteen years to his life (see 2 Kings 20:6).

Zacharias

Like Abraham and Sarah in the Old Testament, the New Testament has its story of people who are too old to have children. I am talking about people for whom it is *biologically impossible* to conceive a child. But, we must remember, prayer is powerful. Zacharias, the elderly priest who wanted a child with his wife, Elizabeth, had an angelic visitation in which the angel said, "Do not be afraid, Zacharias, for your prayer is heard; and your wife Elizabeth will bear you a son, and you shall call his name John" (Luke 1:13, NKJV). This miraculous child, the result of his parents' prayer, became John the Baptist, the one who announced Jesus' coming.

Peter

As a direct result of prayer, Peter was miraculously released from prison, where he was chained and guarded by sixteen soldiers (see Acts 12:4, 6). After his arrest, the people in the church prayed for him fervently and persistently, according to Acts 12:5. God heard their prayers and sent an angel to wake him from his sleep and lead him out of prison. When the angel awakened him, his chains fell off. The angel instructed him to put on his sandals and his coat and to follow him. This situation was so miraculous that Peter thought he was seeing a vision. He followed the angel past the outer guards of the prison, to an iron gate that led into the city. The gate swung open all by itself; the angel disappeared and Peter was free. Miracles do happen when people pray!

On another occasion, a beloved woman named Tabitha died in the city of Joppa. People there heard that Peter was in the neighboring town, so they sent for him and he came. When he arrived, he found many of Tabitha's friends crying in her room, obviously very upset over her death. Acts 9:40 says that "Peter put them all out [of the room] and knelt down and prayed; then turning to the body he said: 'Tabitha, get up!' And she opened her eyes; and when she saw Peter, she raised herself and sat upright." Talk about the power of prayer!

THE POWER OF JESUS' PRAYERS

As we close this chapter, I would like to share with you a truth that God made real to me one day, one that has really encouraged me in my prayer life. It's about the power of Jesus' prayers.

I was so tired of praying and then feeling like something was not right with my prayer life that I finally asked the Lord one day, "Why do I feel like this? I'm praying every day. I'm spending a good amount of time in prayer. Why is it that I come to the end of my prayer time and feel so unsatisfied? I feel like it didn't work. I guess I should be doing something else. Maybe I just need to pray more...." God answered me: "Because you don't feel like you're praying perfect prayers. You don't feel like you're praying right. You don't feel like *you're* right."

I realized that was true; I did not feel that I was "right." I always had a nagging fear that caused me to say to myself: "Well, you know, I'm not praying with enough faith or I'm not praying long enough or I'm not praying about the right things."

God delivered me from that fear when He impressed on me, "And you know what, Joyce? You're right. You're not praying perfect prayers. You're not perfect. That's why you have Jesus as your Intercessor."

Then He continued: "By the time your prayers get to Me, I hear perfect prayers because Jesus intercepts them—that's what an intercessor does. He intercepts them; He interprets them; He fixes them all up; and by the time they get to Me, they sound like perfect prayers prayed by a perfect person."

Once I understood that, my praying became easier because I was out from under the feeling that I had to be perfect. I was free to pray as best I could and trust Jesus the Intercessor to present my prayers acceptably to the Father.

We know that Jesus prays for us. In Luke 22:32, He says to Peter, "But I have prayed especially for you...." In John 17:9, He says concerning His disciples, "I pray for them" (NKJV). In that same chapter, He continues and says, "I do not pray for these alone, but also for those who will believe in Me...," and that means you and me (John 17:20, NKJV). Also, Hebrews 7:25 tells us that "...He is always living to make petition to God and intercede with Him and intervene for them" and Romans 8:34 teaches us that Jesus "is at the right hand of God actually pleading for us as He intercedes." Jesus is our intercessor, and He *lives* to pray for us!

What does an intercessor do? An intercessor stands in the gap that exists between God and an individual. We all have a gap between God and ourselves. In other words, we are not as holy as He is; we are not as perfect as He is; we are not as wise as He is, but Jesus is right there, standing in that gap, bringing God and me—or God and you—together so we can have fellowship with Him and He can answer our prayers. Isn't it awesome to know that as long as our hearts are right and as long as we believe in Jesus, He will intercept, make right, and take care of every imperfect thing we do?

> All of our prayers filter through Jesus' intercession.
>
> ⟶ • ⟵

We need to pray and we need to expect our prayers to be powerful in the spiritual realm—not because of ourselves or our praying, but because of Jesus and His intercession. We will not pray rightly 100 percent of the time, but Jesus does. Part of His ministry is, in the words of Andrew Murray, "the intercession by which our unworthy prayers are made acceptable."[4] All of our prayers filter through Jesus' intercession. He is always interceding for us, making our prayers acceptable to God, and when our prayers are acceptable to God, He hears them and He releases power on our behalf.

SUMMARY

There is no greater power available to any person than the power of prayer. Even the mightiest, most awe-inspiring force on earth is impotent compared to the power of God. We need God's power in our everyday circumstances and situations, and prayer is what connects us to God's power and makes the release of His power possible in our lives.

Many people have wonderful stories about the power of prayer. When you hear or read such accounts, let them encourage you and build your faith. When God moves powerfully in your life, be sure to share with others, so that they too can see how awesome God is and how much power there is in prayer.

We never need to struggle to try to pray perfect prayers because Jesus intercedes for us. His intercession is always perfect and He is always interceding for us, so we can trust that God hears our hearts as we pray and will be faithful to answer. Prayer is powerful, so if you want power in your life, power over your circumstances, power in your relationships, power to make good decisions, power to succeed, power over *anything*, pray!

Prayer Points

→→ Prayer is the greatest power in the universe. It is greater than every other kind of power because it is spiritual and not natural. Prayer releases the power of God into our lives and situations.

→→ Read and listen to testimonies of the power of prayer, and share your own stories. This will build your faith and the faith of others.

→→ Prayer is powerful, even when you feel you must keep praying for longer than you would like and when you think an answer is too long in coming. Do not ever be tempted to doubt the power of prayer!

→→ From the Old Testament days until now, people have experienced the power of prayer.

→→ Jesus is our Intercessor. He will intercept our imperfect prayers and deliver them to the Father as perfect prayers from a perfect person.

5

Praise, Worship, and Thanksgiving

The Bible teaches us about many different kinds of prayer, and in the next several chapters, we are going to take a look at several of them because the more you understand the different types of prayer, the more effectively you can pray. First, I want to focus on praise, worship, and thanksgiving because these are some of the simplest prayers we can pray and they will release great power in our lives. You may not have considered your praise, worship, or thanksgiving to be prayers, but they are—because each of them is a way of expressing your heart to God, a way in which you communicate with Him.

When I use the terms "praise," "worship," and "thanksgiving," I am referring to something deeper and more heartfelt than what many of us do in church. I am talking about communicating with God with all of our hearts, with total honesty, and with great passion. Trying to define *praise, worship,* and *thanksgiving* separately is a challenge because they are similar in nature and they function similarly in the spiritual realm. So, for the sake of simplicity, let me describe "praise" as our response to God for what He has done, is doing, and will do; and let me describe "worship" as our response to who He is. In other words, praise can be considered to relate to God's acts, while worship relates to His character. "Thanksgiving" can be described as a grateful acknowledgment of God's acts and His character.

We often experience all three—praise, worship, and thanksgiving—in the course of a church service or conference meeting. These gatherings typically open with a hymn or a praise chorus; then someone may pray a prayer of thanksgiving and, at some point, people will sing or read something as an expression or form of worship. Sometimes, in these settings, people are really engaged in praising and worshiping God and sometimes they seem to be bored, merely going through the motions or following a prescribed form of outward behavior. But I know that praise, worship, and thanksgiving are so powerful that I must tell you: I yearn to see greater respect for praise and worship in our churches and in our services because I know the power of praising and worshiping God. I encourage you always to be in your seat at church when the service begins unless you have experienced an unavoidable emergency. I believe we should respect times of praise and worship and value them as much as we do the teaching of God's Word. If we are late to a service for some reason, then we should quietly take a seat somewhere in the room and not disturb others who are sincerely trying to worship God.

I long for the day when we walk into conferences or church services and see everybody praising, worshiping, and thanking God with passion, zeal, and total abandon. I am eager for us to look forward to worshiping God, to lay aside our problems and our pressures—and be filled with praise, worship, and thanksgiving, so full in fact that what is in us naturally flows out of our mouths in conversation and song. I want to see the day when we are so captivated by the Lord and so overflowing with praise and gratitude that we are not even tempted during the praise and worship part of the church service to look around to see who is in attendance or what they happen to be wearing!

God responds to that kind of respectful, heartfelt corporate praise and worship. He sends His glory—His manifest presence and power—to people who are truly praising and worshiping Him. And when His glory comes, miracles happen, people are healed, lives are changed, and transformation takes place from the inside out.

> Whatever we are praying for, one of the best ways to start is with praise, worship, and thanksgiving.
>
> ⤚⤜ • ⤛⤙

Isn't that what you are really after in your prayer life? Aren't you praying primarily because you want some kind of change or transformation in some area of your life? If you are praying for a new job, that's change. If you are praying for a loved one to come to know the Lord, that's change. If you are asking God to reveal Himself more to you and to help you grow in spiritual maturity, that's change. If you are praying for your marriage to be healed, that's change. If you are praying for the teenager who lives down the street to stop using drugs and get his life on the right track, that's change. If you are asking God to help you not lose your temper so easily, that's change.

Whatever we are praying for, one of the best ways to start is with praise, worship, and thanksgiving. They will keep our hearts right before God and make a way for change to take place. They are simple prayers, but they are also mighty spiritual dynamics, and it is possible to experience their power in every aspect of our lives.

PRAISE

Many people are familiar with the statement "There's power in praise!" It's true, and when we praise God from our hearts, we exert power in the spiritual realm. God Himself inhabits the praises of His people, according to Scripture (see Psalm 22:3). At my conferences, I make sure I'm in the service as soon as the praise and worship begin because I love to be in God's presence. In fact, before I speak to an audience, I make sure I have entered into praise and worship—not because God needs it, but because *I* need it. I need to express my joy over everything He has done for me and everything He is going to do; I need to engage my heart to focus on Him and my mouth to speak about Him; I need to tap into the power that is released through praise and make sure I have a clear connection with heaven. I do all this because I love God, but also because praise creates an opening in the spiritual atmosphere, which enables people to hear the Word clearly, receive it, and hold on to it through faith.

Just think about it. How many times do we walk into a church service or a conference and feel "blah" when we first arrive, but then feel better after a few minutes of praising God? You see, praise brings a release of our burdens; it takes our focus off ourselves and our problems and puts it on God—and that always makes us feel better.

Not only that, but praise is a form of spiritual warfare. Praising God defeats the devil and the forces of evil (remember the story of Jehoshaphat). Singing or shouting praises can break the power of fear off us and help us to get rid of doubt and unbelief. It will drive away spirits that are not of God. For example, when the spirit of fear attacks us by giving us thoughts that make us afraid, we need to say something like, "I praise you, Lord, and I magnify Your name. You're worthy to be praised. Hallelujah. Thank You, Lord. You're awesome! There is nobody like You!" We can use those words of warfare anytime, anywhere. We can defeat Satan much more quickly by singing a song than by worrying. That's why the Bible is loaded with examples of praise and with instructions and reasons for us to sing and praise God. Just look at some of them:

- "Unto You, O my Strength, I will sing praises; for God is my Defense, my Fortress, and High Tower, the God Who shows me mercy and steadfast love"(Psalm 59:17).
- "Praise the Lord! Sing to the Lord a new song, praise Him in the assembly of His saints! Let Israel rejoice in Him, their Maker; let Zion's children triumph and be joyful in their King! Let them praise His name in chorus and choir and with the [single or group] dance; let them sing praises to Him with the tambourine and lyre!" (Psalm 149:1–3).
- "Rejoice in the Lord always. Again I will say, rejoice!" (Philippians 4:4, NKJV).
- "But you *are* a chosen generation, a royal priesthood, a holy nation, His own special people, that you may proclaim the praises of Him who called you out of darkness into His marvelous light" (1 Peter 2:9, NKJV).

Why does the Bible tell us to sing and praise God? Why does Psalm 149:1 urge us to "sing to the Lord a new song"? Why did

God put music in us? Why did He put songs in our hearts? Because there is power in praise.

PRAISE BRINGS POWER

You may know the story of Abraham, and if not, you can find it in Genesis 12:1—21:7. In a nutshell, God promised Abraham a son, but the problem was that Abraham and his wife, Sarah, were both old—*really* old. He was one hundred years old and she was ninety, so their childbearing years were long gone! But Abraham knew God had spoken and was determined not to focus on the natural impossibility that he and Sarah could have a child. Instead, he planted his faith in God's promise and held on to that promise by praising God. His story is so remarkable that Paul made reference to it in Romans 4:18–21, which says:

"[For Abraham, human reason for] hope being gone, hoped in faith that he should become the father of many nations, as he had been promised, so [numberless] shall your descendants be. He did not weaken in faith when he considered the [utter] impotence of his own body, which was as good as dead because he was about a hundred years old, or [when he considered] the barrenness of Sarah's [deadened] womb. No unbelief or distrust made him waver (doubtingly question) concerning the promise of God, but he grew strong and was empowered by faith as he gave praise and glory to God, fully satisfied and assured that God was able and mighty to keep His word and to do what He had promised."

Look again at verse 18: "[For Abraham, human reason for] hope being gone, hoped in faith that he should become the father of many nations, as he had been promised." This man had absolutely no reason to hope. In fact, if any situation had ever been beyond hope, it would be the possibility of two people past ninety being able to have a child. Nevertheless, Abraham kept hoping; he kept believing God's promise. Verse 19 says that "he did not weaken in faith when he considered the [utter] impotence of his own body." In other words, Abraham looked at his circumstances and was well aware of the odds that were piled against him, but he still did not give up, even though the Bible says that his body was "as good as dead" and that Sarah's womb was barren and "deadened." In the face of a genuine natural impossibility, Abraham did not give in to unbelief; he did not waver in his faith or question God's promise. Instead, "he grew strong and was empowered by faith" as he praised God.

> We gain more and more strength, our faith increases, and the things that are coming against us to defeat us are dissipated as we praise Him.

The same thing will happen to us today when we praise God. We gain more and more strength, our faith increases, and the things that are coming to defeat us are dissipated as we praise Him. That's why we need to be diligent to listen to praise and worship music. We need to play it in our homes and in our cars; we need to learn songs and sing them. Every time we have an opportunity—even a minute or two while walking through a parking lot into a store—to praise and worship God, we need to do it. After a while, praise becomes so natural that it flows out of us without a deliberate decision on our part. We find ourselves singing and thanking God as an automatic response to our awareness of His goodness, mercy, and grace.

Tell the Tale

One of the ways *Vine's Expository Dictionary of Old & New Testament Words* defines "praise" is *telling a tale* or *a narration*. In other words, praising God is simply recounting or telling aloud the great things He has done. If we are doing nothing more than sitting at lunch with a friend and speaking about some wonderful things God has done, we are praising Him. In fact, the Bible says God likes those conversations and when He hears them, He gets out His book of remembrance and records them (see Malachi 3:16). He does not record our murmuring, grumbling, or complaining, but He records the words we speak when praise is on our lips.

Just think about how you would feel if you were to overhear your children sitting around saying, "Oh, man, I tell you, our mom is awesome. We have the greatest mother in the world. There is no mother as great as ours! Don't we have the most incredible mom and dad? They're just the best parents around!" I am sure that if you witnessed such a conversation between your children, you could hardly wait to bless them!

But, on the other hand, what if you walked into a room and your children were saying, "I'm so sick and tired of Mom and Dad. They never do anything for us. They've got all these rules. They don't want us to have any fun. Mom nags us all the time and makes us do our homework. If our parents really loved us, they would give us what we want, not what they think is best."

Our lives with God are no different than the two scenarios I have described above. We are God's children! He hears everything we say and He knows what is in our hearts even when we don't say it. What does He want to hear us talking about? How great He is! How awesome He is! The wonderful things He's done! What He can do! What He will do! What He's probably doing that we do not even know about yet! He wants to hear us praising Him.

Hebrews 13:15 says: "Through Him, therefore, let us constantly and at all times offer up to God a sacrifice of praise, which is the fruit of lips that thankfully acknowledge and confess and glorify His name." We often interpret the "sacrifice of praise" to mean nothing more than praising God when we do not feel like praising Him, and that can certainly be a type of sacrifice. However, I believe the writer of Hebrews is actually making reference to the Old Testament sacrificial system that required the blood of animals to atone for people's sins.

We, however, live in New Testament times, when we no longer need to put slain sheep and goats and bulls on an altar. Instead, the sacrifice—the offering—God wants from us today is to hear right words coming out of our mouths, rising up before His throne. Just as the smoke and the aroma of the animal sacrifices went up before His throne under the Old Covenant, the praise from our hearts rises up as a sacrifice before Him today. In Hebrews 13:15, the Lord was really saying, *The sacrifice I want now is the fruit of your lips thankfully acknowledging Me.*

We need to apply that Scripture to our everyday lives, making sure that we speak God's praises every chance we get. We need to tell people about all the great things He's doing for us; we need to thank Him; we need to tell Him we love Him. In our hearts and with our mouths, we should go through our days saying, "Lord, I love You. Thank You so much for everything You're doing in my life. Lord, I praise You for taking care of my family today. Lord, I even thank You that we have electricity and hot water. Lord, I praise You for working everything out for my good in every situation." We need to be people of praise, acknowledging God "constantly and at all times," continually offering up to Him the sacrifice of praise.

WORSHIP

Vine's Expository Dictionary of Old & New Testament Words says, "The worship of God is nowhere defined in Scripture." Do you know why I think worship is not defined? Because I do not think it can be defined. Worship is so deep; it is so precious and so awesome and it comes from such a deep place within us; it is such a powerful out-pouring of our hearts toward the Lord and it represents such love, gratitude, and devotion that we cannot put it into words. Human language is not rich enough to describe everything that true worship is. In fact, worship is so personal and so intimate that maybe we should even not attempt to limit or define it with our words.

In the absence of a definition of worship, *Vine's Expository Dictionary of Old & New Testament Words* does say that worship "is not confined to praise; broadly, it may be regarded as the direct acknowledgement to God, of His nature, attributes, ways and claims" and that it can mean "to serve," or to "do service to." Some sources also say that to worship means "to kiss," which connotes great affection and intimacy.

Even though we cannot find a definition of worship in the Bible, the Scriptures are clear in their instructions and observations about worship. For example:

- "Give to the Lord the glory *due* His name. . . . Oh, worship the Lord in the beauty of holiness!" (1 Chronicles 16:29, NKJV).

- "O come, let us worship and bow down, let us kneel before the Lord our Maker [in reverent praise and supplication]" (Psalm 95:6).
- "Extol the Lord our God and worship at His holy hill, for the Lord our God is holy!" (Psalm 99:9).
- "I will worship toward Your holy temple and praise Your name for Your loving-kindness and for Your truth and faithfulness; for You have exalted above all else Your name and Your word and You have magnified Your word above all Your name!" (Psalm 138:2).

The Posture of Power

Like praise, worship is so much more than just singing songs. In fact, worship is a condition of heart and a state of mind. We can be worshiping passionately without singing a single note. Worship is born in our hearts; it fills our thoughts and it is expressed through our mouths and through our bodies. For example, we can worship God by dancing, clapping, lifting our hands, playing an instrument, giving tithes and offerings, marching around, or sitting perfectly still, but our actions or our positions are simply reflections of what is in our hearts.

> Worship is a condition of heart and a state of mind.
>
> ⇥ • ⇤

One posture that is often used in worship and in prayer is kneeling. Kneeling is a posture of humility, but it is also a position of incredible power. As an act of humility, kneeling affects us in a positive way because it allows us physically to express our heart's cry of total dependence upon the Lord. To kneel is to say to Him: "I need You, God. I'm submitted to You. I want to follow You and obey You. I can't live without You. I can't do anything without You. I am desperate for You!"

As a power posture, kneeling sends a potent message to the enemy. The devil hates it! When he hears us singing a song, he does not know what's in our hearts, but when he sees us get on our knees or lift up our hands or start clapping or dancing, he gets nervous. A believer filled with worship is his worst nightmare! Although I am not able to stay on my knees for long periods of time, I frequently bow before God and simply say, "Thank You, Lord, for all You have done for me. Thank You for helping me today." Sometimes I stop right in the middle of a busy activity and do that. Sometimes, when I am filming for television, I will worship God this way between filming sessions in my dressing room, all by myself. Sometimes I like to kneel down beside my bed first thing in the morning and simply say, "I love You, Lord. Thank You for all you have planned for me today." I encourage you to develop some of these same habits. Remember, the devil hates praise and worship and he is defeated by it.

The reason he so despises worship is that he was originally the angel in charge of worship in heaven. He was the archangel Lucifer and his body was made of musical instruments. When he became proud and puffed up, God kicked him out of heaven and he fell like lightning (see Isaiah 14:12–15; Luke 10:18). He is still angry with God and will do anything to keep people from truly worshiping Him. Naturally, he doesn't like it that we have his job! But more than that, when the enemy is so opposed to something, we can know for certain that it's good for us, that it exerts power against him in the spiritual realm and that it pleases God.

I admit that I am emotional about my relationship with God. I am enthusiastic, filled with zeal and excitement. I like to be quiet at times, but I also enjoy being expressive in praise and worship. I really encourage you to express yourself in worship, too. Sure, sing. Sing with all your heart, but in addition to that, kneel, bow, dance, clap, or lift your hands in order to push back the enemy, to celebrate God's victory in your life, and to express physically the devotion of your heart toward the Lord in every possible way. God gave you your emotions, so don't be afraid to use them to honor him. I am amazed that people easily accept displays of intense emotion at a ball game, but seem to judge others as "just emotional" when they see enthusiasm expressed during praise and worship.

Put Your Heart into It

The world often thinks of worship as "religion," which could not be further from the biblical concept of worship. When we read about worship in the Bible, we are reading about a personal relationship, about spiritual intimacy, and about passionate expressions of devotion from people who love and worship God with all of their hearts. This is true worship—the kind that bubbles up out of us when we have the fire of God in our lives, when our love for Him spills out all over everything, and when we are zealous and enthusiastic about our dynamic relationship with Him.

According to John 4:23, this kind of worshiper is who God is looking for and the type of worship He wants. The verse says: "A time will come, however, indeed it is already here, when the true (genuine) worshipers will worship the Father in spirit and in truth (reality); for the Father is seeking just such people as these as His worshipers." God is seeking true, genuine worshipers who will really worship Him with all their hearts.

> We should dedicate ourselves to being the kind of worshipers God desires.
>
> ⤝ • ⤜

I have always been a bit saddened by the fact that God has to seek true worshipers. I think there should be an abundance of them and that we should dedicate ourselves to being the kind of worshipers God desires. But I find it interesting that He does not want just anybody to worship Him; He wants *true* and *genuine* worshipers. He is not looking for people who will worship Him out of fear, obligation, or religion, but out of a loving relationship.

E. M. Bounds writes that "religion has to do with everything but our hearts."[1] That is true, but equally true is the fact that true worship has to do with our hearts more than anything else. Obviously, not everybody who appears to be worshiping is a genuine worshiper. True, sincere worship comes out of the heart and out of intimacy with God; that is why worship is so important to our prayer lives.

Worship in spirit and truth is so much more than learned behaviors or habits that cause us to go to a certain place at a certain time and repeat certain rituals. Walking into a building called a church and kneeling at a certain time, standing at other times, repeating certain phrases, or reading from a book can be worship if these activities come from our hearts, but they can be form and legalism if they are nothing but memorized words and actions that are not sincere.

Some churches do not use worship books or prescribed forms of worship, and in such places, we can be tempted to think,

I'm worshiping. I'm looking at the overhead. I'm singing. I'm even clapping! But those things are not worship either unless they come from the heart. God is not pleased because we show up at the same place every Sunday, put in a specified amount of time, and then go home and do not think about Him until the same time next week. Our hearts have to be connected with what we are doing and we have to be focused on Him, or we are not involved in true praise and worship. In true worship, we cannot give God lip service; we have to give Him our hearts, and true worshipers are those who express with their mouths the worship that is in their hearts.

In Matthew 15:7–9, Jesus said: "…Admirably and truly did Isaiah prophesy of you when he said: These people draw near Me with their mouths and honor Me with their lips, but their hearts hold off and are far away from Me. Uselessly do they worship Me, for they teach as doctrines the commands of men." We do not want our worship—or our prayers—to be useless, so in order to keep them fresh, vibrant, and true, we have to keep our hearts in it.

THANKSGIVING

As I wrote earlier in this chapter for the sake of simplicity, we praise God for what He has done, is doing, and will do, and we worship God for who He is. Genuine thanksgiving is a response to both who God is and what He has done, is doing, and will do. It is not only an acknowledgment of these things; it's a *grateful* acknowledgment. It's an expression of true, heartfelt appreciation.

Thanksgiving should be a part of who we are deep down in our hearts; it is a type of prayer and it should flow out of us in a natural way that is pure and uncontrived. Being thankful does not mean merely sitting down at the end of a day, and trying to remember everything we need to be thankful for because we think we have to thank God in order to make Him happy or to satisfy some spiritual requirement or try to get Him to do something else for us. Instead, it means having a heart that is sensitive to God's working in our everyday lives, and just breathing out simple prayers of great thanksgiving every time we see Him working in our lives or blessing us. For example, "Lord, thank You for a good night's sleep" or, "God, I thank You that my visit to the dentist didn't hurt as much as I thought it might," or "Father, thank You for helping me make good decisions today," or "Lord, thank You for keeping me encouraged." God is always good to us, always faithful to us, always working so diligently in our lives. He is always doing something for us and acting in our best interest, so we need to respond by letting Him know we appreciate everything. We should thank God silently in our hearts and we also should voice our thankfulness aloud because that helps us stay conscious and aware of God's love, which He demonstrates through His goodness to us.

Just as the Bible instructs us to praise God and to worship Him, it also gives us reasons to thank Him and teaches us how to offer our gratitude to Him, as shown in the scriptures below:

- "We give praise and thanks to You, O God, we praise and give thanks; Your wondrous works declare that Your Name is near and they who invoke Your Name rehearse Your wonders" (Psalm 75:1).
- "It is a good and delightful thing to give thanks to the Lord, to sing praises [with musical accompaniment] to Your name, O Most High" (Psalm 92:1).

- "Let us come before His presence with thanksgiving; let us make a joyful noise to Him with songs of praise!" (Psalm 95:2).
- "Enter into His gates with thanksgiving and a thank offering and into His courts with praise! Be thankful and say so to Him, bless and affectionately praise His name!" (Psalm 100:4).

It's God's Will

Most Christians want to know God's will. Over the years in ministry, I have observed that a large number of people really are eager to know His will—His will for their personal lives, His will for their families, His will for their ministries or careers. Sometimes people treat God's will like the world's most complicated mystery and say things like, "Well, if I only knew God's will, I would obey" or "I really want to follow God; I'm just not sure what His will is."

> I can give you one absolutely certain way to know and obey God's will for your life: be thankful.
>
> ➤➤ • ◄◄

Let me share with you what at least a portion of God's will is. I cannot tell you whether or not His will is for you to move to Minneapolis or where you are to send your children to school or whether you are supposed to get the lead role in the Easter play at church. But I can give you one absolutely certain way to know and obey God's will for your life: be thankful. Be thankful—all the time, no matter what you go through. That's right; just keep a grateful heart in every circumstance. Sometimes thanksgiving comes easily and sometimes it is difficult, but if you will develop and maintain an *attitude* of thanksgiving, you'll be in God's will. How can I be so certain? Because I have read 1 Thessalonians 5:18, which says, "In everything give thanks; for this is the will of God in Christ Jesus for you" (NKJV).

Now, notice that the verse does not instruct us to be thankful *for* everything; it tells us to be thankful *in* everything. For example, let's say you open the refrigerator one day and see that the light is out and your food is not as cold as it should be. You don't have to start saying, "Oh, God, I thank You that this refrigerator is broken! Father, thank You that our milk has spoiled. Lord, it's such a blessing that the refrigerator went out and I just thank You for that." No, that would be ridiculous, but being thankful in every circumstance means being thankful that you have a refrigerator and that you have food to put in it. It means being thankful that it can be repaired and keeping a grateful heart while you are waiting for it to be fixed. That's what it means to give thanks in everything—and that's God's will. Live that way and you'll be in God's will.

Giving thanks in everything also means to be aware of the common, everyday blessings God gives us—our health, our freedom, our ability to get in the car and go somewhere. We should also thank God all the time for the people that He puts in our lives. He gives us people to support us and do things for us, people to laugh with, people who challenge us, people to impart wisdom, and people with whom to enjoy life.

For example, there is a young woman who travels with Dave and me, and she feels called to a specific ministry that really helps us. We are on the road so much and I like to take everything I even *think* I might want while we are away from home. This lady arrives at our destination several hours ahead of us, gets our luggage (which is sent ahead of us by truck), unpacks for us, and does everything she can to make our hotel room feel like home. When we arrive, our clothes are hanging neatly in the closet and everything is just the way we like it.

If you don't travel much, you may not understand what a blessing this is. If you stay home most of the time, just think about how wonderful it would be for someone to come into your house every few days and put everything away, give you some fresh flowers, and make sure you had everything you needed. If you do spend a great deal of time on the road, you can really understand and appreciate how nice it is to have this young woman on our team. Even though she is called and gifted to help us in this way, and I know she really enjoys it, I found myself thanking God for her not long ago. As I thought about everything she does to serve us and make our lives easier, my heart was filled with gratitude. I said, "Oh, God, thank You for those who help us. God, I'm so thankful! Lord, You've blessed us and helped us so much by giving us good people on the team. I'm so grateful for Your provision in that way."

We need to learn to exercise the privilege of simple prayer in every situation and one way we can do that is to thank God for the people that He puts in our lives. We need to receive and enjoy what He provides, but we should never take for granted the blessings He gives us. Instead, we should always appreciate what He does and make sure that a continual flow of thanksgiving is part of our everyday routines.

CLOSE THE DOOR ON COMPLAINING

E. M. Bounds writes that "gratitude and thanksgiving forever stand opposed to all murmuring at God's dealings with us, and all complaining at our lot.... True prayer corrects complaining and promotes gratitude and thanksgiving."[2] When we maintain an attitude of thanksgiving, we close the door to complaining—which seems to be an ever-present temptation in our lives. I never had to develop a complaining attitude; I was born with one. On the other hand, I did have to develop and nurture a thankful attitude. I learned from Scripture that complaining is evil in God's ears and allows the devil to bring destruction into our lives. Thankfulness opens the door for God to bless us, and complaining opens the door for the devil to curse us.

If we stay busy praising, worshiping, and thanking God, there will be no room for complaining, faultfinding, and murmuring. The Bible says in Philippians 2:14: "Do all things without grumbling and faultfinding and complaining...." And it says in 1 Corinthians 10:9–10: "We should not tempt the Lord [try His patience, become a trial to Him, critically appraise Him, and exploit His goodness] as some of them did—and were killed by poisonous serpents. Nor discontentedly complain as some of them did—and were put out of the way entirely by the destroyer (death)."

A Key to Prayer

Giving thanks is so important to prayer because, like praise and worship, it is something God *responds* to. It's something God loves, something that warms His heart. Anytime we give God pleasure like that, our intimacy with Him increases—and that makes for a better prayer life.

Also, when we are thankful, we are in a position to receive more from the Lord. If we are not thankful for what we have, why should

God give us something else to murmur about? On the other hand, when God sees that we genuinely appreciate and are thankful for the big and little things, He is inclined to bless us even more. Philippians 4:6 says: "Do not fret or have anxiety about anything, but in every circumstance and in everything, by prayer and petition (definite requests), with thanksgiving, continue to make your wants known to God." According to this verse, everything we ask God for should be preceded and accompanied by thanksgiving—and after that, we should thank Him for hearing us and answering our prayers! No matter what we pray for, thanksgiving should always go with it. A good habit to develop is starting all of our prayers with thanksgiving. An example of this would be: "Thank You for all you have done in my life, You are awesome and I really love and appreciate You."

> Everything we ask God for should be preceded and accompanied by thanksgiving—and after that, we should thank Him for hearing us and answering our prayers!
>
> ->- • -<-

I encourage you to examine your life, to pay attention to your thoughts and your words, and to see how much thanksgiving you express. Do you gripe and complain about things? Or are you thankful? If you want a challenge, just try to get through an entire day without uttering one word of complaint. I like what Madame Guyon said, which was basically that "even a sigh indicates we are unhappy with our lives." Develop an attitude of thanksgiving in every situation. In fact, just become outrageously thankful—and watch as your intimacy with God increases and as He pours out greater blessings than ever before.

SUMMARY

Praise, worship, and thanksgiving are some of the simplest prayers we can pray, and yet they are powerful spiritual dynamics. They are types of prayer because they are expressions of our hearts toward the Lord. When we praise, worship, or give thanks, we are talking to God—and that's all prayer really is.

Praise, worship, and thanksgiving enhance and empower our prayer lives because they keep our hearts focused on the Lord instead of on ourselves. They allow us to connect with God in passionate ways and to encounter His presence in our everyday lives. We do not need to wait for a church service or a corporate gathering in order to experience or express praise, worship, and thanksgiving; we can incorporate them into everything we do, all day long.

Prayer Points

→→ Praise, worship, and thanksgiving are types of prayer because they are all ways in which we communicate with God.

→→ Simply stated, praise is our response to God for what He has done, is doing, and will do; worship is our response to who God is. Thanksgiving is a grateful acknowledgment of both God's character and of all the things He has done, is doing, and will do.

→→ Praise releases power in the spiritual realm and it is a form of spiritual warfare that always leads to victory.

➤➤ The Bible never defines worship, but it does show us how worship works. We worship God when we pour out our hearts to Him in a deep, personal, intimate way that reflects our passionate devotion, gratitude, and love for Him.

➤➤ Worship is more than singing songs; it is a condition and a posture of the heart.

➤➤ Complaining, faultfinding, grumbling, and murmuring are dangerous because they open a door for the devil to work in our lives. But thank God, praise keeps that door closed.

➤➤ The Lord is always doing awesome things for us and He is always faithful. We need to be thankful people, continually expressing our gratitude to Him in every situation.

6

Consecration and Commitment

As you have already read, Ephesians 6:18 says, "Pray at all times (on every occasion, in every season) in the Spirit, with all [manner of] prayer and entreaty." We have addressed praying at all times; we have looked at what it means to pray in the Spirit; and we are now in the midst of several chapters on different types of prayer, or as Paul refers to them, "all manner of prayer."

If we pray at all times in the Spirit, we will soon realize that the Holy Spirit will take us through various seasons in our prayer lives; and there are different types of prayer for those seasons. Praise, worship, and thanksgiving are types of prayer that we offer daily, as well as on specific occasions. They are very valuable as spiritual warfare against the devil as a means of keeping our own spirits light and free. Praise prevents heaviness or depression and discouragement. Praise and worship do honor God, but there are times we need to engage in other kinds of prayer for other reasons. I want to continue now by sharing with you about prayers of consecration and commitment, which might also be called "hands-off" prayers because they result in giving our *selves* to God (in the prayer of consecration) and giving our *situations* to God (in the prayer of commitment).

THE PRAYER OF CONSECRATION

I love to lift up my hands in the morning and pray the prayer of consecration found in Psalm 25:1, which says, "Unto You, O Lord, do I bring my life." Those words really define consecration— complete, voluntary surrender to the Lord. In a prayer of consecration, you are saying to Him: "Here I am, God. I give myself to You. Not just my money, but myself. Not just one hour on Sunday morning, but myself. Not just a portion of my day, but myself. Not just my relationships with my 'church friends,' but myself. Unto You, O Lord, do I bring my *entire* life. I lay it on Your altar. Do what You want to do with me. Speak through me today. Touch people through me today. Go places on my feet today. Make a difference in my world through me today. Here's everything about me; here are all the resources You have loaned me; I am not an owner; I'm a steward. Whatever You have let me use, God, really belongs to You, and if You need any of it back, I want to make it all available to You today." That is what we mean when we say, "Unto You, O Lord, do I bring my life." That is what we mean by *consecration*.

When we consecrate something, we set it apart for God's use. Therefore, when we consecrate our lives, we turn our backs on our fleshly desires, worldly values, carnal thinking, undisciplined living, bad habits, and on everything else that does not agree with God's Word. We intentionally put distance between ourselves and ungodly things so that we are prepared and available for God to use us. E. M. Bounds defines consecration as "the voluntary set dedication of oneself to God, an offering definitely made, and made without any reservation whatsoever. It is the setting apart of all

> When we consecrate something, we set it apart for God's use.
>
> ⤐ • ⤏

we are, all we have, and all we expect to have or be, to God first of all."[1] Consecration is not easy, but it is worth the discipline and the sacrifice.

When we consecrate ourselves to the Lord, we should be conscious of giving Him everything that we are, but we should also know that we are giving Him everything that we are not. God shows Himself strong and often most effective in our weaknesses, so we do not need to feel that we must hide them from Him. He knows everything about us and loves us unconditionally, so hold nothing back from Him, not even your weaknesses. Let go of everything as an offering to your Lord and you will be amazed at how free you will feel.

It's Serious Business

Before we go any further with the idea of consecration, I want to make sure you understand that consecrating or dedicating your life to God is not something to be taken lightly. The prayer of consecration is a serious prayer and when it comes from a serious heart, there are serious results. What I mean by "serious results" is that when we say to God, "Take everything about me and do what You want to do in my life," God goes to work. As we know, we all have weaknesses in our lives; so when we consecrate ourselves,

God begins to deal with those things. You see, what we give to God belongs to God, and if He is going to use us, He will need to do a work on the inside of us—and we have to let Him do it.

Consecration is a process and it takes time. The prayer of consecration is simply an invitation for God to change, rearrange, and purify us. When God prepares us for His use, He often starts by cleansing us of the things that do not honor Him, such as improper thought patterns or bad attitudes or habits.

For example, we all know people who have trouble keeping their mouths shut. I can write about this, because I used to be one of them! When those people pray a heartfelt prayer of consecration, God may begin to deal with them in the area of their speech. They will discover that they cannot get away with saying things they once said. They will find themselves more aware of their words so that they can be more careful about what they say. Over time, they will learn to speak in ways that edify and encourage others and honor God. Other people have other problems, and God deals with whatever He needs to deal with in order to make us ready to be used for His purposes.

One way God may need to deal with us is to separate us from some of the people in our lives. For example, we may depend on a friend too much, so much in fact that we do not lean on the Lord as we should. If we cannot maintain balance in relationships, then God will sever them so that we may belong to Him entirely.

Another area in which He may deal with us might be when we have a job or a position at church or in the community, a position that makes us feel important and secure. God wants us to be rooted in Him, not in our positions. He wants us to know we are valuable because He loves us, not because we have a certain title or role to play. God will remove things we cannot keep in balance.

Having friends or positions is not wrong. In fact, God desires that we enjoy both, but He does not want us to depend on them too much. Everything in this world can be shaken and changed in a moment of time, only God never changes. He wants us to depend first and foremost on Him so that we don't get hurt and disappointed by people and things if they should change when we least expect it.

I had a personal experience that is a perfect example of what I am trying to say: I once had a group of friends who meant a great deal to me. I thought they would always be faithful and never hurt me. I also had a staff position at a church, where I taught Bible college and weekly Bible classes. I was well-known in that church and was an integral part of all the inner workings of that organization. I had my little group of friends and my position and I felt good about myself because of them. I did not realize I was overly depen-dent on them or that I was getting my worth and value from them until suddenly I lost both.

My friends did what I thought they would never do. They turned against me and falsely accused me of some terrible things. About the same time, the Lord made it very clear that I was to leave my posi-tion at the church. I felt I had lost everything! I did not understand why it happened or what was going on in my life, but eventually God showed me that what happened was actually part of His answer to my prayers of consecration.

I asked God to take all of me; I gave myself to Him, and I was sincere. I just wasn't expecting some of the

> The process of consecration is not usually comfortable or easy, but it is always good and the benefits are amazing.
>
> ->>- • -<<-

results. There were things in God's way and He had to move them. At first, I was lonely and hurt, but eventually I began to see that my security and value were rooted in my friends and church position and that God actually did me a huge favor in removing them.

If you pray the prayer of consecration, you can expect the fire of God to come and cleanse you and your life. The process of consecration is not usually comfortable or easy, but it is always good and the results are amazing.

Full Consecration

Christians become dangerous to the enemy when they start living consecrated lives that are fully dedicated and sold-out to God. This kind of devotion means we give God everything; we cannot hold anything back. As you know by now, when we consecrate ourselves, everything about us becomes fair game for God to deal with.

If we really are serious about being set apart for God's use, we must ask ourselves if there are any areas of our lives in which we are holding out on God. What little, hidden secret places do we have in our hearts? What are the things about which we say, "Well, God, You can have everything but *that*," or, "Oh, no, God! I'm not ready for *that*!" or, "God, just don't touch *that* relationship yet," or, "Lord, just don't ask me to quit doing *that*"? Full consecration is not saying, "Lord, I'll read my Bible every day; I'll memorize verses and hide Your Word in my heart and pray many hours a day, but please do not ask me to give up my one little favorite vice!" No, full consecration is saying and meaning with all of your heart: "I give myself—entirely—to You, Lord."

I don't mean to sound as if we should expect God to take everything we enjoy away from us, because He won't do that—but everything must be available to Him. He must make the choices about what is really good for us and what is not; our job is to trust Him completely.

God's primary goal in our lives is to make us like Jesus. Romans 8:29 says that He wants us *"to be* conformed to the image of His Son" (NKJV), which means that He wants us to continue to become more like Jesus in our thoughts, in our words, in the way we treat other people, in our personal lives and in our actions. Becoming like Jesus does not happen overnight. It requires a process of consecration and it means that our soulish, carnal, fleshly tendencies have to be eliminated.

Romans 12:1 reads: "I appeal to you therefore, brethren, and beg of you in view of [all] the mercies of God, to make a decisive dedication...." This means that we have to make a choice—a deliberate decision—to give ourselves to God. God has given us a free will, and the only way we will ever belong to Him is to give ourselves freely to Him. He will never force us to love Him or serve Him. He will lead us, guide us, and prompt us, but He will always leave the decision to surrender up to us. God created human beings, not robots, and He will not try to program us to behave a certain way because He has given us the freedom to make our own choices— and He wants us to choose Him. He wants us to lay our lives willingly on the altar every day and say, "God, Your will be done, and not mine." That is one of the most powerful prayers we can pray when we really mean it. It is short and simple, but it represents the kind of full surrender God requires. If God has been dealing with you about anything, I encourage you not to put off surrendering it any longer. In your thoughts, you may intend to surrender at some later time, but remember that good intentions do not equal obedience—and obedience is what God requires.

Present Your Members to God

Paul continues in Romans 12:1 and exhorts us to "make a decisive dedication of your bodies [presenting all your members and faculties]." If we really dedicate our bodies to God, we cannot lie on the couch all day and eat donuts and watch soap operas and think we are living consecrated lives. In order to live consecrated lives, we need to get up in the morning, get out our Bibles, spend time with God, and dedicate ourselves to Him. When we see our bodies as gifts to the Lord and instruments that He wants to use, we will not abuse our bodies; we will not continually fill them with junk; we will not deprive them of proper rest. We will dress appropriately, in ways that honor God; we can dress fashionably *and still* dress appropriately. We must remember that we represent God, not the world.

In order to obey Romans 12:1, we will also need to choose to give the Lord our "members and faculties." In other words, we offer Him our minds, abilities, and emotions. We should not let the devil use our minds. The human mind is his favorite battleground and he will fire thoughts at us all day long. Most of the time, they will be sly, subtle, and deceptive thoughts so that we will find them easy to believe. He will lie and accuse and tell us anything he can think of to steal our joy, rob our peace, and make us feel rotten and unworthy. He fills our minds with ungodly thoughts about other people. We cannot stop him from sending thoughts our way, but we can resist, rebuke, and fight back. Attacking God's people is a way of life for the devil, so prayer also needs to be a way of life for us. To be honest, there are days when I have to cast down a dozen thoughts just in the time it takes to put on my makeup! But, thank God, I know how to do it. One of the best ways I have learned to combat the devil when he gives me wrong thoughts about someone is to begin to pray for that person immediately. When we fill our thoughts with right things, the wrong ones have no room to enter.

> The Word of God gives us power to resist the enemy.
>
> ─➤ • ◂─

How do we stop the lies of Satan? We need to do what Jesus did; open our mouths and say, "It is written..." Then we need to quote a Bible verse that proves what a liar the devil is. For example, if he is telling lies about a certain person, refute those lies by saying, "The Bible says that love believes all things and hopes all things. I am walking in love, and love always believes the best of every person. I have no proof that so-and-so is like that, and I am not going to believe it, devil." The Word of God gives us power to resist the enemy. For example, when the devil tries to tell me my future is dim, I quote Jeremiah 29:11, which states that God has a good plan for my future. One of the reasons we learn the Word is so that we can defeat Satan with it. It is our offensive weapon against him, and we must use it.

When we consecrate our "members and faculties" to the Lord, we also give Him our abilities, our skills, and our talents. Many people use their abilities at work, which means that their professional lives—their integrity on the job, their time management, their stewardship of company resources, and the way they treat their coworkers—should bring Him honor. We need to see ourselves as working for God, instead of working for a boss. We need to go to work every day with the determination to do everything right, with excellence.

If a person goes to work every day and surfs the Internet when no one is watching, he or she is stealing. That is no different than going into the accounting department and taking money. If people have agreed to work a specific number of hours a day for a certain wage, then they need to keep their commitment. We should not try to get away with things we are not supposed to be doing when no one is looking; we should not try to figure out how we can leave early or cut corners without being noticed. People whose lives are consecrated to the Lord know that He is always watching, they are aware that they are living their lives in His presence and they want to please Him with their thoughts and with their actions. They want to live in the light, before God, and to obey Colossians 3:23, which basically says, *Whatever you do, do it unto the Lord with all of your heart, knowing that you will get your reward from God and not from man.*

Here to Make Him Happy

Doing everything unto the Lord with all of your heart is one mark of a consecrated life. It is one way to say, "God, I belong to You." The greatest revelation I could impart right now is that you do not belong to yourself. First Corinthians 6:19–20 says, "Do you not know that your body is the temple (the very sanctuary) of the Holy Spirit Who lives within you, Whom you have received [as a Gift] from God? You are not your own, you were bought with a price [purchased with a preciousness and paid for, made His own]. So then, honor God and bring glory to Him in your body."

We have been bought with a price—the blood of Jesus Christ. God purchased us for Himself, we do not belong to ourselves, and if our lives are consecrated to God, we have deliberately laid down any rights we thought we had. We are not here on earth so that God will have people to please. His job is not to make us happy. On the contrary, we are here to serve Him and to make Him happy and to carry out His purposes on earth. Personally, I cannot think of a greater privilege, nor can I imagine doing anything that would make me happier than fulfilling the call of God on my life.

Some people are so afraid no one else will make them happy that they think they have to do it all for themselves. They believe they have to take care of themselves because no one else will. But the truth is, God really will give us a life we enjoy and He will take care of us. That is what happens if we say, "God, I am not going to live to please myself. I am going to live to please You, believing that if I live for You and Your pleasure, You will take care of me and my happiness."

To the best of our ability, Dave and I have consecrated our lives to the Lord. We have done that in a general, big-picture sense, and we do it regularly in the specific matters we face on a daily basis. We want everything about us to belong to God. We work hard. We travel all the time. We pour our hearts out to other people, and do you know what? God takes such good care of us! He meets every need and makes arrangements for special things we could never, ever experience on our own or provide for ourselves.

For example, it is no secret that Dave loves golf. When we first started traveling, he was in golf leagues and had a Saturday-morning golf group and all sorts of activities that revolved around golf. But as part of consecrating his life to the Lord, Dave had to put his favorite sport on the altar. He had to go to the golf course all by himself when he wanted to play, because he was not home on the weekends when his friends played. That was a sacrifice for him, because golf was something he really enjoyed.

Now, years later, God has blessed Dave so much. He gets to play on most of the best golf courses in the world—often at no charge! He gets to play with some of the professionals, and sometimes they even send him new clubs or the latest golf gadget. Golf was difficult for Dave to give up for God, but he did it willingly. Now God is giving him things he could never have received if he had kept trying to take care of himself. When we give ourselves to Jesus, He gives us favor. Things begin to happen that amaze us and bring us great enjoyment!

Consecration brings blessing. It is an honor to give your life to the Lord; you do not do it to get blessed, but blessings do follow. Setting your life apart for God's use brings Him joy, and He, in turn, will take care of you and help you enjoy your life.

Give It Time

Just as Dave had to wait several years before he was able to play golf the way he does now, the process of consecration and the blessings of a consecrated life have a gestation period for all of us. When God is dealing with us and setting us apart for His use, we have to be patient. He does not waste time when working with us, but He takes as much time as is necessary to do a deep, thorough, lasting work in our lives. We need to be diligent to guard against "fleshly zeal," which means trying to "make something happen," trying to figure it out or trying to accomplish God's purposes in our own strength.

I have seen so many believers attempt to rush God or try to "help" Him as He works in their lives. I have done that myself— and that kind of striving in

> Even when our hearts are dedicated to God, we have to submit to His timing as He continues to purify us so that we can serve Him most effectively.
>
> ✦ • ✦

the flesh absolutely wears people out. Even when our hearts are dedicated to God, we have to submit to His timing as He continues to purify us so that we can serve Him most effectively. We may not understand His timing and we may even grow frustrated or impatient with it. If so, we have to keep our eyes on the prize. The Bible says we inherit through faith and *patience* (see Hebrews 6:12). We honor God when we consecrate our lives to Him, and in order to do that fully, we have to allow Him to take us through the process of consecration on the timetable of His choosing. When we have done so, we will reap rich rewards of His presence and power in our lives, and we will experience the indescribable blessing of being used by God.

I hope you see that the prayer of consecration is not to be prayed lightly without sincerity. But, if you do pray it sincerely, you will never be disappointed with the result.

THE PRAYER OF COMMITMENT

If you have ever met another human being, ever been in a relationship, ever tried to manage your money, ever held a job, ever tried to discover and fulfill God's purpose for your life or grow spiritually—then you have probably encountered some problems. Problems are a part of life, and when you get rid of one problem, you will most likely have another one right behind it! That is true for all of us, and even though we can develop and mature in our abilities to confront, endure, be steadfast, and live in victory, we will always be contending with one problem or another.

If you have problems, then the prayer of commitment is for you. What is the prayer of commitment? Simply put, it is giving our problems to God. It means committing things to Him, releasing the pressures and the problems of life and letting Him work everything out. If we will learn to commit our stresses and situations to God, we will enjoy our lives more, we will be more fun to be around, and we will be happier and more relaxed. God can do more in one moment than we can do through a lifetime of struggles. Nothing is too big for God to accomplish, and nothing is too small for Him to be concerned about. He cares about *everything* that concerns you, so give it all to Him and start enjoying your life.

Give It to God...

Most people respond to problems in a similar way: they immediately begin to try to solve the problem themselves. If that does not work, they pick up the phone to call a friend or someone else they think can fix the situation. But I like to say that we need to run to the throne before we run to the phone! As I wrote earlier in this book, prayer needs to be our first response to every situation.

When does God really begin to intervene in our lives? When we stop trying to live them for ourselves and according to our own good ideas. When does God begin to straighten out our problems? When we give up our attempts to solve them. When does God get involved in our situations? When we quit worrying about them. When does God give us answers? When we finally cease trying to figure everything out for ourselves. Psalm 37:5 says, "Commit your way to the Lord, trust also in Him, and He shall bring *it* to pass," and Proverbs 16:3 says, "Commit your works to the Lord, and your thoughts will be established" (NKJV).

Many times, our "works" are the things we "work" in our minds—our reasoning, our analyzing, and our attempts to figure out what is going on or what we should do. But God says that if we will commit our works to Him, our thoughts will be established. In other words, if we can get our minds to calm down, we will be clearheaded and God can give us ideas and strategies and directions. When we get the wrong thoughts out of our minds, God can give us the right thoughts. When we clear out the bad ideas, God can give us great ideas.

> What does it really mean to commit our ways to God? It means to "roll" them off us and "roll" them onto God.
>
> ⤞ • ⤝

The first step in the prayer of commitment is to stop worrying and reasoning and to commit our works (our thoughts) to the Lord. The prayer of commitment says to the Lord: "God, I give this to You. I give You this problem. I give You this situation. I give You this relationship. I completely release it and let it go. It is too much for me. I cannot handle it. I am going to stop worrying and stop trying to figure everything out—and I am going to let You take care of it. God, I also give myself to You because I can't do anything about myself, either. I give it *all* to you. I give you my weaknesses and problems. I want to change, but You have to change me." It was a great day for me when I finally learned that it was God's job to change me, and my job was to believe!

What does it really mean to commit our ways to God? It means to "roll" them off us and "roll" them onto God. The Amplified Bible expresses it beautifully in Proverbs 16:3: "Roll your works upon the Lord [commit and trust them wholly to Him; He will cause your thoughts to become agreeable to His will, and] so shall your plans be established and succeed." When we roll our problems and human reasonings on God, which means to trust them wholly—completely—to Him, then He changes our thoughts and makes them agree with His will. In other words, His thoughts become our thoughts so that we want what He wants. When that happens, our plans will succeed because they are in complete agreement with God's plans. So many times, we have problems because we try to resist God's will or we do not want to agree with His way, but when we roll those problems onto Him, we end up happy and blessed.

...And Don't Take It Back!

How would you feel if a friend were to give you a birthday present, perhaps a piece of jewelry, at a luncheon in your honor and then followed you home and said, "Oh, may I have that back for a while? I want to wear it tonight." You might think that was strange, but if she returned it the next day and said, "Thanks. It was just what I needed. I know it's yours, so I appreciate your letting me borrow it. I won't ask again," then you would probably tend to believe her. But, if she came back the next day and said, "Could I wear that piece of jewelry to a meeting today and then keep it for a party this weekend? I'll try to return it next week if I don't think of somewhere else to wear it," then you would wonder if she had really *given* it to you in the first place—and she would not have!

Once we have prayed, committed our situations to God, and truly given our problems to Him, we have to leave everything in His hands. But that is easier said than done. We all tend to take our problems back because we are afraid God won't do anything, or we do not think God is acting quickly enough, or we do not like the way He is handling things. Many of us give

> When our problems are resting in God's hands, we are not to go check on them!
>
> ✈ • ✈

our problems to God many times a day. I certainly do, but I have also been known to pray and say, "All right Lord, I put this person in your hands. I give You this situation." Then I walk away and the next thing I know, that person or situation is following me! I quickly find myself thinking about it again, worrying about it again, or the devil has given me a new idea about how to handle it!

How do we keep from taking back things we have already given to God? By learning to rest our cares in Him. The Amplified version of Psalm 37:5 says to roll our cares unto God, and then it says to "repose" each burden on Him: "Commit your way to the Lord [roll and repose each care of your load on Him]; trust (lean on, rely on, and be confident) also in Him and He will bring it to pass." The word "repose" means *to rest*. When something is resting, it should not be disturbed. When our problems are resting in God's hands, we are not to go check on them! We are to leave them alone. At the same time, we need to keep our minds at rest, being fully confident that God will do a masterful job handling what we have entrusted to Him.

First Peter 5:7 says, "Casting the whole of your care [all your anxieties, all your worries, all your concerns, once and for all] on Him, for He cares for you affectionately and cares about you watchfully."

Notice that this verse says we are to cast all of our anxieties, all of our worries, and all of our concerns *"once and for all."* That means we cannot take them back. Once we commit them to the Lord, it's hands off!

My husband's theme in life has been "cast your care." In the early years of our marriage, I worried and he enjoyed life. It made me angry that I had to take care of everything while he just enjoyed himself, but I finally learned that all of my worry was not accomplishing anything good. Instead, it gave me headaches, backaches, neck aches, stomachaches, made me nervous and grouchy, but did nothing beneficial. After years of tormenting myself with worry and anxiety, I finally learned to cast my care also. Actually, I learned that God does not take care of us until we cast all of our care onto Him.

When we are tempted to pick up our problems again in our minds or tempted to try to do something about them in some natural way, we have to stop and say, "No! I can't think about that. I've given it to God once and for all—and I will not take it back! I am not going to try to do anything about this!" We have to refuse to revisit what we commit to God, because that's what the prayer of commitment really means.

SUMMARY

There is no way for us to live as victorious, overcoming Christians apart from trusting God with our lives. When we pray the prayer of consecration, we choose to give ourselves, our entire beings, and everything about us to God. This includes making an intentional decision to give Him our bodies, our minds, our abilities, our weaknesses, and our attitudes and motives. When we give ourselves to Him in this way, we also invite and allow Him to deal with each of those areas in ways that make us holy and more conformed to His likeness.

When we pray the prayer of commitment, we are releasing our problems and concerns to God, trusting Him to take care of them. Once we give our cares to Him, we cannot take them back. God has not designed us to be packhorses for our problems, but He has created us to be able to roll them over onto Him. We are in relationship with Him; He is our Father and our friend; and He is the only one who takes care of every situation.

The prayers of consecration and commitment will bring great freedom to your life, so I encourage you to pray them and pray them often. And remember: nothing is too big and nothing is too small. Pray about everything!

Prayer Points

➤➤ Prayers of consecration involve giving ourselves to God and prayers of commitment involve giving our situations to Him.

➤➤ The prayer of consecration is a complete, willful surrender of ourselves and everything about our lives to the Lord. It means holding nothing back from God and making a deliberate decision to let Him deal with anything He wants to deal with in our lives.

➤➤ Consecration involves not only our bodies, our behavior, and our words, but also our thoughts, attitudes, and motives.

+→ It is an honor to live a consecrated life. It is not always easy, but it does bring blessings we could never imagine.

+→ When we pray a prayer of commitment, we are giving all of our problems to the Lord. The prayer of commitment comes when we realize we cannot run our own lives, control other people, or figure everything out. It means letting God be in charge. When we really commit our problems to God, we cannot take them back; we cannot worry about them; we cannot keep reasoning about them in our minds. We roll them onto God and leave them there.

7

Petition and Perseverance

It seems like everybody, everywhere, wants something. It is hard to find a person who is thoroughly satisfied and cannot think of a single thing to wish for. The Bible says that we have not because we ask not (see James 4:2), and when we want something from God, we are to ask Him for it. The type of prayer we pray when we make requests is called a prayer of petition—and this kind of prayer is important. You see, we partner with Him through prayer. Prayer is simply the means by which we cooperate with Him and work with Him in the spiritual realm in order to get things done in the natural realm. Prayer brings the power of heaven to earth.

Sometimes our prayers seem to be answered quickly and other times we feel we need to persevere until God responds. In that case, we are praying prayers of persistence. God leads us to pray persistently not because He does not hear us the first time we pray, but because He is developing our faith and helping us build our spiritual muscles as we learn endurance through prayer.

One of the reasons we may need to persevere is that evil spirits can oppose the answers to our prayers. We find an example of this in Daniel 10, when Daniel fasted and prayed for twenty-one days until the answer to his prayer came. God sent the answer the first day Daniel prayed, but an evil spirit, the prince of Persia, was hindering the answer. As Daniel refused to give up and continued to pray, God sent Michael the Archangel to do battle with the prince of Persia and victory was secured. Daniel got his answer from God!

We need to petition God and make our requests known to Him and we also need to persist in prayer until the answers are manifest on earth. Both types of prayer are vital and necessary to an effective prayer life.

THE PRAYER OF PETITION

When we ask God for the things we want and need, we are praying prayers of petition. We probably pray this type of prayer more than any other and it is one of the ways Jesus instructed us to pray. He said in Matthew 7:7, "Ask, and it will be given to you; seek, and you will find; knock, and it will be opened to you" (NKJV). If nobody knocks, no doors open. If nobody seeks, nobody finds. If nobody asks, nobody receives.

Because we need to ask in order to receive, our petitions are very important. As we make requests of God, though, we do want to make

> When our requests are in balance with our praise and gratitude, petitioning God is awesome and exciting.
>
> ⤳ • ⤲

sure our petitions do not outweigh our praise and thanksgiving, because we do not need to be asking for more than we are thankful for. Remember that Philippians 4:6 instructs us to "be anxious for nothing, but in everything by prayer and supplication, with thanksgiving, let your requests be made known to God" (NKJV). When our requests are in balance with our praise and gratitude, petitioning God is awesome and exciting. It really is. It is awesome to ask God for something, believe Him for it, and then watch Him bring it to pass in our lives. We may know in our heart that we have received the answer and never need to mention it to God again or we may feel we have to persevere in prayer; either way, we can be sure that God loves to give; He loves to answer our prayers, in His wisdom and His timing and His way. So go ahead—ask!

Petition and Desire

Here's the way I believe petition needs to work. Let's say you're busy serving God; you are obeying His Word; you are seeking righteousness; you are truly seeking first the Kingdom of God, according to Matthew 6:33. The true cry of your heart is to treat people well, to live with integrity, to be wise, and to live in the center of God's will. Now, when a desire arises in you, what do you do? You mention it to God, saying something like, "You know, God, I really need a new car. I know You are good, Lord, and You want us to be blessed, so I pray that You make a way for me to have this car, because I don't see how I'm going to make it happen in my own strength." What do you do next? You go right back to serving God, living the way you were living, and you wait expectantly for God to help you get that new car.

Petition is usually based on desire. I believe that we have to desire something before asking God for it. I believe that God puts the right desires in our hearts, and that we have to know the difference between the desires of our flesh and the true desires of our hearts. I agree with Charles Spurgeon, who observed that, "[God] will direct your desires to the things for which you ought to seek. He will teach your wants...."[1] When God puts a desire within us, we are responding properly to say, "God, I want that," and the Bible says that God will give us the desires of our hearts if we delight ourselves in Him (see Psalm 37:4). But we also have fleshly, carnal desires, desires that are not God-given—and He does not promise to grant those. The proper way to respond to such desires is to release them, to simply let them go. Sometimes a prayer is not answered because our prayers are related to a fleshly desire and are not really being led or inspired by the Holy Spirit (see James 4:3).

We frequently discover that we cannot be certain if our desire is a desire of our heart or our flesh. When that is the case, I simply pray, "Lord, I am asking You for this, but if it is not right for me, then I trust You to do what is best for me." Since I know God is good and I know He loves me and wants good things for me, it would make no sense at all to persist in wanting something that God did not want me to have. Father always knows best!

We need to follow the Holy Spirit as we pray about what we want. We need to allow Him to teach us how to handle our desires, especially when they do not come to pass as quickly as we would like. We must not let a desire get out of balance and become an obsession, and that can happen when our desires are not submitted to God. When a desire for something becomes so strong that we think we cannot be happy without it, that desire has turned into lust—and lust is sin. There is nothing on this earth we cannot be happy without as long as we are in Christ and as long as He really is our joy. Personally, I work toward not allowing any desire to control me and I refuse to lust after anything because I know that whatever God asks me to do without, He will more than compensate for with His presence in my life.

Let me give you a practical example of what it looks like for a desire to get out of control. There are some single women who can hardly think about anything but getting married. They keep telling God, "I have to be married. I have to be married." They ask their prayer group to get into agreement with them, and during the prayer time, everybody asks God to send them husbands. They ask for prayer over and over in this same area. They talk about it all the time. They get depressed and discouraged about it. They have made a decision that they absolutely cannot be happy unless they are married. Do you know what? Those people may stay single forever, and if not, they may end up with someone who makes them wish they were!

There is certainly nothing wrong with a single person saying, "Lord, I'm lonely, and I'd really like to have somebody with whom I can share life. And I am asking that You would bring the right person. I want to be married," or "I need friends." Sure, it's okay to pray about those things, but we need to be diligent to avoid becoming fixated on one desire and allowing it to become the entire focus of our lives. Focus on serving God and obeying Him. Focus on being a blessing to others and you can be sure that whatever God's will is for you will come to pass at the right time. You won't have to struggle, be frustrated or upset. You can enjoy where you are on the way to where you are going.

I am sharing this with you because I really want to help you live a victorious life, and I do not want you to make the same mistakes I have made. I once allowed my desires for my ministry to become inappropriately important to me. All I cared about—and all I prayed about—was my ministry. True, God put a burning desire in my heart to impact people and to preach His Word. A thriving, effective ministry for me was His desire, but I let my own desire for it get out of balance. As a result, I began to pursue what God had given me more diligently than I pursued Him.

Let me share another example. Dave and I have children. If, when we had our first baby, I had stopped paying attention to Dave, he probably would not have wanted me to have more children. But because my relationship with him was deepened because of that baby, then he wanted me to have more if I wanted them.

> God wants us to have anything we can handle—as much of it as we can handle—as long as we keep Him first in our lives.
>
> ⤙ • ⤚

God is the same way. If He gives us something and it separates us from Him, then He will not want to give us anything else. But if God gives us something, and it deepens our relationship with Him, inspiring us to love and worship Him even more than we did before, then He is not bothered by what we ask for. God wants us to have anything we can handle—as much of it as we can handle—as long as we keep Him first in our lives.

At the same time, we are not always smart enough to know the right things to ask for. Jesus said that if we ask for bread, He will not give us a stone, and if we ask for fish, He will not give us a scorpion (see Matthew 7:9,10). But do you know what? Sometimes we think we are asking for bread, when, in reality, we are asking for a stone. In other words, we may be asking for something that we truly believe is right, but God knows that if He were to grant that request, it would be the worst thing He could ever give us. We have the ability, in all innocence, to ask for something that is potentially dangerous without even realizing it. In that case, we need to be glad God does not give it to us! Sometimes we may be asking for something or for a certain person to come into our life, and little do we know that if God said "yes" to that request, it would be like letting a serpent into our house. So we have to trust God enough to say, "You know, God, I have the confidence to ask You for anything. But I don't want anything that is not Your will for me. And I trust You, God. If I don't get it, I will know that the timing is not right or that You have something better for me and I simply have not thought to ask for it yet. But I am not going to get a bad attitude or go pout because You are not giving me everything I want."

We are God's children, and He wants us to be blessed. He wants us to have not only what we want, but what is best for us. We always need to keep that in mind when we pray prayers of petition. If we truly trust God, we must trust Him when He says "no" to our requests as much as we do when He says "yes."

King David wanted very much to build a house for God. God told him that he would not build the temple, but that his son would. David did not have a bad or even a sad attitude. Instead, he got busy helping by giving and collecting finances and supplies from others for the building of the temple.

If God won't let you do or have exactly what *you* want, find out what He does approve of and get busy doing that. Don't spend your life being confused because you do not understand God's ways. We are not meant to understand God; we are meant to trust Him. There is no such thing as trust without some unanswered questions in our lives.

Come Boldly

Romans 8:26 says, "...for we do not know what prayer to offer nor how to offer it worthily as we ought...." Sometimes we do not approach God with confidence because we feel so worthless or condemned or ashamed. Sometimes we do not think He really wants to help us, which is another manifestation of feeling worthless. Some people only pray on days when they think God should approve of them because they have been "good" that day! All of these ideas are lies of the enemy. True, we do not know how to offer our prayers worthily in our own strength, but we do not go to God in our own strength; we go to Him in the righteousness of Jesus Christ. Because Jesus has made us righteous, the Holy Spirit intercedes for us (see Romans 8:26). That, coupled with the fact that Jesus lives to intercede for us (see Hebrews 7:25), should convince us that God will indeed hear our prayers and should give us the courage to approach Him with confidence.

We do not need to tap on heaven's door, walk into His presence with our heads down, saying, "Umm, excuse me, God. Ummm, sorry, but do You have a second? I won't take long, I just wanted to ask You for—well, forget it—well, okay, if You don't mind, could You possibly help me?" No, we need to be secure enough in our relationship with Him to approach Him with boldness. I'll never forget the woman who asked me to pray for her one time. When I agreed, she stopped, looked at me sheepishly, and weakly asked,

"Could I ask for two things?" I assured her that God would be glad to hear all of her requests and that He was not counting.

Approaching God boldly in prayer can be likened to going to a bank to make a withdrawal. If I know that I have fifty dollars in the bank because I deposited it there last week, I will not hesitate to pull up to the drive-through window and cash a $50 check. I know I have the money, it's mine, and I can get it out of the bank if I want to. When I present my check, I fully expect to get my $50. We need to approach God with that same kind of boldness. We need to understand what is available to us because of Jesus and we need to pray confidently, with full expectation that we will receive what belongs to us. God has made incredible provision available to us in Christ and we simply need to ask for the blessings He has already purchased for us. When we struggle with feelings of unworthiness, all we need to do is ask the Holy Spirit to help us, because "the Spirit Himself bears witness with our spirit that we are children of God, and if children, then heirs—heirs of God and joint heirs with Christ..." (Romans 8:16–17, NKJV).

Because we are children and heirs of God, we can do exactly as Hebrews 4:16 says and "fearlessly and confidently and boldly draw near to the throne of grace (the throne of God's unmerited favor to us sinners), that we may receive mercy [for our failures] and find grace to help in good time for every need [appropriate help and well-timed help, coming just when we need it]." One of the main reasons people do not pray and are reluctant to ask God for what they need and want is that they do not feel worthy. They do not feel good about themselves; they do not feel that they are spiritual enough; they do not really think God would listen to them anyway. They are not sure whether or not they have a right to ask God to bless them, because they have "been bad." This happens when they have not grasped the reality of His forgiveness and grace, which allows His blessings to flow even when they have made mistakes.

When we pray prayers of petition, we must understand our position as sons and daughters of God who are made righteous through the blood of Jesus. You see, we so often think our righteousness is based on doing things "right"—saying the "right" words, behaving the "right" ways, or having the "right" attitude. The truth is that we cannot make ourselves righteous. We can make ourselves religious, but we cannot make ourselves righteous. Righteousness has nothing to do with doing everything right; it has to do with the fact that Jesus shed His blood so that we could be cleansed of our unrighteousness. We are only right with God through the blood of Christ. If we will believe that, then we will begin to express that righteousness in our lives, but until we believe it, we will not display it or approach God on the basis of it.

> When we pray prayers of petition, we must understand our position as sons and daughters of God who are made righteous through the blood of Jesus.
>
> ⟶ • ⟵

Throughout the New Testament, we read about the fact that Jesus makes us righteous. Just take a look at some of them:

- "For our sake He made Christ [virtually] to be sin Who knew no sin, so that in and through Him we might become [endued with, viewed as being in, and examples of] the righteousness of God [what we ought to be, approved and acceptable and in right relationship with Him, by His goodness]" (2 Corinthians 5:21).

- "Therefore, as through one man's offense *judgment came* to all men, resulting in condemnation, even so through one Man's righteous act *the free gift came* to all men, resulting in justification of life. For as by one man's disobedience many were made sinners, so also by one Man's obedience many will be made righteous" (Romans 5: 18–19, NKJV).
- "I do not set aside the grace of God; for if righteousness *comes* through the law, then Christ died in vain" (Galatians 2:21, NKJV).
- "For Christ *is* the end of the law for righteousness to everyone who believes" (Romans 10:4, NKJV).
- "Since all have sinned and are falling short of the honor and glory which God bestows and receives. [All] are justified and made upright and in right standing with God, freely and gratuitously by His grace (His unmerited favor and mercy), through the redemption which is [provided] in Christ Jesus" (Romans 3:23–24).

When I teach on righteousness, I like to use the following illustration, and I ask you to give it a try. Sit in a chair; then *try* to sit in the chair. I know that sounds silly, because you are already sitting in the chair. Once you are in the chair, you cannot get into it any more than you already are. The same idea applies to righteousness, except that we cannot do anything to make ourselves righteous. Jesus puts us in the seat of righteousness, and once we are there, we cannot do anything to try to get there again. In Him, we are settled in that place before God. Once we truly believe we are righteous before God because of the blood of Christ, we will begin to behave righteously. However, no number of right actions can ever make us right with God apart from Christ. Affirming this, the Apostle Paul prayed that he would be found and known as being in Christ, having no righteousness of his own, but only that right standing that comes through faith in Christ (see Philippians 3:9).

When we truly understand that we cannot do anything to make ourselves righteous and that we do not have to prove anything to God, we are able to rest in the gift of righteousness Jesus gives to us—and that will make us bold in our petitions and confident in God's desire to answer us. I know that God does not hear or answer my prayers because I am good; He hears and answers because He is good!

THE PRAYER OF PERSEVERANCE

The prayer of perseverance, which is also called the prayer of importunity, is prayer that does not quit. It's prayer that keeps on praying and does not give up. Sometimes you pray a few words or a few sentences one time and then go on about your business; that is not a prayer of importunity. At other times, though, a person or a situation keeps coming back to your heart and you just know you are not finished praying about it. When the Holy Spirit impresses something on you, over and over again, He is probably drawing you to continue to pray in a persistent, importunate way.

One way to persist may be simply to make your request known to God through a prayer of petition and then continue thanking Him for the answer until you see it. You have it by the faith in your heart, you know it will manifest, and each time you think of the situation, you simply say, "Thank You, Lord, that you heard my prayer and the answer is on the way. I know that You will not be late, not one single day." Your prayer of persistence may take the form of persistent thanksgiving.

Another way to persist in prayers is to respond to the "prayer assignments" God gives us. There are many people or situations I pray for once, and that is all. But I also believe God assigns us people to pray for until what He wants to do in them or for them is accomplished. I have prayed for one person, literally, for twenty-five years and will continue to do so until I die or until God releases me, or the person dies or what needs to happen comes to pass. There are actually times when I get tired of praying for this person, but it doesn't matter how I feel, I still find myself praying. I know God has given me this assignment and I will not give up! I believe God is using my prayers to help shape this individual's destiny.

> If God gives you an assignment to pray for someone or something, you will not have to "try" to work up a desire to pray; you will find that you cannot help yourself.
>
> ->> • <<-

There are other times when I feel that I "should" be praying for someone more than I do, but no matter how I feel, they just don't come to mind when I pray. I may also try to pray, but have no desire, or cannot find much to say, and even what I do say is dry and lifeless.

If God gives you an assignment to pray for someone or something, you will not have to "try" to work up a desire to pray; you will find that you cannot help yourself. You find yourself praying for them without even consciously planning to do so.

There are people who are assigned to pray for me. There are probably many I don't know of, but I do know of two. A woman in

Minnesota frequently tells me, "Joyce, you're my assignment." For that reason, she prays for me all the time. Another lady, who is a close personal friend, actually told me that she had taken on many new duties at her church and asked God if she could be released from praying for me all the time—and God would not release her. Her desire to pray for me remained so strong that she could do nothing but pray for me, or she was miserable. I am glad that God has assigned me to intercessors. I need a prayer covering over my life, and so do you.

Regarding prayers of importunity, Andrew Murray wrote: "O what a deep heavenly mystery this is of persevering prayer. The God who has promised, who longs, whose fixed purpose it is to give the blessing, holds it back. It is to Him a matter of such deep importance that His friends on earth should know and fully trust their rich friend in heaven, that He trains them, in the school of answer delayed, to find out how their perseverance really does prevail, and what the mighty power is they can wield in heaven, if they do but set themselves to it."[2]

In my own life, there have been things that I know are God's will because I can see them in His Word. When I pray about them and do not have a breakthrough, I go right back to God and say, "I'm here again. And God, I don't mean to sound disrespectful, but I'm not going to be quiet until I get a breakthrough. I'm not going away. I'm asking You again, Lord, and I am going to keep on asking until I see victory in this area." At times, we must be like the patriarch Jacob, who said to the Angel of the Lord, "I will not let You go until You bless me." God did indeed bless Jacob and said He did so because Jacob was a man who knew how to prevail with men and with God. In other words, Jacob was persistent and would not give up (see Genesis 32:24–28).

When I know God's will, I can pray accordingly and refuse to give up. When the answer does come, I see that perseverance really does prevail and I am encouraged by the mighty power I can wield in heaven through persistent prayer—and so can you.

The Widow Who Wouldn't Quit

One of the Bible's best examples of the prayer of importunity is in Luke 18:1–6:

"Also [Jesus] told them a parable to the effect that they ought always to pray and not to turn coward (faint, lose heart, and give up). He said, In a certain city there was a judge who neither reverenced and feared God nor respected or considered man. And there was a widow in that city who kept coming to him and saying, Protect and defend and give me justice against my adversary. And for a time he would not; but later he said to himself, Though I have neither reverence nor fear for God nor respect or consideration for man, yet because this widow continues to bother me, I will defend and protect and avenge her, lest she give me intolerable annoyance and wear me out by her continual coming or at the last she come and rail on me or assault me and strangle me. Then the Lord said, Listen to what the unjust judge says!"

Jesus' point in this parable is that if an unjust, wicked judge can be worn down, how much more will a just and loving God do for us if we refuse to give up? He will do exceedingly more than we can ever dream of—if we just don't quit. Even when circumstances appear hopeless or problems seem insurmountable, we can overcome if we press in and pray. Romans 8:28 tells us that "all things work together for good to those who love God, to those who are the called according to *His* purpose" (NKJV). This familiar scripture appears in the context of prayer, and I believe the point of this verse is that all things may not work together for good unless we continue to pray. If we will persevere in prayer, then no matter what happens in our lives, all things—no matter how bad the things may be—can work together in God's wisdom and turn out for our good as we keep praying as the situation unfolds.

Jesus said, "And will not [our just] God defend and protect and avenge His elect (His chosen ones), who cry to Him day and night? Will He defer them and delay help on their behalf? I tell you, He will defend and protect and avenge them speedily. However, when the Son of Man comes, will He find [persistence in] faith on the earth?" (Luke 18:7–8).

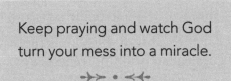

Keep praying and watch God turn your mess into a miracle.

How many lives could be radically different if people had continued to pray when tragedy struck instead of becoming bitter and giving up. Keep praying and watch God turn your mess into a miracle. God wants us to be determined in our prayers. He does not want us to give up on anything. In fact, when He returns to earth, He will be looking for faith that does not quit, prayer that keeps on praying, and people who refuse to give up.

Perseverance Brings Blessings

One reason we are able to persevere in prayer is that we know we will get an answer. We know that God is trustworthy, and that He will not leave us frustrated or our prayers unanswered. I was especially encouraged by this story of persevering prayer and I hope you will be, too.

John and Trish had children from previous marriages, but they believed God had spoken to their hearts and told them that they would have a child together. They prayed about this, and Trish became pregnant. The couple rejoiced over their good news, but soon that joy faded to mourning when Trish miscarried. The couple bounced back, standing on and praying the Word of God back to Him.

"God, you open and close the womb" (see Genesis 29:31, 30:22; 1 Samuel 1:5), John would pray. Trish would add, "Lord, Your Word says in Psalm 21 that when the king asked life from You, that You gave it to him, and You are not a respecter of persons." The couple was asking God for life, and they truly believed that God was going to give them just that—another life.

Soon Trish got pregnant again, only to miscarry a second time. They couldn't believe it. Again? Still, the couple prayed. And again, Trish was pregnant and miscarried a third time. People suggested adoption or simply quitting altogether, but John and Trish could not abandon the belief that God had spoken and promised they would literally have a baby, that Trish would give birth.

Once more, John and Trish conceived, and once more, Trish miscarried. One miscarriage can be hard enough, but four? With the support of their church's intercessors and their pastors, John and Trish continued to stand firm on what God had told them, and they continued praying Scriptures in circumstances that suggested they give up. And again, John and Trish conceived. Trish prayed fervently, "Faith is the substance of things hoped for, and the evidence of things not seen." This time, while praying, God impressed upon her heart Exodus 23:26 (NKJV): "No one shall suffer miscarriage or be barren in your land; I will fulfill the number of your days."

Faithfully, God answered John and Trish's prayer. Trish gave birth to Frances Faith, who is now a delightful testimony to God's goodness, a great blessing to her parents, and a great encouragement to everyone who prayed for them and watched them persevere in prayer.

Importunate, Not Repetitious

I want to make a distinction before we go any further. Importunate, persevering prayer is not the same as repetitive prayer, and I really want to encourage you to pray persistent prayers by the leading of the Holy Spirit—not repetitious prayers that do not come from your heart or that you only pray because you memorized them in Sunday school. It is possible to use your mouth to speak words of prayer that have no meaning behind them at all, and those prayers are nothing but dead works. I could quote the entire Lord's Prayer while I am thinking about something else.

Lip service doesn't do anything for God or accomplish anything in our lives, so even when we pray about the same thing—over and over again—we need to be careful not to fall into repetition. Instead, we need to allow the Holy Spirit to lead us in a fresh way, even when we are addressing a subject about which we have prayed for a long time.

As I previously stated, some people have assignments in prayer, and often the need to be persistent in prayer will accompany that assignment. Sometimes God

> In order to be effective in prayer, it is important for us to learn to discern when to press into more fervent prayer in a situation and when to release it.
>
> ➻ • ⤙

will assign you a person, and the Holy Spirit will put that person on your heart several times a day. That person will stay on your mind and you will have a supernatural energy or desire to pray for him or her often and sometimes very intensely.

We cannot decide what our assignments are. God chooses our assignments, so we need to learn how to be sensitive and obedient to God in this area and follow through. Anything that God energizes us to do is an assignment, even if only for a short time. The prayer of importunity may have less to do with how long we pray than with the determination with which we pray. We may have to pray a prayer of importunity for months or years, but then again, we might have to apply the same kind of determination to a prayer that God answers in a few days. Something or someone may be on our heart all day, for days at a time, or even for several hours one day.

In order to be effective in prayer, it is important for us to learn to discern when to press into more fervent prayer in a situation and when to release it. The fact that we want something really, really bad is not a reason to keep bombarding God with urgent prayers if He has already promised it and asked us to trust His timing. We should not allow our thoughts or emotions to determine what we are persistent about; instead, we are to be led by the Holy Spirit. We need to learn how to tell when there is an anointing (God's ability) on something and when there is not. Here's an easy way to know the difference: If God's anointing is on something, there is an ease to it; there is a flow; there is a grace to stay with it. You can sense the presence of the Holy Spirit as you pray about it. On the other hand, when we have to labor and struggle and strive to pray about a certain matter, there is not an anointing to pray about it.

When you sense the anointing of God on something in prayer, stay with it and don't stop until you sense Him leading you in another direction. Pray persistently every time He leads you to do so. God is infinitely kinder than that stubborn, old judge in Luke 18, and when He sees that you know His will and refuse to settle for anything less, He answers.

None of this means that prayer still cannot be simple. Just because we persist does not mean we have to get complicated. As we pray, we are partnering with God by giving voice to His will in the earth. Prayer requires a commitment; it can definitely be an effort, but does not have to be hard. Prayer is even considered by some to be work, and indeed it is. It is a work in the Spirit that accomplishes tremendous things in the earth.

SUMMARY

Many people pray more prayers of petition than any other type of prayer. God wants us to ask Him for what we need and He loves to bless us. However, we do need to make sure that our requests do not outweigh our praise and gratitude.

When we approach God with a petition, we need to do so with boldness and confidence in our position as His sons and daughters. On our own, we are not worthy to pray, but the blood of Jesus makes us totally righteous before God, so we never need to be timid or ashamed when we pray.

Some prayers require persistence—a persevering attitude that refuses to quit praying until God answers. Perseverance is not arrogant; it is a spiritual dynamic that requires spiritual strength. We must not be lazy in prayer. Sometimes, all God is looking for is someone who will ask—ask boldly and persist until the breakthrough comes.

Prayer Points

- Prayers of petition are prayers in which we make our requests of the Lord. It is awesome to pray and ask God for something, believe Him to do it and see it come to pass, but we need to balance our asking with praise and thanksgiving.

- God will give us the desires of our hearts if we delight in Him. We should not allow soulish desires to get out of balance. Instead, we should surrender our desires to God and let the Holy Spirit lead us as we make requests in prayer.

- Jesus makes us righteous. His sacrifice on the cross puts us in a right relationship with God. Therefore, we can approach God with boldness and confidence when we pray.

- The prayer of importunity is prayer that does not quit. It keeps knocking on the door of heaven with persistence and faith until an answer comes.

- Receive "prayer assignments" from God and let Him use you mightily to keep someone else in His will.

- Learn to recognize the anointing of the Holy Spirit on a specific prayer—a grace, a flow, an ease, and a sense of power as you pray about it. As long as the anointing is there, continue to persevere. When it lifts, release the matter and thank God for hearing and answering your prayer.

8

Intercession and Agreement

Prayer is a personal relationship, an intimate activity that takes place primarily between God and an individual. But, as believers, we do not exist in a vacuum. We are part of God's family; we are connected to the body of Christ, and part of the power of the Christian life is found in our relationships with other people. God uses them to sharpen us, to strengthen us, to help us, to celebrate with us, and to walk with us through the ups and downs of everyday life.

Just as our relationships are an important part of our social lives, they are equally or more important in our prayer lives. Sometimes we pray *for* the people around us and sometimes we pray *with* them. When we pray for them, we are praying prayers of intercession, and when we pray with them, we are praying prayers of agreement. Both types of prayer are extremely powerful and we need to understand them and know how to operate in them.

THE PRAYER OF INTERCESSION

Intercession is simply praying for someone besides yourself. It is crying out to God on someone else's behalf and taking their needs to Him in prayer. Intercession is one of the most important kinds of prayer because many people do not pray for themselves or do not know how. Why? Because they have no relationship with God. There are also times when circumstances are so difficult, stress is so high, the hurt is too great, things are so confusing, that people do not know how to pray for their own situations. And there are times when people have prayed and prayed and prayed for themselves and they simply have no strength left to pray.

There are all kinds of reasons people cannot or do not pray, but what is most important is when we encounter these people or become aware of a believer who cannot pray, we step in for them before

> I encourage you to draw nearer to God by joining Jesus in His ministry of intercession.
>
> ->>- • -<+-

God and pray on their behalf as the Holy Spirit leads. For example, I once visited a friend who was in the hospital suffering with cancer. She had fought a valiant fight and prayed like a warrior, but she reached a point where she was not strong enough to pray the way she wanted to and she said, "Joyce, I just *cannot* pray anymore." She needed her friends to pray for her—not just to *pray* for her, but to really pray *for* her—to pray in her place because she could not.

Both Andrew Murray and Watchman Nee write about intercession as a "priestly" function—as a believer's opportunity to participate in Jesus' ministry of praying for people. Watchman Nee says,

"We stand before the Lord to pray for other people. Actually this is fellowship with the Lord in His high-priestly function. How He Himself intercedes unceasingly for His people and their needs."[1] Andrew Murray writes that a priest "does not at all live for himself. He lives with God and for God.... He lives with [others] and for [others]. His work is to find out their sin and need, and to bring it before God, to offer sacrifice and incense in their name, to obtain forgiveness and blessing for them, and then to come out and bless them in His Name."[2]

I encourage you to draw nearer to God by joining Jesus in His ministry of intercession. Your family and friends need your prayers; your neighbors and coworkers need your prayers; the people of your church, your community, and the world need your prayers. We live in difficult days and we must pray for one another. Your intercession is the most powerful, most valuable gift you can ever give to those around you and it will make an eternal difference in their lives and in yours. There may be times when you are the only person on earth praying for someone else—and your intercession can change that person's entire life.

Standing in the Gap

A gap is a space between two things; it keeps two objects, two spaces, two entities, or two people from being connected to each other. When I preach in foreign countries, there is a gap between the audience and me. There may be a physical gap if I am on a platform; there may be a cultural gap; but I am most concerned about the language gap. If I want the people to understand me, I need a translator, someone to stand in the language gap for me so that I can communicate the message effectively. The translator has to work on my behalf so that the gap can be eliminated and the people can comprehend what I am saying.

Ezekiel 22:29–31 talks about standing in the gap—and I think this passage contains one of the saddest statements in the Bible: "The people of the land have used oppression and extortion and have committed robbery; yes, they have wronged and vexed the poor and needy; yes, they have oppressed the stranger and temporary resident wrongfully. *And I sought a man among them who should build up the wall and stand in the gap before Me for the land, that I should not destroy it, but I found none.* Therefore have I poured out My indignation upon them; I have consumed them with the fire of My wrath; their own way have I repaid [by bringing it] upon their own heads, says the Lord God" (emphasis mine).

God was basically saying, "I needed somebody to pray, and I couldn't find anybody who would, so I had to destroy the land." All He needed was *one* person to pray, and the whole land could have been spared. Do you see how important intercession is? Just one person could have made a major difference in an entire country and saved the entire place through prayer! We need to be willing to pray; we need to be sensitive to those times when the Holy Spirit is leading us to intercede and we need to obey. We never know when our prayer might be the very one needed to fill a gap and result in connecting God's power with a desperate situation.

God Changes His Mind

You can see from the story in Ezekiel that intercession is mighty and that one person's prayers could have saved many others. But do you know that intercession can also change God's mind? As a result of prayer, God can actually reconsider something He had planned to do.

Remember this story? "The Lord said to Moses, Go down, for your people, whom you brought out of the land of Egypt, have corrupted themselves; they have turned aside quickly out of the way which I commanded them; they have made them a molten calf and have worshiped it and sacrificed to it, and said, These are your gods, O Israel, that brought you up out of the land of Egypt!" (Exodus 32:7–8).

What happened was Moses went up Mount Sinai to get the Ten Commandments and was gone longer than the people wanted him to be. In the absence of their leader, they forgot the Lord, gave in to their fleshly desires, and decided to melt all their jewelry to make a golden calf and worship it. God spoke to Moses on the mountain and said, essentially, *You better get back down there, because the people have really gotten themselves in a mess. And I'm angry about it.* (Thank God, Psalm 30:5 says that His anger only lasts a moment, but His mercy is forever!)

The story continues: "And the Lord said to Moses, I've seen this people, and behold, it is a stiff-necked people; now therefore let Me alone, that My wrath may burn hot against them and that I may destroy them; but I will make of you a great nation" (Exodus 32:9–10).

It's a good thing Moses was a godly man, or he might have said, *Terrific idea, God! Forget about them, and do something great with me.* Instead, Moses began to intercede for the people because he cared so much about them. The Bible says, "Moses besought the Lord his God" (Exodus 32:11). That means he would not leave God alone. But God had already said, *Leave me alone. Don't come pray-*

ing, because if you do, I'm going to have to hear you. But Moses persisted: "Lord, why does Your wrath blaze hot against Your people, whom You have brought forth out of the land of Egypt with great power and a mighty hand?" (Exodus 32:11). Moses refused to give up because the issue was not settled in his heart. He loved the people; he knew the nature of God; and he knew the character of God. On top of that, he knew that God really loved the people and did not really want to leave them stranded.

So how did Moses approach this situation as He prayed and talked to God about it? He actually asked Him to change His mind (see Exodus 32:12) and basically said, *Now, come on, God. You don't want Your reputation to be ruined among the Egyptians. You don't want them to say that You aren't able to deliver Your people. You don't want them to think You just let Your people suffer and die out in the wilderness. Come on, God, this is not about us, this is about You. I'm just asking You, God, to deliver them, not for themselves, because they are really rascals, but for the sake of Your name. I really don't want Your reputation to be affected by all this, so, God, why don't You just go ahead and deliver them so that everybody knows You're great?* (see Exodus 32:12, 13).

The Bible says God changed His mind. Exodus 32:14 actually reads: "Then the Lord turned from the evil which He had thought to do to His people." That's part of the purpose and the power of intercession. We *can* make a difference when we pray!

Intercession Makes a Difference

Throughout this book, I hope you have been learning from various stories and examples how much power there is in prayer and what a great difference prayer makes in people's lives when we pray for them. Let me share one specific and very practical situation in my life in which intercession really made a difference. I was having great difficulty disciplining myself to exercise. I am normally a disciplined person, but I just could not seem to stay on a regular exercise program. Frankly, I hated it! Exercise was absolutely the worst kind of bondage for me. Now, of course, Dave has been exercising all of his life. So his great discipline was always lurking nearby, condemning me every day. On top of that, every doctor I went to wanted to know: "Are you exercising?" And I always had to say, "Well, no." Worst of all, I kept seeing more of my body move from where it was supposed to be to places it was definitely *not* supposed to be. When I looked in the mirror, I asked myself, "Where did Joyce go?" And when I finally realized I *was* the woman in the mirror, I asked, "What do we do about all this 'dimply' stuff?" The answer was always the same: exercise. So I groaned and grumbled and started all kinds of exercise programs, which only lasted until my muscles became sore. Then I would stop the program, because I did not enjoy intentionally making myself uncomfortable.

Then a very anointed friend of ours called me and said: "Joyce, I feel like God's put it on my heart to pray for you for one thing that you want personally—not anything to do with your ministry, just something you want."

Well, I know this man to be a powerful intercessor, so I thought: *I'm going to think this over carefully, because I'll probably get whatever he prays for.* I thought and thought and came to the conclusion that I would ask him to pray for me to be able to develop the discipline to exercise. I knew I needed to because I want to be around for the long haul. I want to be around to aggravate the devil until Jesus comes back! So I finally responded, "I want you to pray that I'll be able to discipline myself to stick with a good exercise program."

Simply sharing that weakness with that intercessor and saying, "I cannot discipline myself in this area" was incredibly powerful and very freeing. After he began to pray for me, I was able to exercise—consistently and in a disciplined way—for the first time in my life. Not long after I started, I even got to the point that I could say, "I'm beginning to actually enjoy exercising."

A Burden to Pray

Sometimes, as you are praying for others, you will get what is called a burden, or a prayer burden, or an intercessory burden. A burden is something that comes to your heart and feels weighty and important; it is something you cannot shake. Sometimes you do not even know what the burden is or you do not fully understand it; you only know that you *have* to pray.

I had a prayer burden not long ago. I was trying to watch something on television, a program I really

> A burden is something that comes to your heart and feels weighty and important; it is something you cannot shake.
>
> ➤➤ • ◄◄

wanted to watch. But I had a hard time concentrating on the show and just felt weepy. I could not figure out what was wrong with me, but my insides seemed to be saying, "Ugh!" So I turned off the television, lay facedown on the floor, and started to pray and weep before the Lord. Suddenly, a young lady came to my mind. I knew that she was going through a rough time, and for about fifteen minutes, I prayed and interceded and cried and prayed for her. Once I did that, after I prayed through it, the burden lifted. I got back up, watched my movie, and everything was fine.

Let me share something about a prayer burden: you cannot make it up and you cannot fake it. But if you try to ignore a prayer burden, you will not be able to find relief. If you have never experienced anything like what happened to me and you do find yourself with a prayer burden at some point, do not start wondering if something is wrong with you. God does not give me burdens like that often; most of my prayers are just simple, normal, ordinary prayers. On the other hand, some people seem to get a prayer burden every time they close their eyes. I have a good friend who is an intercessor, and every time she begins to pray, within five minutes, she is bawling like a baby. She has a different kind of call than I do, but I do not feel unspiritual when I pray with her. When God gives me a burden, I respond appropriately; but when He does not, I do not feel condemned or start wondering if there is something wrong with my spiritual life.

As intercessors, we must learn how to get our assignments from God, and know how to distinguish whether something is a real burden from God or not. Also, intercessors do not try to do what God has called someone else to do; they simply obey God by faithfully praying for the things for which God is calling them to pray and they stick with it until the burden lifts.

We all have the ministry of intercession, the responsibility to pray for others as God leads. Some people are called and especially gifted in the ministry of intercession and we might say that they stand in the spiritual office of an intercessor. They may pray for others many hours every day or several times a week. They often speak of God waking them up at night to pray. These people may experience things in prayer that others do not, but remember that

God is teaching us to pray as individuals. We don't have to be intimidated by someone else's experience in prayer.

Find Your Place in Prayer

Every believer is called to pray and intercede, but not everyone is called into the "spiritual office" of an intercessor. For example, I believe God has called Dave as an intercessor for America. He seems to have an "official" assignment from the Lord to pray for our country, a true burden for national issues and affairs, a longing to see revival in our land and a deep sustained interest in the things that concern the United States. He diligently studies American history and stays informed about what is going on in the government of our country. There is also an unusual fervency that accompanies his prayers. That's what I mean by a person who functions in the office of an intercessor.

Since 1997, I have watched Dave pray and cry and bombard heaven on behalf of the United States. I do not weep over our nation the way he does, but that does not mean I do not care or that I do not pray for our leaders. It simply means that I cannot force myself to have Dave's passion, because that passion is God-given. It also means that God is using Dave and me as a team; He has Dave playing one position and me playing another. If I start to wonder what is wrong with me because I do not intercede the way Dave does, I end up under condemnation—and that will keep me from fulfilling what God has called me to do. However, if I stay confident in my position and focus on being excellent in it, our team wins every time. God does not assign everything to everyone. The Holy Spirit divides things up the way He sees fit and all we need to do is our part.

When Not to Pray

Do you know that sometimes we can pray for someone and be opposing God's will? Believe it or not, there are times when we are not supposed to intercede for a person. God told Jeremiah in Jeremiah 7:16, "Therefore do not pray for this people [of Judah] or lift up a cry or entreaty for them or make intercession to Me, for I will not listen to or hear you."

Sometimes, through our prayers, we can protect people and keep the enemy away from them. But there are times when the enemy needs to get close enough to them that they have to go through something unpleasant because that difficulty is the very thing that will turn them to God. This is important, because the enemy wants us to think we are in sin if we are not praying for someone. He will use the fact that we are not interceding to heap condemnation on us and to keep us from praying the way God wants in that situation. That is why we must be led by the Holy Spirit. He may not tell us to pray for someone very often, but when He does, we need to know His voice, resist the enemy, and obey.

A Most Powerful Prayer

One of the most powerful prayers you can pray is a prayer for your enemies. If you want to see someone who is mighty in prayer, look for the person who will intercede for an enemy. I believe that God blesses us

> If you want to see someone who is mighty in prayer, look for the person who will intercede for an enemy.
>
> ->- • -<-

tremendously when we intercede for those who have offended or betrayed us.

Remember Job? He had to pray for his friends after they had really hurt and disappointed him. But immediately after he prayed, God began to restore his life. In fact, God gave him back twice as much as he had lost (see Job 42:10)! Praying for someone who has hurt us is so powerful because, when we do, we are walking in love toward that person and we are obeying the Word of God.

What does Jesus tell us to do in Matthew 5:44? He instructs us to pray for our enemies, saying, "Love your enemies, bless them that curse you, do good to them that hate you, and pray for them which despitefully use you, and persecute you"(KJV). When you think about the people who have used you, abused you, harassed you, and spoken evil of you, bless them; do not curse them. Pray for them. God knows that blessing your enemies is not easy and that you may not feel like doing it. But you don't do it because you feel like it—you do it as unto the Lord. Choosing to pray and bless instead of curse is so powerful in the spiritual realm, and God will do great things in your life as a result of it.

THE PRAYER OF AGREEMENT

When you have been praying about something and do not seem to be making any progress, you may need to get someone to pray in agreement with you. That kind of unity is a powerful spiritual dynamic, and according to Psalm 133, it is good and it garners God's blessing.

When two or more people come into agreement, Jesus Himself promises to be with them, and His presence exerts more power than we can even imagine in our lives and in our circumstances. He says in Matthew 18:19–20: "Again I tell you, if two of you on earth agree (harmonize together, make a symphony together) about whatever [anything and everything] they may ask, it will come to pass and be done for them by My Father in heaven. For wherever two or three are gathered (drawn together as My followers) in (into) My name, there I AM in the midst of them." God is also with us as individuals, but our power increases as we come together in unity and agreement. The Bible says that one can put one thousand to flight and two can run off ten thousand (see Deuteronomy 32:30). I like that kind of math!

Because God's blessing rests on unity and His presence is with those who agree in His name, the enemy works diligently to divide people, to bring strife into relationships, to provoke anger and jealousy, and to keep people at odds with each other. We need to understand the power of unity and agreement, and though we do need private times of intimate communion with God, we also need to exercise the power of praying in agreement with others.

Living in Agreement

The prayer of agreement is only effective when those who come into agreement in prayer are living in agreement in our natural, everyday lives. Living in agreement does not mean we cannot ever have our own opinions about anything, but it does mean that there is harmony, mutual respect, and honor in our relationships. It means there is an absence of the things that cause division and strife—like selfishness, anger, resentment, jealousy, bitterness, or comparison. Living in agreement is like being on the same ball team—everyone works together, supports and encourages each other, believes each other, and trusts each other as they all pursue the same goal and share the victory.

My husband, Dave, and I live in agreement. That does not mean that we never have differing opinions or that we never disagree about anything. It does mean, though, that we are committed to avoiding strife and division in our relationship, that we sometimes have to "agree to disagree," and that we honor and respect each other.

Likewise, I live in agreement with the people at Joyce Meyer Ministries. I am not intimately involved in every decision made, but I have communicated my heart to the people who work for us. When they make decisions, they do so in agreement with the vision that God has given and I have expressed to them. In this way, all of us are praying and working in agreement with the God-given purpose for the ministry, and we are experiencing great blessings and being used to bless others beyond anything we ever imagined.

Just as I want you to know what it means to live in agreement, I also want you to know what living in agreement is *not*. For example, we cannot gossip about the pastor all week and then ask him to agree with us in prayer for healing if we get a bad report from the doctor. We cannot scream at our children every day, nag them, or continually point out their faults and then say we will agree with them in prayer for a good grade on a test at school. We cannot talk behind a coworker's back and then ask that person to agree with us in prayer to keep our jobs when we know layoffs are imminent. We cannot fight with our spouse all the time, complain about them to our friends, and then, when they lose their job, say, "Well, let's just pray in agreement that you'll get another job soon." We cannot hold unspoken resentment toward a family member for years and then ask that person to pray in agreement for both of us to be mightily blessed when the time comes to read grandfather's will.

Maintaining unity and harmony does require effort, but the power released when people pray who live in agreement is worth it. God is honored when we commit to live in unity because He knows it is not always easy. Be a maker and maintainer of peace and you will be called a son of God (see Matthew 5:9).

Pray in Agreement; Pray to God

In Luke 18:10–11, we read about two men who went up to the temple to pray. One was a Pharisee and the other one was a tax collector. Jesus said, "The Pharisee took his stand ostentatiously and began to pray thus before and with himself: God, I thank You that I am not like the rest of men—extortioners (robbers), swindlers [unrighteous in heart and life], adulterers—or even like this tax collector here." Then he went on to list all of his good works.

What I like about this passage is that the Bible does not say the Pharisee was praying to *God*. It says he went into the temple to pray, but he prayed "thus before and with *himself.*" Here we read about a man who appeared

> Agreement is incredibly powerful, but it has to be pure, and it has to come from a place of humility.
>
> ⤞ • ⤝

to be praying, and yet the Bible says he was not even talking to God; he was talking to himself! I think sometimes we also pray to impress people, maybe even to impress ourselves. Let's be honest: we can be impressed with our own eloquence. When we are praying in agreement with someone else or with a group of people, we have to be very careful that we are not preaching to the other people and that we are not simply trying to sound superspiritual, but that our prayers are led by the Spirit and that we are really sharing our hearts with God. Agreement is incredibly powerful, but it has to be pure, and it has to come from a place of humility.

Multiplied Power

Jesus has promised that if two people on earth agree about something, God will bring it to pass (see Matthew 18:19). As I have already shared, He answers prayers of agreement when the people who are praying are already expressing agreement in their everyday lives. He so appreciates those who pay the price to live in agreement, unity, and harmony that He says to them essentially, "When you get together like that, My power is released among you. The power of your agreement is so dynamic that you're going to break through—no doubt about it. I'll do it."

You see, agreement is so powerful that it is a principle of multiplication, not addition. That is why the Bible says that one person can put a thousand to flight and two can do ten thousand (see Deuteronomy 32:30). If agreement were based on addition, one would put a thousand to flight and two would put two thousand. But unity commands God's blessing—and God's blessing brings multiplication. For that reason, the prayer of true agreement is a strong and mighty force in the spiritual realm.

Not long ago, I heard a story about a young man who prayed the prayer of agreement with the pastors of his church. It is a great testimony to the power of this type of prayer, and I believe it will both help you understand how to pray in agreement with others and encourage you to do so.

Alan was twenty-one years old when he felt in his heart that God wanted to send him a wife. To many, he was entirely too young to be thinking of such a commitment, but after talking with his pastors, they also agreed that it was the Lord who was leading him to believe for an answer to this request. He was walking in a close, accountable relationship with his pastors, practicing the principle of living in unity.

Because he understood and believed in the prayer of agreement, and to demonstrate that he was completely serious about his prayer, Alan called one of his pastors every day to pray for his wife. Alan prayed, "God, the Bible says that You put the single in families, and I am asking You to send me my wife in Your perfect timing."

On the other end of the telephone, his pastor would come into agreement with Alan's request. "Lord, I agree with Alan," he would say, "and Your Word says that if any two of you agree on earth about anything that they may ask, it shall be done for them by My Father who is in heaven. So, Lord, we agree and believe that Alan's wife will come quickly in Jesus' name."

Within six short weeks, God answered Alan's prayer. With uncanny certainty, he knew that his wife was to be a young woman he had met months earlier. Until that point, neither had any interest in the other, but after Alan and his pastor began to pray every day, feelings began to change in both Alan and the girl.

At first, they both dismissed it, as Alan was certain that surely the Lord would not answer so quickly. He expected God to send his wife months, if not years, later. Even so, he was still prepared to pray every day for his bride to come, but six weeks seemed a bit ahead of schedule! After rebuking the feelings for a time, both realized that truly God was leading them to wed. The two courted for seven months before they married.

Looking back, Alan directly connects their marriage to the nights where he faithfully called his pastor, and they agreed that God would send and bless a mate for him. The couple has now been married more than two years, are expecting their first child, and are serving God together wholeheartedly.

Let me be quick to say that everyone who prays the prayer of agreement for a spouse may not meet his or her mate as quickly as Alan did. Remember that Alan was asking God to bring his wife in God's perfect timing, and it just so happened that God chose to answer quickly.

All of us can experience the power of the prayer of agreement, just as Alan did. Personally, I have also experienced the power of agreement in many areas of my life and ministry. I know that the prayer of agreement is indeed a type of prayer that releases multiplied power, and I am believing that praying this way will have tremendous results in your life.

SUMMARY

As believers, we live as part of a family—God's family. Relationships are at the core of the Christian life and we are to help each other, encourage each other, share with each other, and bear each other's burdens. We are also to include one another in our prayer lives by praying *for* and *with* other people.

When we pray for other people, we are practicing a type of prayer known as intercession. When we intercede, we are also joining Jesus in His ministry and we are cooperating with Him as He intercedes in heaven for those of us on earth. Intercession can truly change the course of a person's life and we are privileged to be able to pray for the people around us. We never need to devalue the power of our prayers; just one person's prayers can make a major difference!

Not only can we pray for people, we can also pray with people in the prayer of agreement. Harmony in relationships leads to unity in prayer, which releases great power in people's lives and situations. Andrew Murray writes that "[God] gives us a very special promise for the united prayer of two or three who agree in what they ask."[3] That promise is the power, the comfort, and the guidance that is available in His presence as we pray. God's power, comfort, and guidance are available to you. He wants you to experience them in powerful and personal ways—and so do I.

Prayer Points

→→ Intercession is prayer for other people. When we intercede, we stand in the gap between God and another person.

→→ God can change His mind as a result of intercession.

→→ In intercession, let the Holy Spirit lead and cooperate with what He is doing in the lives of the people for whom you are praying. When you have a burden to pray, pray until it lifts. If you sense for some reason that you are not to pray about a situation, trust God in that and do not force yourself to pray.

→→ We all need to find our place in prayer and be faithful to fulfill the intercessory assignments God gives us.

→→ Some of the most powerful prayers we can pray are prayers for our enemies.

→→ A powerful spiritual dynamic comes into play when people who are living in agreement begin to pray in agreement.

➤➤ Living in agreement includes harmony, purity, honor, and humility in a relationship. It requires the absence of strife, jealousy, resentment, anger, and bitterness.

➤➤ The prayer of agreement brings the power of multiplication and the blessing of God into a situation._

9

The Word and the Spirit

In the past several chapters, we have examined several different types of prayer. Whatever type of prayer we pray—whether it is a prayer of consecration or commitment, petition or perseverance, intercession or agreement, praise, worship, or thanksgiving, God's Word is an essential ingredient. Our prayers are always effective when we "remind" God of His Word and pray in faith that He is able to perform what He has spoken.

I also believe that to be most effective, prayer needs to be "in the Spirit." As I mentioned in chapter 3, different groups of people throughout the body of Christ have different ideas about what "praying in the Spirit" means, but most Christians seem to agree that it means to allow the Holy Spirit to lead us as we pray instead of praying whatever we want to pray. I have a personal conviction about "praying in the Spirit," which I will elaborate on later in this chapter, but more than anything else, I believe that we all should endeavor to the best of our ability to let the Holy Spirit inspire and empower our prayers.

We need both the Word and the Spirit in our prayers in order to stay balanced and strong in our spiritual lives. If people seek supernatural experiences or even become excessive in spiritual matters, they may become deceived and be too emotional or even flaky. At the same time, if we focus on the Word without also being sensitive to the Spirit, we can become legalistic and dry. When we have the Spirit and the Word together, we can live solid lives that are balanced—grounded in truth and graced with joy and power. We need the solid foundation of the Word of God and we need the enthusiasm and excitement of the Spirit. Praying in agreement with the Word and praying in the Spirit keeps us praying according to God's will. It also causes our prayers to be effective and bears great fruit in our lives. Whatever you do, I encourage you to fill your prayers with the Word and let the Holy Spirit lead. You will see tremendous results.

PRAYING GOD'S WORD

Isaiah 62:6 instructs us to "remind" God of the promises He has made to us and one of the best ways to do that is to pray His Word back to Him. That verse says, "I have set watchmen upon your walls, O Jerusalem, who will never hold their peace day or night; you who [are His servants and by your prayers] *put the Lord in remembrance [of His promises], keep not silence*" (emphasis mine).

God's Word is extremely valuable to Him and should be to us as well. In fact, the Amplified Bible renders Psalm 138:2 as follows: "I will worship toward Your holy temple and praise Your name for Your loving-kindness and for Your truth and faithfulness; for You have exalted above all else Your name and Your word and You have magnified Your word above all Your name!" This verse indicates that God magnifies His Word even above His name. If He honors it to that extent, we need to make a priority out of knowing the Word, studying the Word, loving the Word, getting the Word deeply rooted in our hearts, esteeming the Word more highly than anything else, and incorporating the Word in our prayers.

When we honor the Word and commit ourselves to it, as I have just described, we are "abiding" in it. Jesus said in John 15:7, "If you live in Me [abide vitally united to Me] and My words remain in you and continue to live in your hearts, ask whatever you will, and it shall be done for you." As we can see from this verse, abiding in the Word and allowing the Word to abide in us is directly related to confidence in prayer and to having our prayers answered. When we pray the Word of God, we are less likely to pray for things not in God's will for us.

> Abiding in the Word and allowing the Word to abide in us is directly related to confidence in prayer and to having our prayers answered.
>
> ⇥ • ⇤

Andrew Murray writes, "Nothing can make strong men but the word coming to us from God's mouth: by that we must live. It is the word of Christ, loved, lived in, abiding in us, becoming through obedience and action part of our being, that makes us one with Christ, that fits us spiritually for touching, for taking hold of God."[1] He also says, "It is abiding in Christ that gives the right and power to ask what we will: the extent of the abiding is the exact measure of the power in prayer."[2] Jesus Christ is the living Word (see John 1:1–4), and as we abide in the Word, we abide in Him—and that brings unspeakable power to our prayers.

Word-Based Prayers

God's Word is such a treasure. It is filled with wisdom, direction, truth, and everything else we need in order to live purposeful, powerful, and successful lives. We need to incorporate the Word in our prayers, confessing it over every circumstance and situation. The word "confess" means *to say the same thing as*, so when we confess the Word, we are saying the same things God says; we are putting ourselves in agreement with Him. If we really want a deep and vibrant relationship with God, we need to agree with Him, and nothing will help us do that like confessing the Word. Our confession strengthens our knowledge of the Word and our faith in God, which increases the accuracy and effectiveness of our prayers.

In order to confess the Word, we need to know the Word, because we can only agree with God when we know what He has done and what He has said. I often encounter people who are asking God to give them something they already have or to make them something they already are, and I want to say, "Stop praying that way! God has already finished the work you are asking Him to do." Prayers that ask God for something that He has already given us are totally unnecessary. When we pray God's Word back to Him, or put Him in remembrance of it, we need to do so in the proper way, which is to declare what the Word says He has done, instead of asking Him to do something He has already done. For example:

- Instead of praying that we will hear God's voice, we need to thank Him that we do hear (see John 10:27).
- Instead of praying that we will be set free, we need to thank God for already setting us free (see Galatians 5:1).

- Instead of praying and asking God to have a good plan for our lives, we need to thank Him for already having a good plan (see Jeremiah 29:11).
- Instead of praying that God will make us righteous, we need to thank Him that He already has (see 2 Corinthians 5:21).
- Instead of praying and asking God to bless us, we need to thank Him that we are already blessed with every blessing (see Ephesians 1:3).
- Instead of praying that we will be accepted, we need to thank God for already accepting us in Christ (see Ephesians 1:6).

Model Prayers

I believe that the way people pray and the things they pray about reveal so much about their character and spiritual maturity. There was a time when my prayer life did not indicate much spiritual maturity. Even though I was a born-again, baptized-in-the-Holy-Spirit preacher, my prayers were pathetically carnal. When I prayed, I had a list of requests I thought God had to say "yes" to before I could be happy—and all of them were natural things: "Lord, make my ministry grow. Give us a new car; do this; do that. Make Dave change. Make the kids behave," and so on.

In response, God simply said to me, "I want you to examine the prayers of Jesus and the prayers of Paul. Then we'll talk about your prayer life." Of course, there are many prayers throughout the Bible, especially in Psalms, but God told me to pray the prayers of Jesus, which are found in the gospels and the prayers of Paul, which are found in the Epistles.

When I began to pray the way Jesus prayed and the way Paul prayed, I discovered that there really is no more powerful way to pray than to pray the Word of God because it shows us what is important to Him. Just take a look at some of Jesus' prayers:

- "Father, forgive them, for they know not what they do" (Luke 23:34).
- "Sanctify them [purify, consecrate, separate for Yourself, make them holy] by the Truth; Your Word is Truth" (John 17:17).
- "I in them and You in Me, in order that they may become one and perfectly united, that the world may know and [definitely] recognize that You sent Me and that You have loved them [even] as You have loved Me" (John 17:23).
- "But I have prayed especially for you [Peter], that your [own] faith may not fail" (Luke 22:32).
- "Father, I thank You that You have heard Me" (John 11:41).

I also want us to pay particular attention to some of Paul's prayers. By the time I read his prayers in Ephesians, Philippians, and Colossians, I was reduced to tears. I felt so bad about the carnality of my prayer life, and Paul's prayers affected me so powerfully that I have not been the same since. I saw that Paul never prayed for people to have easy lives or to be delivered from difficulties. Instead, he prayed that they would be able to bear whatever came their way, that they would walk in the Spirit, that they would be stead-fast, that they would endure and that they would be living examples of God's grace to

> Paul never prayed for people to have easy lives or to be delivered from difficulties.
>
> →→ • ←←

other people. He prayed about the things that are important to God, and I can assure you from experience, He releases incredible power to us when we pray that way.

In Ephesians 1:17, Paul said, "[For I always pray to] the God of our Lord Jesus Christ, the Father of glory, that He may grant you a spirit of wisdom and revelation...." Following this example, we also need to pray for a spirit of wisdom and revelation—and that needs to be one of our primary requests. In fact, I believe that asking God for revelation—spiritual insight and understanding—is one of the most important prayers we can pray. Revelation means "to uncover," and we need to ask God to uncover for us everything that belongs to us in Christ. We need Him to reveal and uncover the truths of the Word revealed to us so that we will understand how to pray for ourselves and for others. When someone tells you about a biblical principle or a spiritual truth, that is a piece of *information.* But when God helps you understand it, it becomes a *revelation*—and revelation is something no devil in hell or no person on earth can take away from us. Revelation is *ours* because it is God-given.

We also need to ask the Lord continually to give us insight into spiritual mysteries "in the [deep and intimate] knowledge of Him," as indicated by the end of this verse. Paul continued in Ephesians 1:18 that it was his desire that the "eyes of your heart" (which I consider to be the mind) would be "flooded with light, so that you can know and understand the hope to which He has called you." I still pray these words often: "God, show me the great hope that I have in You, so I don't become discouraged in my life."

In the next verse, Paul said, "And [so that you can know and understand] what is the immeasurable and unlimited and surpassing greatness of His power in and for us who believe..." (Ephesians 1:19). In simplest terms, he was saying, *I pray that you would know the power that is available to you as a believer.* This is the kind of prayer I am praying over you as you read this book, because I want you to experience the awesome, unlimited power that is available to you as you commune with God through prayer.

In Ephesians 3:16, Paul prayed, "May He grant you out of the rich treasury of His glory to be strengthened and reinforced with mighty power in the inner man by the [Holy] Spirit [Himself indwelling your innermost being and personality]." We need to be praying for this on a regular basis. We need to be saying, *God, grant me strength and power in my inner man, and let the Holy Spirit indwell me and flow through my personality.* That kind of prayer will transform us.

I also love Ephesians 3:19, in which Paul prayed, "...that you may be filled [through all your being] unto all the fullness of God [may have the richest measure of the divine Presence, and become a body wholly filled and flooded with God Himself]!" We need to be praying that we will be so full of God that there will not be room in our lives for anything else.

Also, Paul prayed about the love of God. He said, "May you be rooted deep in love and founded securely on love.... [That you may really come] to know [practically, through experience for yourselves] the love of Christ" (Ephesians 3:17, 19). He longed for people to know God's love personally—not just to hear about it from other people, not just to listen to a sermon about it, but to really know the love of God for themselves. One of the most life-changing prayers we can pray for other people is that they will really know God's love in a powerful, personal way. Paul did not pray that people would love God; he prayed that people would know and have revelation of God's awesome love.

Paul continues this theme of love in another epistle: "And this I pray: that your love may abound yet more and more and... display itself in greater depth..." (Philippians 1:9). Do you know what he is saying? *I want to see you loving each other. I want to see it. I don't want to just hear about it; I want to see it. Get it on display and let people see how you love one another. Put your love on exhibit and let it grow.*

In Philippians 1:10, Paul also asked that those for whom he prayed would not cause other people to stumble. He prayed that they would learn to prize and choose what was excellent, to learn what had real value in life, and to seek after those things. He prayed that they would be stable and that they would continue to show forth the fruit of righteousness during tough times.

He said in Colossians 1:11, "[We pray] that you may be invigorated and strengthened with all power, according to the might of His glory, [to exercise] every kind of endurance and patience (perseverance and forbearance) with joy." In other words, *No matter what you are going through, stay happy. No matter how long the trial takes, withstand it—and don't mistreat other people when you're going through it. Be victorious.*

Why did Paul pray the way he did? Because he was praying about things that are important to God. I encourage you to get out your Bible and look at Paul's prayers in Ephesians, Philippians, and Colossians. Then, either write them down or type them and study them; pray them for yourself and for other people; let them sink into your spirit. Realize

> Understand and pray the things God wants you to pray, realizing that He will take care of the things that are important to you.
>
> ⤜ • ⤛

that not one time in any of these prayers did Paul ask for anything in the natural. Do you know why? Because Matthew 6:33 says, "But seek first the kingdom of God and His righteousness, and all these things shall be added to you" (NKJV). And Psalm 37:4 says, "Delight yourself also in the Lord, and He will give you the desires and secret petitions of your heart." Be like Paul. Understand and pray the things God wants you to pray, realizing that He will take care of the things that are important to you.

It is not wrong to petition God for things for yourself. We have already established that God says we have not because we ask not. He said, "Keep on asking and it will be given you" (Matthew 7:7). What we ask God for is important. I don't believe that 90 percent of our requests should be for worldly, natural things and only 10 percent for spiritual things. Once again, all things should be kept in balance, otherwise we open a door for Satan to work in our lives (see 1 Peter 5:8).

How to Pray the Word

Perhaps you have never heard the phrase "pray the Word" and are wondering how to do it. I think praying the Word, or "praying the Scriptures," as some people say, is the simplest form of prayer available to any believer. All it takes is reading or memorizing words in the Bible and praying them in a way that makes them personal or applies them to someone else. I believe the

> God's promises are for you; they are for every believer— and He loves it when we know His Word and pray it back to Him.
>
> ⇥ • ⇤

best way to do this is to preface the Scripture by saying, "God, Your Word says (insert Scripture) and I believe it."

If you were praying Jeremiah 31:3 for yourself, you would say something like this: *God, Your Word says that You have loved me with an everlasting love and that You have drawn me with loving-kindness. I thank You for loving me so much and for continuing to draw me closer to You with such kindness. Help me, Lord, to be conscious and aware of Your love for me.* If you were praying that same Scripture for your friend Susie, who had been struggling to believe God really loved her, you would say something like, "God, Your Word says that You have loved Susie with an everlasting love and that You have drawn her with loving-kindness. God, You know that Susie hasn't felt very secure in Your love lately, so I am asking You to override her emotions with the truth of this promise."

I know a woman named Beth who has a great testimony of praying God's Word for a personal need. She had a desire to advance in her profession. After she worked at one company for quite a while and realized she had little opportunity for a higher position, she applied at another company and was hired in a position of greater influence, responsibility, authority, and opportunities to do the work she enjoyed. She spoke with her boss and gave two weeks' notice before she planned to begin her new job. He filled her position immediately, giving her job to her assistant. Within five minutes after she had given her notice, her new employer called and said, "Stop! Do not give your notice. Our company is being sold and we may not have a job for you after all."

Her assistant refused to step back into the assistant's position, and that boss agreed that the assistant should be given the job as planned, although he agreed to let her stay for four weeks instead of two. Beth desperately needed a job, and she could not afford to lose pay for time off to spend looking for other employment. So, she asked God to impress upon her heart a specific Scripture that she could pray and claim as a promise from His Word.

God's promises are for you; they are for every believer—and He loves it when we know His Word and pray it back to Him. He led her to Jeremiah 24:6: "For I will set My eyes on them for good, and I will bring them back to this land; I will build them and not pull them down, and I will plant them and not pluck them up" (NKJV).

Beth began to pray this Scripture several times a day, walking the parking lot of her current place of employment during breaks and lunchtimes, saying, "Lord, I know and declare that You have set Your eyes upon me for good. I am praying that You will bring me back to this land, that You will build me and not pull me down, that You will plant me and not pluck me up." When she prayed "bring me back to this land," Beth was specifically asking God to "bring her back" to the place she had been working and not to "pluck" her up from that company. She asked, in addition, that she would not miss one day of work or pay.

On her last day of work, at the end of four weeks, Beth did not have a job. She submitted her name to another department in her company, but heard nothing. Still, she continued to pray and believe that God would not pluck her out of that company. At a few minutes before 5:00 P.M. on her last day, as she was gathering her belongings to leave the office, her phone rang. She received a job offer from the other department in her company—along with these words: "We really hate to rush you, but is there any chance you could start working for us first thing tomorrow morning?"

Everything turned out just as she had prayed from God's Word. He did "bring [her] back into [that] land; [He] did not pluck [her] up"; and she knew that His eyes were indeed set upon her for good, knowing her need and making sure that she did not miss a single day of work.

I have heard many stories like this one, and I have had many similar experiences. Let me encourage you, when you are in times of crisis or need, to ask God to impress a Scripture upon your heart and to help you pray it. As you do, I believe that your confidence in God's Word will grow, your faith will increase, and you will experience the awesome joy of answered prayer.

Prayers of the Word for Your Everyday Life

God's Word is designed to help us, direct us, and encourage us in our everyday lives and we can find Bible verses or passages to pray in every situation. At times, we can find verses or passages that give us remarkably specific, detailed direction, and at other times, we need to take a nugget of wisdom or a general spiritual principle and apply it to the matter with which we are dealing. For example, listed below are several common, specific circumstances and emotions with which the enemy threatens us and corresponding verses to pray in each case:

- When you or someone you love is sick, you can pray the last phrase of Exodus 15:26, which says, "I *am* the Lord Who heals you," and Psalm 103:2–4, which says, "Bless the Lord, O my soul, and forget not all His benefits: Who forgives all your iniquities, Who heals all your diseases, Who redeems your life from destruction, Who crowns you with lovingkindness and tender mercies" (NKJV).

- When you are going through a season of difficulty or something that is wearing you out, you can pray Isaiah 40:29 (NKJV) and 31, which say, "He gives power to the weak, and to *those who have* no might He increases strength" and "But those who wait for the Lord [who expect, look for, and hope in Him] shall change and renew their strength and power; they shall lift their wings and mount up [close to God] as eagles [mount up to the sun]; they shall run and not be weary, they shall walk and not faint or become tired." You can also pray Lamentations 3:22–23 which says, "It is because of the Lord's mercy and loving-kindness that we are not consumed, because His [tender] compassions fail not. They are new every morning; great and abundant is Your stability and faithfulness."

- When you need to know God hears your prayers, you can pray Psalm 6:9, which says, "The Lord has heard my supplication; the Lord receives my prayer," and Psalm 55:17, which says, "Evening and morning and at noon I will pray, and cry aloud, and He shall hear my voice" (NKJV).

- When your mouth is getting you in trouble, you can pray Psalm 141:3 which says, "Set a guard, O Lord, over my mouth; keep watch over the door of my lips" (NKJV). You can also pray Psalm 19:14, which says, "Let the words of my mouth and the meditation of my heart be acceptable in Your sight, O Lord."

- When you are afraid, you can pray Isaiah 41:10, which says, "Fear not, for I *am* with you; be not dismayed, for I *am* your God. I will strengthen you, yes, I will help you, I will uphold you with My righteous right hand" (NKJV). You can also pray Joshua 1:9, which says, "Be strong, vigorous, and very courageous. Be not afraid, neither be dismayed, for the Lord your God is with you wherever you go."

- When you are stressed out and under pressure, you can pray Psalm 55:22, which says, "Cast your burden on the Lord, and He shall sustain you; He shall never permit the righteous to be moved" (NKJV), and Isaiah 26:3, which says, "You will keep *him* in perfect peace, *whose* mind *is* stayed *on You,* because he trusts in You" (NKJV).

- When you are struggling financially, you can pray Psalm 34:9-10, which says, "Oh, fear the Lord, you His saints! *There is* no want to those who fear Him. The young lions lack and suffer hunger; but those who seek the Lord shall not lack any good *thing*" (NKJV). If you have been faithful in giving, you can also pray Philippians 4:19, which says, "And my God shall supply all your need according to His riches in glory by Christ Jesus" (NKJV).

- When you are faced with a decision and do not know what to do, you can pray Proverbs 3:5–6, which says, "Lean on, trust in, and be confident in the Lord with all your heart and mind and do not rely on your own insight or understanding. In all your ways know, recognize and acknowledge Him, and He will direct and make straight and plain your paths." You can also pray Isaiah 42:16, which says, "I will bring the blind by a way they did not know; I will lead them in paths they have not known. I will make darkness light before them, and crooked places straight. These things I will do for them, and not forsake them" (NKJV).

- When you are concerned or discouraged about the future, you can pray Jeremiah 31:17, which says, "There is hope for your future," and Jeremiah 29:11, which says, "For I *know* the thoughts and plans that I have for you, says the Lord, thoughts and plans for welfare and peace and not for evil, to give you hope in your final outcome."

- When you are having problems with your children, you can pray and remind God of His Word in Isaiah 54:13, which says, "All your children *shall be* taught by the Lord, and great *shall be* the peace of your children" (NKJV). You can also pray Romans 15:13, which says, "Now may the God of hope fill you with all joy and peace in believing, that you may abound in hope by the power of the Holy Spirit" (NKJV).

- When you are not sure what God is doing with you or what is going on in your life, you can pray Psalm 37:23, which says, "The steps of a [good] man are directed and established by the Lord when He delights in his way [and He busies Himself with his every step]," and Isaiah 55:8–9, which says, "For My thoughts are not your thoughts, neither are your ways My ways, says the Lord. For as the heavens are higher than the earth, so are My ways higher than your ways and My thoughts than your thoughts."

I realize that the examples above do not cover every single area of our lives, but I hope you can see from them that God's Word does provide answers, direction, and prayer strategies for every situation we face. I strongly encourage you to search the Scriptures for yourself and to memorize and meditate on as many

> God's Word does provide answers, direction, and prayer strategies for every situation we face.
> ⤜ • ⤛

verses and passages as you possibly can. This way, God's Word will be "hidden" in your heart and you will have a deep well of wisdom and truth to draw from so that you can include the Word as a vital part of your prayers.

PRAYING IN A PRAYER LANGUAGE

Some Christians believe in praying in a personal prayer language that is given by the Holy Spirit (praying in other tongues). This practice is also called speaking in tongues. I certainly respect people who do not believe in this spiritual gift, but I want to address it in this chapter because there are many people who do. Personally, I believe that we desperately need all of the gifts of the Holy Spirit operating in the church today and that the gift of a prayer language is available to every Christian. I believe these gifts are given to us so that we can exercise and experience the power of God in the midst of a dark world and the uncertain times in which we live. I believe we need everything the Holy Spirit offers us: we need words of wisdom and knowledge; we need faith; we need gifts of healings; we need miracles; we need to be able to see and minister prophetically; we need to be able to discern the spirits that are at work around us; and we need different kinds of tongues and interpretations of tongues (see 1 Corinthians 12:8–10).

I will say to you what Paul said in his letter to the Corinthians: "I thank my God I speak with tongues..." (1 Corinthians 14:18, NKJV). In fact, I pray in tongues often because it is such a source of strength, it builds me up inside and strengthens me spiritually. It increases my sensitivity to the leading of the Holy Spirit and keeps me in the Spirit instead of in my mind or in my emotions. I assure you that praying in a prayer language releases incredible power to those who receive and exercise this gift of the Holy Spirit.

The Power of a Prayer Language

Part of the power of praying in a prayer language (praying in other tongues) is that it is a means by which we speak spiritual secrets and mysteries to the Lord. First Corinthians 14:2 says, "For one who speaks in an [unknown] tongue speaks not to men but to God, for no one understands or catches his meaning, because in the [Holy] Spirit he utters secret truths and hidden things [not obvious to the understanding]." When we pray in a prayer language, our minds do not comprehend what we are praying and that causes our prayers to be pure, untainted by the influence of our carnal thoughts and our reasoning. In 1 Corinthians 14:14, Paul affirmed this when he wrote: "For if I pray in an [unknown] tongue, my spirit [by the Holy Spirit within me] prays, but my mind is unproductive [it bears no fruit and helps nobody]."

When we pray in tongues, we are not only praying prayers our own minds do not understand, we are also praying in a language that Satan cannot understand. Furthermore, we are often praying great things over our lives and the lives of others—things so great we would hardly be able to believe them if we understood what we were saying. Praying in tongues is also a way to pray correctly at times when we really do not know how to pray. Romans 8:26 says, "...we do not know what we should pray for as we ought..." (NKJV). When that is the case, we can pray in a prayer language. These prayers of the Spirit will communicate accurately because they are given by the Holy Spirit, and the Holy Spirit is the one Who intercedes through us.

I believe in the power of praying in tongues (a language that is not a person's native tongue or that they do not have natural knowledge of). It has made a tremendous difference in my prayer life, as well as in my practical, everyday circumstances. It brings the power of the Holy Spirit to bear on every aspect of our lives and enables us to walk through life with supernatural wisdom, supernatural grace, and supernatural

> When we pray in tongues, we are not only praying prayers our own minds do not understand, we are also praying in a language that Satan cannot understand.
>
> ->- • -<-

strength. I received this gift from God in 1976 during a time of intense seeking. I sincerely believed God had more available to me than I was experiencing as a Christian. I surrendered to Him, and He filled me with His Spirit and enabled me to speak in other tongues, even though I had only briefly heard of this experience at that time.

Literally thousands of people all over the earth pray in a prayer language and I personally believe it is available to all. Some people fear other tongues because their minds do not understand; some have been taught against speaking in tongues (and the practice of other supernatural gifts), some may have the mistaken idea that these gifts disappeared with the early church. Still, others merely need teaching in this area. We cannot put our faith in something we have never heard of.

I want to encourage you to study this topic more for yourself. None of us should accept the doctrines of men without searching the Scriptures for ourselves. A person does not need to speak in tongues to go to heaven. The Bible doesn't even tell us that speaking in other tongues is the greatest gift (actually, Paul told us that love is the greatest gift of all). I personally know people who do not speak in other tongues and they have godly character. I also know people who do speak in other tongues and they remain very selfish, unloving, and carnal.

Speaking in tongues is not a guarantee of spiritual maturity, but it does give us an opening in the spiritual realm and an ability to tap into the secrets and mysteries of God. It gives us an ability to pray accurately when we don't know how to pray and is a way that we can edify and build ourselves up in faith.

SUMMARY

One sure, simple way to pray effective prayers that align with God's will is to pray the Word. God values and honors His Word, and in Isaiah 62:6, He invites us—even urges us—to put Him in remembrance of it. We need to know the Word so that we understand what God has promised us and so that we do not keep asking Him to do things He has already done.

Another sure way to pray effective prayers is to pray in the Spirit, which is being led by God's Spirit and/or praying in other tongues. We may be led by the Spirit of God to pray in our known language or in other tongues. Such prayers take place spirit to Spirit with God; they speak mysteries in the spiritual realm, they are free from the influence of our fleshly thoughts, and they are unintelligible to the enemy. When we pray in other tongues, our minds do not comprehend their meaning, but our spirits bear witness of their accuracy and power.

The Word and the Spirit are an unbeatable combination in any situation—especially in our prayers. So, pray the Word and be led by the Holy Spirit!

Prayer Points

→→ Praying God's Word is an especially effective way to pray. It keeps us mindful of God's promises, aligned with His truth and in agreement with His heart.

→→ When we see in the Word that God has already given us something, we need to declare it and thank Him for it, instead of asking Him for it.

→→ Paul did not pray for people to be spared trials or troubles. Instead, he prayed that they would see—have revelation of—what God has already done. He also prayed that they would be able to endure whatever they encountered, they would live in the power of the Spirit, they would be steadfast, and they would be walking testimonies of God's grace to other people.

→→ We can find a Scripture to pray in every situation life brings. The Bible does not include verses that specifically address all the details, but it does provide wisdom, principles, and general direction to help us know how to pray in all kinds of circumstances.

→→ Many Christians believe in praying in a prayer language called other tongues, which is a spiritual language that our minds do not comprehend and that Satan cannot understand.

➤ I believe that praying in this type of supernatural prayer language makes an enormous difference in a person's prayer life. It brings supernatural wisdom, supernatural power, and supernatural strength to our lives, to our decisions, and to the everyday situations we face.

10

Keys to Powerful Prayer

→→ One of my prayers for you is that your prayers will be powerful and effective, and that you will be able to talk with God in ways that successfully bring His heart and His plans into your life and the lives of the people around you. The Bible says, "The effective, fervent prayer of a righteous man avails much" (James 5:16, NKJV). If we want to pray effective prayers that avail much, then we need to know what God says about them, because all of our prayers are not necessarily successful. For example, sometimes we want something so desperately that we fail to pray according to God's will—and those prayers are not effective. Sometimes we are so angry or so hurt that we pray prayers that are based on our emotions instead of on God's Word or His heart—and those prayers are not effective, either.

Through His Word, God tells us what to do in order to pray powerful, effective prayers, and I would like to explore some of His instructions in this chapter. As I have written previously in this book, powerful prayers do not result from following formulas or abiding by certain principles. Powerful prayers are based on God's Word; they are simple, sincere, and filled with faith; they have nothing to do with rules or guidelines; they have everything to do with the attitudes of our hearts.

OBEY GOD

One of the most important aspects of our Christian lives—and a condition for effective prayer—is obedience, which reveals our love for God. We simply will not make progress with God or excel in prayer unless we are willing to obey Him. Disobedience of any kind, on any level, is sin. Just as sin will always keep us from praying successfully, obedience to God will make a way for our prayers to truly be effective and fruitful.

Over the years, I have had many opportunities to obey God. One such time, when obedience seemed especially challenging, was when I received my call into ministry in 1976. At the time, I was working a full-time job, plus trying to raise three children and be a wife. I had very little time for anything except survival, but I desperately needed to begin preparing for the teaching ministry God was putting on my heart.

God began to deal with me to take a step of faith and quit my job so I could spend several hours each day studying and praying. I would be putting it mildly to say I was afraid. Petrified would be more accurate! First of all, I had very little experience trusting God to meet my financial needs. God was calling me to a new level of faith, but I was accustomed to taking care of myself and found it difficult to be obedient.

Our monthly bills exceeded my husband's income by $40, which meant we would need not only to trust God for the money, but also for anything extra that came up like car repairs, home maintenance, clothes, and other things we needed.

With our financial situation in mind, I decided to quit my full-time job and get a part-time job. That was my way of obeying God and still having assurance that our needs would be met. In other words, I was not willing to trust Him *fully*. I was offering a sacrifice instead of obedience. That is not pleasing to God, nor is it true obedience.

A few months went by and my new part-time job was not going well. Normally, I was a very good employee, but I could not seem to do anything right on the new job. To make a long story short, I finally ended up getting fired (something that had never happened to me before) and realized through that incident that God was serious when He said, "Quit your job; trust Me to meet all your needs and start preparing for the teaching ministry."

Over the next few years, I learned so much about God's goodness by watching Him meet our needs in miraculous ways, month after month. The things He did may not have appeared miraculous to someone else, but they were to me. I remember keeping a list of items I needed and was asking God to provide. On my list were new dishrags and dish towels. You can imagine my amazement when a friend showed up at my front door saying, "I hope you don't think I am crazy, but I felt that God wanted me to get you new dishrags and towels, so here they are."

Had I not taken that step of faith years ago, I could not trust God for the finances we need to run the ministry today. As one preacher said, "You have to believe God for your socks before you can believe Him for a new house or car." As we take steps of obedience, we learn to trust God. We gain experience in trusting Him, and that increases our confidence.

Let me caution you not to try to do what I did just because it worked for me, but be willing to do whatever God is asking you to do. Radical obedience will lead you into an exciting life with God, a life that will thrill and amaze you.

I encourage you to make up your mind that you are going to be extremely, even radically, obedient to God. First John 3:22 says: "We receive from Him whatever we ask, because we [watchfully] obey His orders." Does that mean we have to be perfect? No. It is true that God in His grace will bless those who make mistakes, but we should not be satisfied to stay the way we are. God blesses us even though we are not perfect, but at the same time, our hearts need to be longing for growth and improvement. We cannot knowingly, deliberately, and habitually sin and then expect God to give us a life filled with His blessings. Our attitudes need to send God a message that says: "I don't want to stay this way. I want to grow. I want to change and I'm pressing toward that mark. While I'm on my way, I know I won't get everything right, but You are so gracious and merciful that I can still believe You will bless me while I keep maturing." On the other hand, if we wallow in disobedience, knowing we are disobeying God, then we really do not need to be blessed because if God blesses us in the midst of that attitude or behavior, we will not want to change or grow.

We hurt ourselves every time we do not obey God. For example, if God has told us to go and apologize to somebody and we are too stubborn to say, "I'm sorry," we are hurting ourselves and

> Make up your mind that you are going to be extremely, even radically, obedient to God.
>
> ⇥ • ⇤

negatively affecting our prayer lives. But when we do obey God, we position ourselves for answered prayer and great blessings. Just look at what the Bible says about the good things that come to those who obey.

Those who sin but have a repentant attitude can be blessed. We must admit our sins, confess them, and be willing to turn from them. However, if people love their sin and are unwilling to turn from it, they will live under God's chastisement until they see the light.

- "Now therefore, if you will obey My voice in truth and keep My covenant, then you shall be My own peculiar possession and treasure" (Exodus 19:5).
- "Observe and obey all these words which I command you, that it may go well with you and your children after you forever, when you do *what* is good and right in the sight of the Lord your God" (Deuteronomy 12:28, NKJV).
- "The Lord your God will make you abound in all the work of your hand, in the fruit of your body, in the increase of your livestock, and in the produce of your land for good. For the Lord will again rejoice over you for good as He rejoiced over your fathers, if you obey the voice of the Lord your God, to keep His commandments and His statutes which are written in this Book of the Law, *and* if you turn to the Lord your God with all your heart and with all your soul" (Deuteronomy 30:9–10, NKJV).
- "If they obey and serve Him, they shall spend their days in prosperity and their years in pleasantness and joy" (Job 36:11).

- "...Obey My voice, and I will be your God, and you shall be My people. And walk in all the ways that I have commanded you, that it may be well with you" (Jeremiah 7:23, NKJV).
- "If you keep My commandments, you will abide in My love, just as I have kept My Father's commandments and abide in His love" (John 15:10, NKJV).

BE CONSISTENTLY RIGHTEOUS

God promises in His Word that He will hear our prayers if we seek to be faithful in our walk with Him. Proverbs 15:29 says: "The Lord...hears the prayer of the [consistently] righteous (the upright, in right standing with Him)." What does it mean to be "consistently righteous"? Simply put, I think the best way to be consistently righteous is to refuse to compromise.

A person who compromises is someone who tends to go along with what everybody else wants to do, even though it may not be totally right. A compromiser knows when something is not right, but does it anyway and hopes to get away with it. We compromise when we know in our hearts—and even have the conviction of the Holy Spirit—that we should not say, should not do, should not buy, or should not eat something and respond with: "Well, I know I shouldn't say this, but...," "I know I shouldn't eat this, but...," "Well, I know I shouldn't buy this, but...," "I know I shouldn't do this, but...," and "I know I shouldn't stay up this late, but..." What are we really saying with our *I-shouldn't-but*'s? We are saying, "God is showing me what to do, but I'm going to do what I want to do." In that case, we can only blame ourselves if we do not see the results we would like.

When we refuse to compromise, though, and devote ourselves to being consistently righteous, God hears our prayers and promises other blessings as well, such as:

- "...the desire of the [uncompromisingly] righteous shall be granted" (Proverbs 10:24).
- "The [uncompromisingly] righteous shall flourish like the palm tree [be long-lived, stately, upright, useful, and fruitful]" (Psalm 92:12).
- "Light is sown for the [uncompromisingly] righteous... and joy for the upright in heart" (Psalm 97:11).
- "...the Lord loves the [uncompromisingly] righteous (those upright in heart and in right standing with Him)" (Psalm 146:8).

Even though the Bible clearly affirms the blessings of righteousness, people in our modern society seem to want us to compromise, and if we refuse, they may call us legalistic and rigid. Even some Christians will accuse us of being legalistic if we try to live holy lives. I would rather go overboard trying to be holy than to go overboard taking a bunch of liberties that I do not need to be taking or that will get me in trouble! It is easy to be swept away with the world,

> If we are going to obey God . . . we will have to overcome the opinions of people around us and dedicate ourselves to being consistently righteous.
>
> ⤜ • ⤛

but God is looking for those who push against the downhill moral slide the world seems to be in and live pure and holy lives—lives that are without compromise!

If we are going to obey God (and remember, that is a key to powerful prayer), we will have to overcome the opinions of people around us and dedicate ourselves to being consistently righteous. What does a consistently righteous person do? A consistently righteous person tries to do what is right all the time. Now, some people only try to do what is right when they are in trouble or when they need a miracle. For instance, they think, *We should go to church this week because we need God to help us!* Or, for example, *We need a healing, so we better not gossip!* It is amazing how "holy" we can act when we need a breakthrough, but the consistently righteous person tries to do what is right all the time—not just when he or she needs something from God. The consistently righteous person regularly does what is right because it is right, because it honors God, because it reflects a heart of humility and a desire to obey God—and God likes that!

KEEP ON PRAYING

James 5:16 says, "The earnest (heartfelt, continued) prayer of a righteous man makes tremendous power available [dynamic in its working]." Notice that an earnest prayer, which is the prayer that makes tremendous power available, is heartfelt, *continued* prayer.

One of the keys to powerful prayer is to ask God for what we need and to continue to pray until we experience His tremendous power working on our behalf or in our situation. We need to press through in prayer and not give up so easily!

Soon after Jesus taught His disciples to pray, He encouraged them to be persistent in prayer by saying, "Ask and keep on asking and it shall be given you; seek and keep on seeking and you shall find; knock and keep on knocking and the door shall be opened to you. For everyone who asks and keeps on asking receives; and he who seeks and keeps on seeking finds; and to him who knocks and keeps on knocking, the door shall be opened" (Luke 11:9–10). Jesus wants us to persevere in prayer; He wants us to ask boldly and importunately. That does not mean we ask disrespectfully; it means we ask reverently but confidently. When we pray and keep on praying, He promises that our prayers will be effective and that we will indeed receive the answers we need.

Refuse to Give Up

You may remember from the chapter on persistent prayer that Jesus once told a parable about an importunate widow who continued to ask for justice from an unjust judge. The Bible says His purpose in telling this story was to emphasize that we "ought always to pray and not to turn coward (faint, lose heart, and give up)" (Luke 18:1). Essentially, this woman had said, "You better do something for me, or you will get awfully tired of hearing me." Do you remember what happened? She got what she was asking for!

Matthew 15:22–27 tells the story of another person who was persistent in her request and received an answer: "And behold, a woman who was a Canaanite from that district came out and, with a [loud, troublesomely urgent] cry, begged, Have mercy on me, O Lord, Son of David! My daughter is miserably and distressingly and cruelly possessed by a demon! But He did not answer her a word. And His disciples came and implored him, saying: Send her away, for she is crying out after us. He answered, I was sent only to the lost sheep of the house of Israel." Note that this woman was not an Israelite, but she came to Jesus anyway: "But she came and, kneeling, worshiped Him and kept praying, Lord, help me! And He answered, It is not right (proper, becoming, or fair) to take the children's bread and throw it to the little dogs. She said, Yes, Lord, yet even the little pups (little whelps) eat the crumbs that fall from their [young] masters' table."

This woman had much faith that Jesus could help her. Basically she was telling Jesus, "You don't have to do anything big for me. If I can just get a few crumbs, that will be enough." Because of the persistent faith that proved she was not going to give up, Jesus responded to her and granted her request.

Bartimaeus was another person in the Bible who was persistent in his asking. He cried out to Jesus and kept on crying out until Jesus paid attention to him. This blind beggar shouted continually, "Jesus, Son of David, have pity and mercy on me!" I can just imagine people saying, "Man, shut up! Leave Him alone! You're making a ruckus here. You're making a scene. Be quiet!" But the Bible says that when people told this blind man to keep still, he "kept on shouting out all the more" (Mark 10:47–48). Praise God! He knew that Jesus was his only hope, so he refused to quit crying out to Him. As a result, Jesus stopped what He was doing and healed Bartimaeus right on the spot.

One of the main reasons people do not experience victory in prayer (as well as in other areas) is simply that they give up too soon. Paul and Silas were found still worshiping and praising God in their jail cell at midnight (see Acts 16:25–26). Many people would have given up and gone to sleep much earlier. Our motto should be: "Never give up." A person who refuses to quit is one whom Satan cannot defeat.

I encourage you not to give up praying, no matter what. It is Satan who wants you to throw in the towel and give up right now! He wants you to say:

- "I'll never be blessed."
- "I guess I wasn't called into ministry after all."
- "Well, I guess I'll never have a better job."
- "I'll never graduate from college."
- "I guess I'll never be able to move away to a better place."
- "I'll never get married."
- "I'll never have anything."
- "I'll always be in debt."
- "I'll never lose weight."
- "I'll always be the one who gets left out."

Attitudes like those illustrated above are likely to guarantee that we will not receive anything! Instead, we need to be saying, "I know who I am in Christ. I know, God, what You did for me and I intend to be an overcomer because Your Word says that I can be. I am more than a conqueror through Christ. Greater is He who is in me than he who is in the world. I can do all things through Christ Who strengthens me. I refuse to eat ashes and dust all of my

> Any type of prayer that God inspires and leads us in will be powerful if we pray it and keep on praying until our answers come.
>
> ⤞ • ⤝

life. I am going to have everything God wants for me. I'm coming up out of this pit and I'm going to do great things in Jesus' name." That type of prayer and confession agrees with God's Word, and prayed persistently, it will be powerful and yield great results. In fact, any type of prayer that God inspires and leads us in will be powerful if we pray it and keep on praying until our answers come. Remember, just thanking God that your answer is on the way is a type of persistent prayer. Keep letting God know that you believe His promises and trust Him to be faithful.

BE PROPERLY RELATED TO AUTHORITY

Proverbs 28:9 says a startling thing about what happens to our prayers when we are not properly related to authority: "He who turns away his ear from hearing the law [of God and man], even his prayer is an abomination, hateful and revolting [to God]."

Our modern society is absolutely filled with rebellion. I have observed that many, many people have trouble relating to authority. To start with, look at the role reversals we have in our families. I believe that women are equal to men; I believe women can hold respectable positions in the world and make good money; obviously, I also believe that women can be used by God, but none of these beliefs has anything to do with the order—the authority structure—God has established for the home.

The Bible says that a wife should submit to her husband as unto the Lord. That does not mean she submits to sin. For example, her call to submission to her husband doesn't mean she has to watch a pornographic movie because he wants her to. But we wives need to have an attitude of submission, an attitude of respect, toward our husbands. If husbands would obey the Word and love their wives as Christ loves the Church, and if wives would embrace true, godly submission, I believe marriages would last—and be happy—and I believe families would be stable, safe, and joyful places. This would be the case because we would all be living in obedience to God's Word, honoring the authority He places in our lives for the purpose of keeping us safe, secure, and satisfied.

At one time, my attitude toward my husband was rebellious due to a fear of being taken advantage of. I thought I had a good excuse, but God would not allow me to stay in rebellion just because of past bad experiences. He let me know that unless I submitted to my husband and had a respectful attitude toward him, that my bad attitude would hinder my prayers. No matter what our excuses may be, God cannot bless willful, conscious disobedience. Once I understood what I was doing and knew how to secure God's grace and power to change, God expected me to do so. It was not easy, but had I refused, I would be stuck at that place still going around and around the same mountains of defeat and frustration.

Even as the lack of true biblical submission is absent in many marriages, submission to spiritual authority is practically nonexistent. Hebrews 13:17 makes clear the biblical command to be properly positioned under spiritual authority, saying, "Obey your spiritual leaders and submit to them [continually recognizing their authority over you], for they are constantly keeping watch over your souls and guarding your spiritual welfare, as men who will have to render an account [of their trust]. [Do your part to] let them do this with gladness and not with sighing and groaning, for that would not be profitable to you [either]."

Often when a pastor tries to bring some kind of correction, people tend to become upset and want to leave the church—and that is not right. Paul corrected people often; that was part of his job as a spiritual leader and it remains a responsibility for spiritual leaders today. Paul said: "Not that we have dominion [over you] and lord it over your faith, but [rather that we work with you as] fellow laborers [to promote] your joy" (2 Corinthians 1:24). If we will understand and believe that spiritual authority exists to promote our joy, we will embrace it, and when we do, our joy will increase and our prayers will be effective.

We simply cannot grow up or mature without correction. If we are rebellious toward office policy, company rules, government guidelines, traffic laws, or toward any other form of authority, then we have more serious attitude problems than we might think. Being rebellious is not something to be proud of; it is something we need to be diligent to eliminate from our attitudes and behaviors! Why? Because if we refuse to submit to earthly authority, then we will not submit to God's authority. That is called disobedience and it will keep our prayers from having power.

God placed me in someone else's ministry for several years before He allowed me to start my own ministry. In the other ministry, I had to learn how to come under authority. That was not easy

> We are not fit to be *in* authority until we know how to come *under* authority.
>
> ⇥ • ⇤

for me, because I'm a pretty strong person. I did not always agree with the decisions that were made and I did not always feel I was treated fairly, but one of the lessons God taught me is that we are not fit to be *in* authority until we know how to come *under* authority. I also learned that God will promote us at the right time if we keep a good, godly attitude during challenging times.

You might want a pay raise or a promotion at work, yet you regularly gossip and say critical things about your boss. This is a form of rebellion. God once told me, "Joyce, you can do what you are asked to do and still have a rebellious attitude." Submission is not an act we put on: it is an attitude we should have.

The anointing of God (His presence and power) is a form of authority. If we want to operate in a greater anointing—a stronger authority from God—then we have to submit to the authority under which God places us before He moves us on to a new level of leadership. In our ministry, the people who lead worship are extremely anointed. If they were rebellious toward Dave and me, I do not believe the anointing on their lives would be as strong as it is. By the same token, if I were not submissive to my husband, I do not believe the anointing of God would be as strong on my life as it is. In our marriages, in our spiritual lives, in our professional lives, and in any other realm in which authority is in place, we must be properly related to that authority in order to experience answered prayer and God's favor in our lives.

Many people would experience tremendous breakthroughs in prayer if they would simply stop being so rebellious. We do not have to express an opinion about everything; we do not have to have an idea about everything; we do not have to make comments about everything. When we begin to submit to authority, we have to stop saying things like, "It's not fair that they make me punch a time clock." Well, too bad. Just go in and punch the thing anyway. We have to stop grumbling about what we do not like and just do those things. We cannot complain and say, "Well, I don't want this lunch hour. I want another lunch hour." We just need to do what we are told to do because someone in a position of authority has told us to do it. We need to do it because our Lord has asked us to. We don't live to please people, but to please the Lord.

An attitude of honor and submission toward authority needs to permeate our everyday lives—because remember, God puts authority in place in order to keep us safe and to promote our joy. He gives us both spiritual authority and natural authority and it is just as important to obey natural authority as it is to obey spiritual authority. So, if somebody asks you not to sit somewhere, don't sit there. If there is a "no parking" zone, don't park there, even "just for a minute." If the only parking space available is a handicapped space and you are not handicapped, don't park there even if it means having to walk a long way! If a red light flashes "Do not walk," then don't walk. Don't cross the street anyway simply because you cut your time too close and are in a hurry. If there is a sign saying "Please put your grocery cart back here when you unload your groceries," then take your grocery cart and put it back there when you unload your groceries. Don't leave it out in the middle of the parking lot to bump into someone else's car!

You may be thinking, *Well, those things can't make any difference. That's all little stuff. I've got big problems.* You do have big problems and you will keep your big problems if that's the way you feel about the "little stuff"! We all keep our big problems until we learn that our little, everyday attitudes and mind-sets add up to create either big troubles or big blessings.

Behaviors similar to the ones I have just described reflect a sloppy attitude toward authority, which essentially says: "I'm going to do what I want to because I don't think you're right." We do not have to think someone or something is right. All we need to do is obey the rules, and if we do, God will bless us. On the contrary, if we have a stiff-necked attitude about authority, we are not going to be blessed and our prayers will not be effective. Remember the strong words of Proverbs 28:9: "He who turns away his ear from hearing the law [of God and man], even his prayer is an abomination, hateful and revolting [to God]."

FOCUS ON OTHERS

Another key to powerful prayer is to focus on others and not obsess about our own needs. We can pray for ourselves and we can pray for radical blessings for ourselves, but we need to avoid praying for ourselves all the time. Prayers of self-indulgence—selfish, self-centered prayers—are not effective, so we really need to make sure that we spend time praying for other people. I am constantly hearing about four or five people who need prayer, and just when some of those prayers are answered, I will become aware of other people to pray for. Your life is probably similar. You hear of someone who recently lost a loved one, someone who needs a job, somebody who needs a place to live, somebody who just received a bad report from the doctor, someone whose child is sick, or somebody whose spouse just walked out. People have all kinds of needs, and they need our prayers. God wants us to pray for one another with loving, selfless attitudes because our prayers cannot be answered otherwise. I want to challenge you to ask God to give you someone for whom you can pray. Initially, you may not even know what to pray for, but sometimes, if you just get quiet in His presence and ask, He will begin to show you things and help you pray. I wrote about praying for others in the chapter on intercession and I personally know this type of prayer to be extremely valuable, rewarding, and effective. It is important to understand that God places priority on people, and as we learn that, people will become our priority also.

BE GOOD TO PEOPLE

Proverbs 21:13 says: "Whoever stops his ears at the cry of the poor will cry out himself and not be heard." This means that when I do not pay attention to people in need and do not do anything to help them, then God may not be inclined to answer my call for help when I have a need.

Being good to people extends beyond our inner circle of friends and family to our communities. There are some very serious situations going on in our own cities. I remember reading a statistic one time that said the average age of a homeless person in St. Louis was seven years old. In my city! Do you know what my response to that might have been twenty years ago? I would have said, "That is really pathetic." But now, I become aware of realities such as that one and say, "I'm going to do something about that!" People might say, "It's easy for *you* to say that, Joyce; you've got a big ministry and access to lots of people who can help." You may not have some of the resources we

> I believe a lot of our prayers go unanswered because we do not treat others well and we do not extend mercy or compassion to the difficult situations around us.
>
> ⟶ • ⟵

have in the ministry, but you have the same ability to pray that I do. You can give an offering to ministries that are trying to help and meet needs. You can go and volunteer a little bit of time. All of us can do something if we really want to.

I believe a lot of our prayers go unanswered because we do not treat others well and we do not extend mercy or compassion to the difficult situations around us. Isaiah 58:6–9 gives the true picture: "[Rather] is not this the fast that I have chosen: to loose the bonds of wickedness, to undo the bands of the yoke, to let the oppressed go free, and that you break every [enslaving] yoke? Is it not to divide your bread with the hungry and bring the homeless poor into your house—when you see the naked, that you cover him, and that you hide not yourself from [the needs of] your own flesh and blood? Then shall your light break forth like the morning, and your healing (your restoration and the power of a new life) shall spring forth speedily; your righteousness (your rightness, your justice, and your right relationship with God) shall go before you [conducting you to peace and prosperity], and the glory of the Lord shall be your rear guard. Then you shall call, and the Lord will answer; you shall cry, and He will say, Here I am." All the prophet Isaiah is really encouraging us to do is to be good to people. The result? God Himself will say to you, "Here I am. What do you need? What can I do for you?"

We can receive a tremendous harvest just by being nice! What do I mean by that? Well, for example:

- Don't be rude.
- Let somebody go ahead of you in the grocery store line.
- Let somebody have a parking place you wanted.
- Don't make big issues out of little things.

- Don't throw a fit every time your spouse asks you to pick up your dirty socks or asks you to take out the garbage—just pick up the socks or take out the trash and be gracious about it.
- Speak kindly to your children.
- Say "thank you" to retail clerks, service people, bank tellers, and others who help you.
- Smile.
- Give an older person your seat if no more seats are available.

It is very important to God that we treat people well. If you have ever been mistreated, then you know how painful that is. You may be in a situation right now in which you are being mistreated or you are mistreating someone else. If you want to pray powerful prayers—if you want God's ears to perk up at the sound of your voice—you will have to treat people well and be good to them.

FORGIVE

If we want to pray prayers that are powerful, we simply must have clean hearts when we approach God—and one sure way to be clean before Him is to make sure that we have forgiven everyone who has hurt or offended us. Forgiveness is not easy, but it is a prerequisite for effective prayer. Jesus instructs us, in Mark 11:25: "And whenever you stand praying, if you have anything against anyone, forgive him and let it drop (leave it, let it go), in order that your Father Who is in heaven may also forgive you your [own] failings and shortcomings and let them drop."

Although Jesus' disciples were familiar with His teachings on forgiveness, they still found it a challenge. Peter asked Him one day,

"Lord, how many times may my brother sin against me and I forgive him and let it go? [As many as] up to seven times?" (Matthew 18:21). Jesus essentially said:

> Forgiveness is manifested mercy; it is love in action.
>
> ➤ • ◄

"No. How about seventy times seven?" The number "seven" represents completion or perfection, so all Jesus was really saying was: "Keep on forgiving, and keep on forgiving and keep forgiving until it works."

Even though we know we must forgive, forgiving those who hurt us is not easy because our emotions are involved. In order to forgive, we must realize that forgiveness is not something we feel, it is a decision we make. Anytime we make right decisions, our feelings will eventually follow, but it may take some time before they do.

When we have been hurt, we feel that opening our hearts again to the people who hurt us will be impossible. We want to shut them out of our lives and avoid them if at all possible. These are natural reactions, but they are not God's way. God forgives us daily and He expects us to forgive others.

I remember a time when Dave really hurt my feelings and I could not seem to open my mouth to talk to him, let alone be friendly. As usual, the Holy Spirit was pressing me to behave in a godly way, but I had no strength to do it. I went to my office at home, where I frequently pray, and told God, "I am not coming out of here until You give me the grace to go out and talk to Dave as if he had never hurt my feelings. I know he didn't hurt me on purpose and I want to drop it and let it go."

I not only prayed, but I looked up several Scriptures on forgiveness and the danger of staying angry. Before long, I felt my heart softening and opening up to Dave again. I was able to go out of the room and resume my normal relationship with him.

I encourage you to pray when you need to forgive. Don't just "try" to forgive, but depend on God to give you grace, which enables you to do the hard things in life. Too often we "try" without going to God for help. When we do that, we are operating on our own. We must remember that Jesus said, "Apart from Me [cut off from vital union with Me] you can do nothing" (John 15:5).

Prayer opens the door for God to work, so when you need to forgive, pray until you're released from the anger you feel and then to be obedient to God.

When we forgive, we are being Christlike; we are acting as God acts—because He is a forgiving God. Forgiveness is manifested mercy; it is love in action—not love based on a feeling, but love based on a decision, an intentional choice to obey God. In fact, I believe forgiveness is the highest form of love. And I believe that love is so important to powerful, effective prayer that I have devoted the next chapter to that subject. Forgiveness and love go hand in hand and expressing them honors and glorifies God, puts us in agreement with Him, and causes us to obey His Word—which all bring great power to our prayers.

BE EXPECTANT

There was a time in my prayer life when I was about to burst with expectation. Every time I prayed, I prayed with tremendous faith, fully expecting God to do exactly as I requested. Then for some reason, I lost that "edge" to my prayer life and my sense of expectation began to fizzle out. But God did not let me stay that way for long. He began dealing with me, encouraging me to be aggressive again in my expectations and to express them in prayer, expecting Him to do great things in the earth and in my life. I am not talking about "name-it-and-claim-it" prayers that people can say every time they see something they want; I am talking about prayers that are filled with God-given expectation, God-given desires, and God-given vision—prayers that are prayed in faith from a pure heart.

As I returned to an aggressive attitude in my expectations, I said things like, "God, I am expecting favor everywhere I go today. I am expecting favor from You and favor with everyone with whom I come in contact." I prayed prayers such as, "God, I am expecting good news today. I am expecting to be amazed at the great things You do." It was amazing how many times the phone rang on those days and I picked it up to hear something incredibly encouraging. Sometimes people even said, "Joyce, I've got good news for you!"

I have learned that many people do not pray for good news because they are so afraid of bad news! That's not a godly attitude. If we want to see the power of God released in our lives, we need to have attitudes that are pleasing to Him. We need to have positive expectations instead of negative ones. Our basic approach to life needs to align with faith and hope and good expectations, because the Bible says that without faith it is impossible to please God (see Hebrews 11:6) and that hope will never disappoint us (see Romans 5:5). There is nothing negative about God; there is nothing in Him or in His actions that will ever disappoint us; everything He does is for our good—so that's what we need to expect as we

> If we want to see the power of God released in our lives, we need to have attitudes that are pleasing to Him.
>
> ➤➤ • ◄◄

pray. We should not pray and then *wonder* if God will do anything at all; we should pray *expecting* God to do even more than we have asked.

I encourage you confidently to expect big things from God. Many Christians can quote Ephesians 3:20 as the verse that says God "is able to do exceedingly abundantly above all that we ask or think" (NKJV). But I want you to see that verse from the Amplified Bible. It says that God "is able to [carry out His purpose and] do superabundantly, far over and above all that we [dare] ask or think [infinitely beyond our highest prayers, desires, thoughts, hopes, or dreams]." Did you catch that? God can do "superabundantly, far over and above all" that we would ever dare to ask or even *think* to ask and *infinitely beyond* our "highest prayers, desires, thoughts, hopes, or dreams." Now that is amazing—and that should give us all the confidence we need in order to pray expectantly. Personally, I would rather pray big prayers with great expectations and receive half of what I prayed for than to pray little puny prayers without any faith and get it all!

There is another important phrase in Ephesians 3:20 and we need to pay attention to it. Some translations place it before all the superabundant things God can do for us and some place it afterward. Either way, it's necessary; and it says, "according to the power that works in us" (NKJV). The Amplified Bible says that God can do so much more than we can even ask or imagine "by (in consequence of) the [action of His] power that is at work within us." What is the power that works in us? It is the power of God, and it comes through simple, believing prayer.

When we have power, we are able to pray expectantly, but at the same time, expectancy carries its own kind of power—the power of hope, the power of faith. God's power is released when we pray in faith, trusting and believing Him, because faith pleases Him. Expectancy is an attribute of faith. Faith reaches out into the spiritual realm and expects God's supernatural power to show up and do what no person on earth could do. Doubt, on the other hand, is afraid nothing good will happen; it does not please God and is not something He tends to bless. We are powerless when we live with doubt, disappointment, and a lack of confidence in God.

Just think about a time when you were not really sure God would come through for you. You were not able to pray very powerful prayers, were you? Now recall a time when your heart trusted completely in God and you knew that He would come through for you. You were able to pray then with a certain sense of power, weren't you? That's the power of expectation in prayer. Even if things don't work out exactly the way you hoped they would, trust God to know what is best and keep expecting Him to do great things.

SUMMARY

We want our prayers to be powerful and effective. When we pray, we really want to know that we are partnering with God to make a difference in someone's life or in a situation. In order to pray successfully, we need to understand the keys to effective prayer, which include: obedience to God, being consistently and uncompromisingly righteous, persistence, being properly submitted to those in authority over us, praying for others more than we pray for ourselves, treating people well, extending forgiveness just as we have been forgiven, and praying with expectation. As we endeavor to incorporate these attitudes and actions in our prayer lives, we will experience the joy of effective, answered prayer.

Prayer Points

➤ Obey God. Obedience reveals our love for God and is an important condition for effective prayer.

➤ Be consistently righteous, which means to refuse to compromise. God hears the prayers of the consistently righteous and He blesses uncompromising righteousness in awesome ways.

➤ Keep on praying. Pray persistently under the Spirit's direction, and do not give up until the answer comes.

➤ Be properly related to authority. A heart that can submit to natural authority and to spiritual authority can also submit to God. God's authority is designed for our welfare and it promotes our joy.

➤ Focus on others. Selfishness will hinder our prayers, but focusing on others is a key to praying successfully.

➤ Be good to people. Treating people well is important to God and keeps us in obedience to His Word.

➤ Forgive. Forgiveness is the highest form of love, and according to Mark 11:25, it is a prerequisite to God hearing our prayers.

➤ Be expectant. Expectation is a powerful spiritual dynamic. God loves to answer expectant prayers!

11

Above All

In the preceding chapter, we looked at several keys to effective prayer and in this chapter, I want to address one specific key that I believe both includes and supercedes all others. We can apply every prayer principle imaginable and meet every possible condition, but if we do not meet this one, our prayers will be like a noisy gong, clanging against the ceiling of heaven. What is this all-important key to answered prayer? Walking in love.

Jesus made it clear that love is His number one priority when He said, "I give you a new commandment: that you should love one another. Just as I have loved you, so you too should love one another" (John 13:34). The Apostle Peter writes: "And *above all* things have fervent love for one another, for *'love will cover a multitude of sins'*" (1 Peter 4:8, NKJV, emphasis mine). In other words, we are to have genuine, pure, fervent love for others above everything else we do. If we can only manage to do one thing in our lives, it should be to love other people. Of course, it is impossible to truly love others without knowing God, loving Him, and knowing that He loves us. In the context of loving Him, receiving His love and extending His love to other people, we will find that our prayers are rich, vibrant, effective, and rewarding.

FAITH WORKS THROUGH LOVE

Many people think great faith is the number one sign of spiritual maturity. But I believe that walking in love is the true test of spiritual maturity and I know that it is essential to an effective prayer life. Our love walk energizes our faith walk, and when these two spiritual dynamics of faith and love work together, our prayers will have tremendous results. We cannot pray effective prayers without having faith in God, but love demonstrates and expresses our faith. If we love God, we have faith in Him.

The Bible teaches that faith works through love. Galatians 5:6 says that what really counts is "faith activated and energized and expressed and working through love." Love is not talk or theory; it's action. In fact, the Bible says that we cannot be walking in love if we see a brother in need, have what it takes to meet his need, and will not do anything to help him (see 1 John 3:17).

Jesus also said all the law and all the prophets are summed up in love when He declared: *"'You shall love the Lord your God with all your heart, with all your soul, and with all of your mind.' This is the first and great commandment. And the second is like it: 'You shall love your neighbor as yourself.'* On these two commandments hang all the Law and the Prophets" (Matthew 22:37–40, NKJV). Jesus gave these words to people asking which commandment was the most important. They were basically saying to Him: "Just give us the bottom line, Jesus." In response, He said: "Okay. You want the bottom line?

You want to fully obey all the law and all the prophets? Then love Me and love people." End of story. It's that simple. Jesus let people know that walking in love is

> Trying to walk in faith without love is like having a flashlight with no battery.
>
> →→ • ←←

at the heart of living a life of faith. Trying to walk in faith without love is like having a flashlight with no battery. We must be sure that we keep our love battery charged at all times. Otherwise our faith will not work!

I believe Christians can run into problems when we do not diligently pursue walking in love as a vital part of our faith and relationship with God. We want to be blessed; we want to be healed; we want successful ministries, but we do not seem to desperately want to seek and pursue walking in love and the fruit of the Spirit. I believe Satan is seeking to build a stronghold of cold love in the hearts of believers. He wants us to have hard stony hearts that do not sense, feel, or care about the needs of other people. He wants us to be selfish and self-centered, thinking, *Somebody do something for me,* without ever reaching out to do anything for anybody else. He knows that faith works through love and that without love, our faith amounts to nothing. We need to know that too and be careful to develop a strong love walk as we seek to grow in faith and in other areas of our spiritual lives.

WHAT LOVE IS

What does it mean to have the kind of faith that works through love? It means that we love people who do not seem to deserve to be loved. It means that when someone deserves for us to stay angry with them, we forgive—even if we believe our anger is justified. It means there are going to be times when we would love to talk about what someone did to us, but we choose to cover their offense instead because the Bible teaches us that "love covers a multitude of sins" (1 Peter 4:8).

Love also means we give to people unconditionally, with no strings attached. We don't think they owe us anything when we give to them; we simply give because we walk in love—and that's what people do when they really love someone. Walking in love means we begin to have a heart like God—generous, kind, merciful, forgiving, compassionate, always believing the best, always encouraging, always helping, never giving up.

First Corinthians 13 is often read at weddings because it so beautifully describes real love. It does apply to husbands and wives, but it also applies to everyone who seeks to walk in love in any kind of relationship—with siblings or extended family, with people at church, with friends and acquaintances, with coworkers and people we may not know, but encounter as we go about our daily activities. We are to love people wherever we go and whatever we do—from running errands to checking out at a grocery store to working to banking to attending sports events to putting children to bed at night or waking them up in the morning.

First Corinthians 13 teaches us that love is patient. A person who walks in love is not quick-tempered or easily angered. Love is kind, which means that a person who walks in love is good to people; that person is considerate, gentle, and giving. Love is long-suffering. In other words, it can put up with something and put up with it and put up with it and put up with it—it's impossible to wear out real love! Love is not easily offended, which means that a person who walks in love is not touchy and gets over things quickly. That person does not hold grudges or seek revenge; love forgives and forgets. Love always believes the best about people; it does not default to the negative or think, *You're out to get me! You must not like me because you did not speak to me when I came in. I knew you didn't really like me!* Love is not rude. A person who loves does not push other people out of the way while trying to buy a book on love! No, love prefers other people. If someone is in a grocery store line with two full carts, and someone else is standing behind with two items, love backs off and lets the other person go first. If somebody has been waiting for a parking space for five minutes, and just about the time it's empty, a little old man who can barely see above the steering wheel pulls up, love lets him have the parking spot.

Love sacrifices; love meets needs; love gives and gives and gives and gives and gives. Real love does not have to be talked into giving; it is always looking for opportunities to express itself. Love edifies. It does not tear down; it lifts up. Love encourages. Love listens. Love is seen or not seen in how we treat people. Love is the law of the kingdom and the nature of God. It is the demonstration of our faith in God and the secret to effective prayer.

What Love Is Not

Now that you are beginning to see what real love is, let me also describe what love is *not*. Walking in love does not mean you have to become a doormat for everybody and allow people to abuse you and use you. That is not good for anyone. Love sometimes has to be tough enough to break off a relationship if you know that a person's mistreatment of you is hurting them even more than it is hurting you. Loving someone does not mean that you have to be walked on all your life, but it does mean that there are going to be times when you will stick with somebody you would rather get away from. It means seeking and incorporating the heart of God for other people as you relate to them and applying His wisdom in your relationships.

Sometimes love has to be tough in order to be real and we need balance in this matter of giving to others in love. We should not keep giving to somebody who never does his part. We are not wise to keep giving to people who will not work when they are able, or to people who do not try to take responsibility for their lives. For example, if a person had a grown child still living at home and that person refused to work and simply took advantage of the rest of the family, true love from the parents would not allow them to continue living that way. The most loving thing the family could do would be to put the grown child into a position where he or she had to work and be responsible.

> Walking in love does not mean you have to become a doormat for everybody and allow people to abuse you and use you.
>
> ⤚ • ⤙

I have decided that if I have tried to help someone for years and they are still not helped, then they really do not intend to change and they are just using me and my resources. Everyone deserves a chance and we can be used by God to give them one, but they still have to make a choice. If they are offered a way out and still choose to stay in their messes, we might as well go help someone who will truly benefit.

Allowing people to use us does not help them, but helping them be responsible does. The Bible teaches us in Proverbs 1:3

to "receive instruction in wise dealing and the discipline of *wise* thoughtfulness…" (emphasis mine). There comes a time when giving to someone is not the best thing for them, when it is not wise. Sometimes it is a sacrifice for me not to meet the need of a person I love and care for. It would be easier for me to give them what they want rather than let them do without. But the God kind of love is not moved emotionally; it follows wisdom.

WE'RE USELESS WITHOUT IT

We need to pray about our love walk, asking God to help us grow and mature in love and to enable us to love people the way He wants us to. I have been studying the love walk for years because I finally got it through my head that my life and ministry would have no power at all if I did not walk in love. I spend a lot of time on platforms with microphones and cameras rolling, but the most important thing is how I live my life off the platform with no microphones and no cameras. That determines what happens when I am in those visible, public settings. When I speak before people, I do not put on a show; I simply want to help them get their lives straightened out if they are in a mess and to encourage people to develop a more mature relationship with God. If we pretend to love people when we are in public, but mistreat them behind closed doors, then according to Scripture, we are nothing more than a big noise, a useless nobody, a whitewashed tomb full of dead men's bones (see 1 Corinthians 13:1, 2; Matthew 23:27).

I don't have anything to offer people except the anointing of God on my life. I am not fancy. I don't sing or do other things that might thrill people. I simply tell people like it is—the truth of

God's Word—when it comes to living in victory and obeying God in practical ways. I tell people how to change so they can enjoy their lives more and I tell them how to grow spiritually. I teach God's Word in a practical way that helps them in their everyday lives. By God's grace, this ministry reaches millions of people around the world, but I have to have God's anointing in order to do what He has called me to do—or I am finished. I have learned that I will not carry God's anointing if I do not walk in love, because God does not anoint the flesh (our own desires and selfish attitudes or behaviors).

You see, when the anointing oil was poured on the priests in the Old Testament, none of it could be put on their bodies—only their heads. God does not anoint carnal behavior. We really must walk in love because that aids and increases the anointing on our lives, and the anointing is what enables us to do what God has called us to do. Again, God's anointing is His presence and power and that enables us to do with ease what we could never accomplish with any amount of struggle on our own. We all need God's anointing. A person does not have to work at a so-called "spiritual" job to need God's anointing. We need it to parent, to survive in the world, to be good friends, on the job, and literally in everything we do.

For years, I was an obnoxious, smart-aleck preacher who would mouth off to my husband at home and then walk up to the pulpit thinking I was a great woman of God. I did not know how to treat people well. I was impatient; everybody had to do things my way or I was going to get upset. Nobody could correct me; nobody could tell me anything; nobody could have any input into my life because I was "the woman of God"—the president of what we then called "Life in the Word."

During that time, things were not happening in my life and ministry the way that I felt they should. I was not seeing the growth I desired for the ministry, and I was not seeing the power of God that I really knew was available. Our meetings were satisfactory because the Lord had graced me with a gift of teaching, but we did not experience the presence of God and the ministry of the Holy Spirit as we do now. I was frustrated and felt unfulfilled. I knew something was missing and finally realized that it was God's presence. Through a long series of God's dealings with me, I finally understood that I had to develop a strong love walk. I realized that God is very concerned about the way we relate to other people because He wants us to love them. The love walk is foundational to everything else we do.

First Corinthians 13:2 says, "And if I have prophetic powers (the gift of interpreting the divine will and purpose), and understand all the secret truths and mysteries and possess all knowledge, and if I have [sufficient] faith so that I can remove mountains, but have not love (God's love in me), I am nothing (a useless nobody)." That's a pretty strong statement: "If I don't walk in love, I am a useless nobody."

> The love walk is foundational to everything else we do.
>
> ⤝ • ⤞

If we want to be useful, we need to really think about this truth and start walking in love as the Bible encourages us:

- "Walk worthy of the calling...bearing with one another in love" (Ephesians 4:1–2, NKJV).
- "Hold fast the pattern of sound words which you have heard from me, in faith and love which are in Christ Jesus" (2 Timothy 1:13, NKJV).

- "And above all things have fervent love for one another, for *'love will cover a multitude of sins'*" (1 Peter 4:8, NKJV).
- "And walk in love, as Christ also has loved us and given Himself for us" (Ephesians 5:2, NKJV).

BE A BLESSING

One of the best ways to walk in love is to be a blessing to other people or simply to help them. There are so many different ways to bless and help people, and many times we can start by just being nice. For example, when we hear that someone has a problem, we need to go beyond saying, "Oh, what a shame!" without taking action. Instead, we need to pray and say: "God, if there is something I can do to help, would You show me what it is?" When we learn that a friend is ill, God might lead us to help by offering to drive that person to a doctor's appointment. When we hear about a family who has lost their home and all of their belongings in a fire or a weather-related disaster, the least we can do is to look around our own homes and go through our closets to see what we can give them. Obviously, no one person can address every single problem on earth, but we can pray and ask God what He would have us do in order to express His love by being a blessing to the people around us.

One of our managers sold his house before the house he was moving into was ready. When I heard he was going to stay in a hotel for a week or two, I started looking for a place for him to live. My son-in-law got involved and started helping me. We found a couple who were moving out of their apartment. They had a week left on their lease and offered to let our manager and his family stay there for that week. Well, at the end of the week, their house still was not complete enough for them to move into. They still needed a little more time. Then my daughter came to me and said: "Would you like us to let them stay with us until their house is finished? Would that be okay?" Now, my daughter and her husband already had four children—and they did not need five more people in their house. But my daughter knows how to be a blessing and she knows that sometimes we have to make ourselves uncomfortable in order to bless somebody else. She was willing to sacrifice some personal comfort in order to walk in love.

If we will concentrate on being a blessing to others, then God will see to it that we are also blessed. We do not need a special word from God before we do something for someone! We can learn what people want and need simply by listening to them or observing them. Look for people in your church who seem to be a little lonely. Look for the person who always comes to the services alone and think about how you would feel in that situation and invite that person to sit with you. Watch for a single mother who has four children hanging on her and looks like she's barely going to make it through the day. Give her $50 and tell her to take her family out to lunch—or offer to babysit her children so *she* can have a quiet lunch. If you overhear someone saying, "My hair is so stringy and awful; I need a perm, but I just don't have the money," hand her $100 and tell her she now has the money to get that perm. Be creative in your thinking as you seek to bless others.

You might say, "Joyce, I don't have $100." My answer to you is to start giving what you do have and you will get to the point of having $100 to give anytime you need it. We often give up when we hear of a need because we do not have what it takes to meet the entire need. Don't let what you don't have stop you from giving what you do have. Don't let what you cannot do stop you from doing what you can do! Stay active, be a blessing, and do something. Otherwise, you will end up doing nothing and that is a total waste of God's ability in your life.

I know you may be thinking, *What about me? I've got needs myself and nobody is doing anything for me.* As long as you keep that attitude, nobody *is* going to do anything for you. You may have to start by giving sacrificially, but you will get to the point where you can give out of your abundance. But unless you start where you are, you will never get to where you need to be.

Sometimes God will put it on our hearts to give people things they do not even really need. They may even have more than we do, but they may need encouragement. They need to know that someone is thinking about them, that someone cares. If you give somebody something—I don't care if they don't even want it—it will bless them. Even if they cannot use it, the fact that we give to them will bless them and us, too.

Sometimes we give somebody something that meets a specific need and sometimes we give them a seed. The Bible says that God gives seed to the sower and bread to the eater (see 2 Corinthians 9:10). People send me many things that I will not use personally, but I can use them for seed, so I give them to someone else. When someone gives us something we cannot use, we should still receive it as a gift, but then use it as a seed with which to bless someone else. I frequently give things to people and say, "If you can't use this

> Sometimes we give somebody something that meets a specific need and sometimes we give them a seed.
>
> →→ • ←←

or don't like it, use it as seed to be a blessing to someone else." Even if they do pass along the gift, they are still blessed because I thought of them.

We need to decide to be a blessing in every situation, and to everyone we meet. Being a blessing may be as simple as smiling at a clerk in a checkout line or it may require doing something that is inconvenient or something we would really rather not do for someone. It may cost time or money, but whatever it takes, we need to understand that walking in love is critical to our relationship with God and essential to an effective prayer life, so we need to seek ways to bless others everywhere we go.

LOVE LOOKS TO GIVE

The Bible gives us the greatest example of the type of sacrificial giving that says, "I'm giving the very best I have." God the Father, out of His love for us, gave His only begotten Son. But when we are faced with an opportunity to give away something, we can be easily tempted to say, "I can't give that! It's the only one I have and I might need it someday." The reality is that many of us keep things we have not used for years. When we do need those things, we usually cannot find them or we realize they do not work anymore or they are so covered with dust that we do not recognize them! Instead of hoarding things, we should use them and then, when we believe we are finished or may not need them again for a few years, go ahead and give them to people who need them now. Then if we do need them later on, God will see that we have them. God's Word teaches that we should use our excess to meet the needs of others, and then when we have a need, their excess will help meet our needs. Remember, we reap only what we have sown. Each time we give to someone in need or simply to bless them, we are assuring ourselves that our needs will be met later on.

I have an elderly mother and an elderly aunt. God has clearly shown me that it is my duty to take care of them in a manner that depicts the way I would want to be cared for in my old age. I may never need any care, but if I do, I have already sown seed for my harvest.

I challenge you to prune (cut back or trim away) your possessions. Walk around your house; gather the things you have not used in a year or two and put them in a box to give away. You might think, *I worked hard for that stuff. I may need that someday.* Do you know what happens when you prune a bush? It grows! If you start pruning your possessions on a regular basis, you will have more than you'll know what to do with and then you will find out you need bigger boxes all the time to carry off all the stuff you are not using. That principle works in my life all the time. When I bring in things, I prune everything else I already have; then I get more stuff and have to prune that. Then people give me more things and then I prune again. That's a cycle of blessing. I am blessed; then I bless others; then I am blessed again; so I bless others some more, and on it goes.

I have had the joy of pruning and giving away many of my clothes. I need a lot of clothes and the way to get them is to give away some of what I have on a regular basis. What a joy it has been for me to give away some of these perfectly good clothes to women who just need a blessing. There are days when I can walk around my office and see perhaps twelve ladies wearing clothes that I used to have. The clothes are a blessing to them, and that blesses me because I was able to participate in blessing them.

We need to stop this nonsense of clinging to our possessions. Instead, we need to express our love by having open hands that refuse to hoard, but are always eager to give to others. Love looks for places to give. Love is aggressive in giving. Love thinks about how it can bless somebody. Love does something nice on purpose.

If I were a carpenter, I would have equipment to help me do carpentry work. If I were a doctor, I would have equipment to help me practice medicine. Similarly, I have learned that if I am going to be a lover of people, I also need equipment, which often comes in the form of material goods that can bless others. If at all possible, I need to be prepared before people's needs come to my attention. Let me suggest that you think about keeping some money with you, money set aside just to give to people who need a blessing. Keep gift certificates to restaurants, grocery stores, or shopping centers handy. When you go to church, work, or family gatherings, take your blessing box with you in your car just in case you need some seed to sow into someone's life.

What I am talking about is radical, outrageous, aggressive, on-purpose giving. Instead of buying groceries, clothes, books, or movie tickets for ourselves all the time, we might buy some of these items for other people, too. Most of us do not need to look very far before we see someone who needs something, and we just need to bless one another. Galatians 6:10 instructs us to "...be mindful to be a blessing, especially to those of the household of faith [those who belong to God's family with you, the believers]." Also, we need to ask God to show us when we may need to give to strangers or unbelievers so that we can share His love with them. No matter who the recipient is, love gives. It cannot stand not to!

LOVE DOES NOT PLAY FAVORITES

I believe love requires us to treat all people basically the same and to have an attitude that honors everyone equally. That does not mean having a best friend or a group of best friends is wrong, but I do believe it is wrong to consider

> I believe love requires us to treat all people basically the same and to have an attitude that honors everyone equally.

some people to be in a "lower" category than others. We should be very careful not to make people feel left out or rejected.

Jesus obviously did some things with Peter, James, and John that He did not do with the other disciples, but I do not think that was because He loved those three more than the rest. I think He simply saw in them something that He could work with, something beyond what He saw in the others. I believe He spent more time developing and pouring Himself into Peter, James, and John because He recognized in them such a great capacity to receive His ministry, perhaps a greater capacity than the others. Even though Jesus spent so much time with Peter, James, and John, and even though He invested so much of Himself in them, I do not think He ever mistreated anyone or treated one person better than another.

Scripture is very clear that God has no favorites. Acts 10:34 says, "God shows no partiality and is no respecter of persons." The Bible also says, "God is not impressed with the positions that men hold and He is not partial and recognizes no external distinctions" (Galatians 2:6). And in James 2:1, the Bible provides excellent teaching on how to regard others: "My brethren, pay no servile regard to people [show no prejudice, no partiality]. Do not [attempt to] hold [and] practice the faith of our Lord Jesus Christ [the Lord] of glory [together with snobbery]!"

We know that a snob is someone who thinks he or she is better than other people. People who are snobs may consider themselves "above" others because they have more money than most, more education than some, or a professional position that commands more worldly respect than other stations in life. Such people may decide not to associate with others who do not have similar or equal status. Snobs do not want to be acquainted or associated with people they deem somehow "beneath" them for some reason. That kind of attitude is called "pride"; it is sin, and it will keep a person from walking in love. It will also hinder answered prayer. The Bible says in Psalm 10:17 that God hears the desires of the humble and in James 4:6 that He gives grace to the humble, but He resists the proud and haughty.

We need to value the things that make us different from one another and to realize that everybody does not have to be just like we are in order for us to be friends with them. As a matter of fact, one of the healthiest things we can do in life is to have a wide variety of friends so we begin to understand that the whole world is not like our neighborhood, our church, our workplace, or any other environment in which we live.

I encourage you to do everything you can to walk in love deliberately. You can do that by refusing to play favorites, by not giving in to the temptation of pride, and by positioning your heart to love and honor all people equally, treating them as God's unique and special creations and valuing them for the people He has made them to be.

LIVE THE GOLDEN RULE

Another biblical principle that will help us walk in love and reap great results when we obey it is found in Matthew. Matthew 7:7–11 says: "Keep on asking and it will be given you; keep on seeking and you will find; keep on knocking [reverently] and [the door] will be opened to you. For everyone who keeps on asking receives; and he who keeps on seeking finds; and to him who keeps on knocking, [the door] will be opened. Or what man is there of you, if his son asks him for a loaf of bread, will hand him a stone? Or if he asks for a fish, will hand him a serpent? If you then, evil as you are, know how to give good and advantageous gifts to your children, how much more will your Father Who is in heaven [perfect as He is] give good and advantageous things to those who keep on asking Him!"

Matthew 7:12 says: "So then, *whatever you desire that others would do to and for you, even so do also to and for them,* for this is (sums up) the Law and the Prophets" (emphasis mine). I think sometimes we approach Matthew 7:7–11 as one subject and Matthew 7:12, which is known as "the golden rule," as an independent thought. We may think Matthew is suddenly going in a different direction, but he is basically saying: *If you ask and keep on asking, it will be given to you, but now here comes a condition: so then, if this is what you want to see happen—however you want other people to treat you, treat them that way first.* This tells us that loving others is a condition of answered prayer! Remember, our faith won't work without love.

The institution of marriage in the United States is in great danger and I think the reason is really quite simple. I believe that, many times, strife begins when neither party will be humble enough and mature enough to be the first one to apologize or the first one to give in. We usually treat people they way they treat us, but according to the Bible, we should be treating them the way we desire to be treated.

No one wants to be the first one to say, "I'm sorry." They think, *Well, if you're not going to be good to me, I'm not going to be good to you. If you're not going to show me respect, I'm not going to show you respect. If you don't ever do anything for me, I'm not going to do anything for you.* When one person waits for the other to make amends—and the other one does not—offenses accumulate, anger builds, harsh words are spoken, and relationships become deeply troubled.

If a husband and wife were walking in love by obeying the golden rule, both of them will think, *I wish my spouse would bring me more gifts and he doesn't, so I'm going to start buying him gifts. I wish my spouse would just give me more compliments and pay a little more attention to me, but he doesn't, so I'm just going to start complimenting him all the time and showing him all kinds of affection.*

These same principles apply to other relationships besides marriage. There is always a possibility for strife in other family relationships, at work, among parents on the Little League team (and among the Little Leaguers themselves!), on church committees, and everyplace where people are trying to accomplish something together. Treating others as we would like to be treated in every situation will reduce strife and lead to strong, fruitful relationships in which people do what God has called them to do and enjoy Him together.

> Treating others as we would like to be treated in every situation will reduce strife and lead to strong, fruitful relationships.
>
> ➤➤ • ◄◄

Live by the golden rule: whatever you want other people to do for you, do for them. If you want friends, be friendly. If you want gifts, give something away. If you want people to encourage you, find people and encourage them. If you want people to pray for you, pray for others. You may think encouragement, prayer, friendliness, and gift giving are little things, but it's the little things people don't do that destroy relationships. At the same time, it's the little things that also build up relationships. So whether it's a big thing or a little thing, treat people the way you want to be treated. That's a never-fail way to walk in love.

I am sure we all believe that God the Father heard and answered Jesus' prayers, but let us also remember that Jesus walked in love, literally, at all times. Even on the cross, while suffering intense pain, He said, "Father, forgive them for they know not what they do." He kept on giving right up to the ultimate sacrifice, which was His life.

SUMMARY

One sure way to make certain that our prayers are effective is to walk in love. Truly loving other people encompasses so many heart attitudes that are pleasing to God. Above everything else, God honors the heart that truly loves Him and loves other people. In fact, our faith in Him works through love and we express our love for Him by loving other people. Love is God's nature, and the more we demonstrate love to others, the more we become like Him. As we walk in His ways and imitate Him by loving others, our relationship with Him deepens and is strengthened and our prayer lives are enriched.

Prayer Points

-›- We are to love God above everything else and then to have fervent love for others.

-›- Faith works through love.

-›- First Corinthians 13 describes love.

-›- Love does not require anyone to be abused or to be treated as a doormat or to take responsibility for people who will not take responsibility for themselves as best they can.

-›- Without the love of God flowing in our lives, our ability to effectively help others is hindered.

-›- Love does not hoard or cling to things. One of the best ways to express love is to be a blessing to others.

-›- Love does not play favorites or act snobbishly, but values everyone.

-›- When we walk in love, we will treat others as we like to be treated.

-›- People who walk in love never quit; they love until they draw their last breath.

12

Fourteen Hindrances to Answered Prayer

Now that you have learned some of the keys to effective prayer, I want us to look at some hindrances to answered prayer. We need to know not only what to do, but also what *not* to do when we pray. If we are going to invest our time and energy in prayer, we want to do everything within our power to get good results!

Naturally, some of the hindrances to answered prayer will be the opposite of keys to effective prayer (for example, forgiveness is a key to effective prayer, and unforgiveness is a hindrance to prayer). I want to include some of those "opposites" in this chapter anyway because we need to understand not only how the positive elements of an issue increase effectiveness in prayer, but also how its negative aspects cause problems in our prayer lives.

1. PRAYERLESSNESS

I know this sounds simple, but our prayers are not answered when we do not pray. Several times in this book, I have referenced

James 4:2, which says, "You do not have, because you do not ask." That sounds simple, I know, but it is true. We have to ask for what we want and need. Sometimes we work on situations in our minds, or talk about them with our friends, or wish or hope, but we do not pray. Thinking, wishing, hoping, and talking with others are not prayer; only *prayer* is prayer. When we have a need or a situation that concerns us, we are only praying when we talk to God about it.

Did you know that God is waiting for us to make requests of Him in prayer? Matthew 7:7 and Isaiah 65:1–2 tell us that He is ready to act for us if we will only pray.

I once had an employee who often complained about how much work he had to do. I don't think he even realized he was complaining, but he was irritating me. I fussed and fumed over it in my heart; I got aggravated; I thought negative thoughts. I actually began to complain about my employee who was complaining! Then one day I realized I had never actually prayed about his negative attitude, so I simply asked God to cause him to stop complaining about his workload and to be thankful and positive.

The very next day when I saw the man, he made the first positive comment I had heard in a long time about his job. He mentioned that he had some time to rest and things were getting better. Wow! God was ready to help us, but His hands were tied until someone prayed. My prayerlessness was just as wrong as my employee's complaining. I was hindering God by being too passive to open a door for Him to work. I thought about the problem, resented

> Don't let prayerlessness hinder God from working in your life and the lives of your loved ones.
>
> ⤜ • ⤛

the problem, talked about the problem, and got aggravated about the problem, but literally months went by before I prayed. As soon as I did, God intervened.

Learn from my mistake and don't let prayerlessness hinder God from working in your life and the lives of your loved ones.

2. LACK OF BOLDNESS

Not only do we need to pray in order to have our prayers answered, we also need to pray boldly, which means without fear and unreservedly. Jesus has made a way for us to approach God with boldness because He made us righteous through His death on the cross. Because of what He has done for us, we can go to God with total confidence and pray unashamedly, knowing that He loves us, hears us, and will answer our prayers in the best possible way.

When we understand that we can rightfully approach God with boldness, we will be able to overcome the enemy's attempts to make us feel condemned and we will become daring in our prayers. We will no longer buy into the enemy's lie that causes us to say to ourselves, *Well, I know God can do great things, but I find it hard to believe He will do them for me.* We think such thoughts because we do not think we are worthy, but we must always remember that Jesus has made us worthy, and when we approach God boldly, we can count on Him to be merciful to us (see Hebrews 4:16). Mercy means that God will give us what we do not deserve and bless us when we do not deserve to be blessed—if we are bold enough to ask. We ask in Jesus' name, not in our own name. That means we are presenting to the Father all that Jesus is, not all that we are. We are nothing without Jesus!

Ephesians 3:20 tells us that God is able to do more than we could ever dare to hope, ask or think, so we need to determine to be daring and to avail ourselves of all He can do by asking boldly!

When people ask me to do something for them, I respond better if they approach me with confidence. I want them to be respectful and thankful, but not fearful. Confidence breeds confidence. In other words, when people approach me with confidence, their confidence gives me confidence that they can handle what they are asking for. However, if they come in fear, I am hesitant to partner with them in anything, because where fear exists, the devil has an open door to bring defeat.

Don't ask God for less than you would like to. Be bold and be confident. Ask Him for great things and open the door for Him to show just how great He really is.

3. SIN

Psalm 66:18 says, "If I regard iniquity in my heart, the Lord will not hear me." In other words, sin that we are aware of and refuse to deal with is a hindrance to answered prayer. None of us are perfect. We may all have something in our lives that displeases God, but it may be unintentional and we may not even realize it. Once God convicts us of sin and makes us aware of it, we must deal with it. Otherwise, we are regarding iniquity in our hearts, and in that case, God will not hear us.

If we have sin hidden in our hearts, we cannot pray with confidence that God will answer. However, if we ask Him to reveal those hidden sins, He will. When He does, we must respond if we want to keep the lines of communication open with Him. For example, if He brings to mind a situation in which we did not tell the truth, we cannot think, *Oh, that's no big deal. It was just an innocent little white lie.* We cannot take something He shows us and sweep it under the rug or decide it does not really matter. Instead, we have to admit that we have sinned, repent for lying, and receive His forgiveness.

More often than not, what we call "little things" end up causing us major trouble because we allow them to grow into sinful habits and patterns. When God reveals sin in our lives, we need to stop what we are doing and repent. We need to revere Him so much that we take Him seriously—immediately! This means we do everything within our power to make sure that our relationship with Him is clean and pure and unobstructed by sin. Otherwise, our prayers will go unheard and unanswered.

4. PRAYING OUTSIDE OF GOD'S WILL

Not praying according to God's will, of course, keeps our prayers from being answered. One of the best ways to make sure we are praying in the will of God is to pray the Word as much as we can. What I mean by that is we need to use a verse, a passage, or a principle in God's Word to back up what we are praying.

We will not find Scriptures that address all of our needs or wants in detail. For example, we will not find a verse that tells us specifically to go buy a new car, but we will find Scriptures that tell us God will meet our needs. If a new car is a legitimate need, we can pray and believe that God's will is to meet that need.

Sometimes there are things we want to pray for, but we are not sure whether those things are God's will for us, according to scripture. In those cases, we simply need to ask God to give it if it is His will to do so, and to help us be satisfied with His decision.

On the other hand, there are other things we know to be part of God's will because He does specify them in His Word. For instance, 2 Peter 3:9 says that He is "...not willing that any should perish but that all should come to repentance" (NKJV). Therefore, we know that we are praying within His will when we pray for people to be saved.

When we pray in agreement with God's will, we *will* have what we ask for. We may have to wait, because God's timing is part of His will, but it will come. We can say, "It's mine. I may not see it yet, but it belongs to me, so it's on its way."

I am sure we all ask for things amiss at times, but God knows our hearts. I

> God's timing is part of His will.
>
> ⇥ • ⇤

believe that if He cannot give us what we ask for, that He will give us something better if we keep a good attitude.

5. PRAYING WITH THE WRONG MOTIVES

You know that James 4:2 says, "You do not have, because you do not ask," but I want you to also see the verse that follows. It says, "[Or] you do ask [God for them] and yet fail to receive, because you ask with wrong purpose and evil, selfish motives. Your intention is [when you get what you desire] to spend it in sensual pleasures." A motive is the "why" behind the "what." It is why we do what we do. In prayer, the reason we pray is much more important than the words we say. God looks at our hearts, and when He sees an impure motive, He cannot answer prayer.

Having a pure heart that truly loves God and loves people is always an acceptable motive to the Lord. Selfishness is unacceptable; revenge is unacceptable; manipulation and control are unacceptable; jealousy is unacceptable; pride is unacceptable. In fact, everything that is selfish and unloving is an unacceptable motive.

I will admit that there was a time when I prayed and prayed for God to help my ministry grow because I thought having a large, influential ministry would make me feel important. Do you know what happened? The ministry did not grow at all! In fact, it did not even begin to grow until my motives had been purified, the selfishness had been eliminated, and I could truthfully say that I only wanted the ministry to grow so that I could help more people.

Similarly, we may want to get our way in a situation and ask God to change someone's heart to be in agreement with us without even considering what might be best for the other person. God won't answer those types of selfish prayers. We might ask God to have someone apologize to us when, in reality, God wants us to apologize. Whatever happened may not have been our fault, but God still wants us to humble ourselves and be the ones to make peace. Why would He do that? Because humility is more valuable to us in the long run than having our feelings soothed because someone apologizes to us.

We need to be asking God to purify our hearts on a regular basis so that we can pray with the right motives. We need to honestly examine our motives. A lot of things changed in my life when I began to ask myself why I was doing what I was doing. Likewise, many of my prayers changed when I became more sensitive to the motive behind them. Taking a look at our motives can be painful, but it must be done if we truly desire to live before God with pure hearts.

6. DOUBT AND UNBELIEF

We know that faith in God is foundational to answered prayer, so it stands to reason that doubt and unbelief—which are opposites of faith—will keep our prayers from being answered. Faith is a powerful spiritual dynamic, and it is something God responds to and blesses. But our faith is not without opposition. Satan will attack our minds with doubt, unbelief, and questioning, and when he does, we need to check in with our hearts and see what they say. We can believe something in our hearts even when our minds question it, and we need to go with what is in our hearts and not with what is in our heads. We are not supposed to believe our doubts; we are supposed to doubt our doubts and believe our God.

One of the keys to overcoming doubt and unbelief is found in Hebrews 12:2, which says: "Looking away [from all that will distract] to Jesus, Who is the Leader and the Source of our faith...and is also its Finisher...." Many times, doubt and unbelief start with distraction. When we are distracted from God's promises or God's ability to come through for us, then we begin to doubt. We start thinking more and more about our problems or our challenges, and then our faith begins to diminish. But we need to do what Hebrews 12:2 says to do and keep looking to Jesus. In order to resist doubt and stay in faith, we need to stare at Him, at His goodness, at His ability to help us, at His love for us, and merely glance at our problems. We do not deny the existence of problems, but we do refuse to pay too much attention to them.

Keeping our eyes off everything that would steal our faith or distract us from what God says is the antidote to doubt and unbelief. We have to remember that He is the Source of our faith and He finishes what He starts—so there's no reason to doubt.

The Apostle James said that when we doubt, we become double-minded and the double-minded man receives nothing he asks for from God because he is unstable in all of his ways (see James 1:6–8). We need to decide what we believe and not change our minds when our circumstances begin to waver. We need to remember that John 11:40 promises that we will see the glory of God if we will only *believe*!

7. WORRY

Another reason people do not have their prayers answered is that after they pray, they worry. Philippians 4:6 says, *"Do not fret or have anxiety about anything,* but in every circumstance and in everything, by prayer and petition (definite requests), with thanksgiving, continue to make your wants known to God" (emphasis mine). Anxiety, which is another

> Anxiety . . . means spending today trying to figure out tomorrow or spending today fearing tomorrow.
>
> ->>- • -<-

word for worry, means spending today trying to figure out tomorrow or spending today fearing tomorrow—and we are not to have anxiety about anything.

When we pray and then worry, we are not exercising trust in God. We are not fully releasing our burdens or needs to Him; we are "taking them back" and working them over in our minds. When we insist upon keeping our hands on the situations we pray about, and not letting God have them completely, He does not have much freedom to answer our prayers. We say we trust God, but we want to have a backup plan just in case God does not come through for us. Worry is meditating on our problems, but we are told to meditate on God's Word, not our problems.

The opposite of worry and anxiety is peace, and if we are going to live in peace, we need to learn how to live our lives one day at a time. Jesus says in Matthew 6:34, "So do not worry or be anxious about tomorrow, for tomorrow will have worries and anxieties of its own. Sufficient for each day is its own trouble." In other words, Jesus is telling us not to spend today worrying about tomorrow. All of our "todays" have enough trouble—and we only have enough grace and enough energy to deal with today. Just as each day has its own trouble, each day has its own supply of grace. God does not give us grace today to live tomorrow. We need to make the most of the grace we have today, refuse to be anxious about tomorrow, determine to leave our prayers in God's hands, and not take our problems back by worrying.

8. LACK OF GRATITUDE

A lack of gratitude is a hindrance to answered prayer. As I wrote in chapter 5, why should God do more for us if we are murmuring about what He has already done? By the same token, if we genuinely appreciate His goodness and have hearts that are thankful for all He has done, He will be inclined to continue to bless us.

A lack of gratitude indicates that something is not right in a person's heart. The reason people grumble and complain is not that they do not have what they want; it is that they have a character problem. People of godly character are thankful, always appreciative of what God does for them. Thanksgiving keeps us focused on God.

On the other hand, a lack of gratitude causes people to never be satisfied and to talk about their discontent. I don't think anything opens the door for the enemy to influence a person's life like murmuring and complaining, because we are agreeing with him when we grumble. However, when we speak words of thanksgiving, we are agreeing with God because the Bible is full of Scriptures that instruct us to be thankful and not to complain. A thankful person is a powerful person, and when we are thankful, God is able and willing to do more for us than He has ever done before.

We can "be" thankful even if we don't particularly "feel" thankful. We can feel wrong and still choose to do what is right. Until we learn this dynamic principle, there is no hope of truly walking in the Spirit.

The Apostle Paul, who knew much suffering during his life, and certainly had reason to complain about some of his circumstances, said this: "I have learned in whatever state I am, to be content: I know how to be abased, and I know how to abound" (Philippians 4:11–12, NKJV). In other words, we need to stay thankful in every situation, no matter how we feel. True gratitude is not only being thankful when things are going well, but also remaining steadfast when dealing with life's struggles, obstacles, and disappointments. When God sees that we are thankful no matter what, He can answer our prayers.

9. NEGATIVE CONFESSION

We can render our prayers ineffective with negative confessions. When we allow doubt and unbelief to take root in our minds and then begin to speak negatively, we can hinder our prayers. When we pray and ask God to do something and then turn around and say, "I am afraid God will not come through for me," that is a negative confession.

The words we speak are powerful, more powerful than we realize. In fact, Proverbs 18:21 says, "Death and life are in the power of the tongue, and they who indulge in it shall eat the fruit of it [for death or life]." In other words, we will have what we say, so we need to be speaking positively, not negatively.

Isaiah 53:7 says about Jesus, "He was oppressed and He was afflicted, yet He opened not His mouth" (NKJV). Jesus "opened not His mouth" and did not speak negatively because He knew that He could thwart or delay God's plan by speaking negatively at the wrong time. Sure, His trials were difficult—unimaginably grueling—but He did not complain.

We need to be able to make the same statement about ourselves—that when we are going through hard times, we open not our mouths. We do not complain; we do not murmur; we do not speak ill of others; we do not doubt God with our words. You see, our words do not exist independently of who we are. Instead, our words represent who we are because they reveal what is in our hearts. Matthew 12:34 says, "For out of the abundance of the heart the mouth speaks" (NKJV). When our hearts are full of doubt, we will make negative confessions, but when they are filled with faith, our words will reveal our faith and trust in God. When God hears a prayer followed by a negative confession, He does not respond.

> When our hearts are full of doubt, we will make negative confessions, but when they are filled with faith, our words will reveal our faith and trust in God.

But when He hears a prayer that is accompanied with words that express confidence in Him, He delights to answer.

10. FAILURE TO FOCUS

Another reason prayers are not answered is that we do not stay focused when we pray and we are not diligent to keep our hearts connected to heaven. Before we know it, we are saying words that have little meaning or we are distracted by the many pressures or activities of life. We end up not concentrating on talking to God, not really paying attention to Him—and that's not a good way to have a prayer answered!

One of the best stories I know about focus has to do with taming lions. When a lion trainer goes into a cage with a lion, he takes three things with him: a whip, a stun gun, and a stool with three or four legs on it. He holds the stool with the legs pointing toward the lion. Why? Because a lion cannot focus on more than one thing at a time. When the lion sees more than one leg on the stool, he actually "freezes" and cannot move to attack the trainer.

I believe we are like the lions and can be paralyzed, in a way, when too much comes at us at one time. When we cannot focus, we are not effective or productive. The Bible says in Proverbs 4:25–27, "Let your eyes look right on [with fixed purpose], and let your gaze be straight before you. Consider well the path of your feet, and let all your ways be established and ordered aright. Turn not aside to the right hand or to the left. . . ."

If we do want to receive from the Lord—if we do want our prayers answered—we need to learn to stay focused not only in prayer, but also in life. We need to know what God has called us to do, prioritize that, focus on that, pray about that and watch as God answers our prayers and does great things through us.

Know what God has called you to do; be responsible for and pray consistently concerning those things. No one's prayers have as much effect on your life, family, and ministry as yours do. When Paul told Timothy to give himself to his ministry, to "throw himself wholly" into his duties (see 1 Timothy 4:15), he was telling him to stay focused. Prayer is like a laser beam. It is powerful, but you must stay focused in an area until the desired results are accomplished. Whatever God assigns you to do, stay focused! Focused prayer is powerful prayer!

11. NOT CARING FOR PEOPLE IN NEED

E. M. Bounds writes, "Compassion stands beside sympathy for others, is interested in them, and is concerned about them" and that "prayer belongs to the compassionate man."[1] If we want our prayers to be answered, we need to be compassionate and kind to the poor. I have referenced Proverbs 21:13 before, but I want to emphasize it again: "Whoever stops his ears at the cry of the poor will cry out himself and not be heard." That verse speaks for itself. If we want God to hear our prayers, we need to care for those who are less fortunate than we are.

First John 3:17–18 says, "But if anyone has this world's goods (resources for sustaining life) and sees his brother and fellow believer in need, yet closes his heart of compassion against him, how can the love of God live and remain in him? Little children, let us not love [merely] in theory or in speech but in deed and in truth (in practice and sincerity)." We close our hearts or stop our ears when we hear about people who are needy, for several reasons. First, we may think someone else should take care of them. I want to tell you that someone else should not take care of them; the Church of Jesus Christ is called and commissioned by God to care for the poor and needy. The government is not called and commissioned, the government is not anointed by God—but His people are. Second, we may be afraid to get involved because we think someone will take advantage of us. Well, we need to refuse to let that happen. We need to be led by the Holy Spirit, do what we know is right, and serve others well without allowing ourselves to be exploited. Third, we may be just plain lazy. Laziness is not a good reason to ignore the commands of Christ, so we need to get up and do something about the needs around us.

We may be aware of so many needs that we feel overwhelmed, or even worse, we may become hardened to hearing about them simply because we hear of so many. Today, tragedy and disaster fill the newspapers and television broadcasts. We continually hear about terrible diseases, accidents, earthquakes, tsunamis, fires, floods, landslides, tornados, hurricanes, and other disasters.

God has equipped us with compassionate hearts and we are told in 1 John 3:17 not to close our hearts of compassion when we see needs. Satan would like for our love to grow cold. As a matter of fact, Matthew tells us that love grown cold will be a sign of the Last Days. Matthew 24:12 says that "the love of the great body of people will grow cold because of the multiplied

> Don't ignore the needs you hear about by closing your heart or letting your love grow cold.
>
> ➤➤ • ⭠⭠

lawlessness" and wickedness in the land. The best way to combat hardness of heart and a stronghold of cold love is to stay active helping those who are less fortunate than you are. Don't ignore the needs you hear about by closing your heart or letting your love grow cold. Instead, respond to them.

The Book of James reveals the secret to having pure religion before God which is to "visit orphans and widows in their trouble..." (James 1: 27, NKJV). Those two categories of people (orphans and widows) are very important to God and they are mentioned often in the Bible, but I believe the phrase "orphans and widows" is also a way to describe anyone who is hurting, lonely, oppressed, or in need of anything. When we do not extend the love of God to people like this, our prayers will be hindered. We need to be a blessing to people, but especially to the poor and needy and to the orphans and widows. If we will do that, we will be expressing the love of God and He will answer our prayers.

I have referenced Isaiah 58:6–9 before in this book, but I want you to see it in the context of the current chapter. "[Rather] is not this the fast that I have chosen: to loose the bonds of wickedness, to undo the bands of the yoke, to let the oppressed go free, and that you break every [enslaving] yoke? Is it not to divide your bread with the hungry and bring the homeless poor into your house— when you see the naked, that you cover him, and that you hide not yourself from [the needs of] your own flesh and blood? Then shall your light break forth like the morning, and your healing (your restoration and the power of a new life) shall spring forth speedily; your righteousness (your rightness, your justice, and your right relationship with God) shall go before you [conducting you to peace and prosperity], and the glory of the Lord shall be your rear guard. Then you shall call, and the Lord will answer; you shall cry, and He will say, Here I am...."

12. REBELLION

Being rebellious toward authority will keep our prayers from being answered. As you read earlier in this book, a submitted heart, which is the opposite of a rebellious heart, is tender toward God and eager to obey Him. A rebellious person, on the other hand, will intentionally disobey—and God does not bless disobedience as we've already discussed.

I am so convinced that rebellion hinders my prayer and my relationship with God that I would be afraid to ever walk onto a platform and begin to teach God's Word if I had been knowingly rebellious toward my husband and had not apologized to him and to God. I would not do that because I would be in sin and the enemy would be able to devour me. I have to stay under the covering God has given me; we all need to stay under the authority He has put in our lives so that our hearts will be right toward Him and our prayers will be answered.

13. UNFORGIVENESS

You already know that I believe walking in love, which includes forgiving people, is the most important condition for effective prayer. In the same vein, I also believe that unforgiveness is probably the number one reason prayers are not answered. I would venture to say that more ground is given up in a believer's life through unforgiveness than through anything else. God's Word contains many Scriptures that emphasize the importance of forgiveness, which is nothing more than treating others the way God treats us. I do not think we can find any clearer biblical command to forgive than Ephesians 4:32, which says that we are to forgive "one another [readily and freely], as God in Christ forgave you."

> I also believe that unforgiveness is probably the number one reason prayers are not answered.
>
> ➤➤ • ◄◄

Because we live in a fallen world full of people who are as imperfect as we are, we cannot avoid being hurt, offended, victimized, or betrayed. We will have reasons to be angry, but unresolved anger turns to bitterness and unforgiveness—and that will hinder our prayers. In fact, Ephesians 4:26 says, "When angry, do not sin; do not ever let your wrath (your exasperation, your fury or indignation) last until the sun goes down." We simply cannot hold on to anger and harbor unforgiveness in our hearts if we want God to answer our prayers.

Jesus makes this point plain in Mark 11:25, when He says, "And whenever you stand praying, if you have anything against anyone, forgive him and let it drop (leave it, let it go), in order that your Father Who is in heaven may also forgive you your [own] failings and shortcomings and let them drop." In other words, whatever we have against anyone must be forgiven. No matter how major or how minor an issue seems, we have to let it go. We do not wait until we feel like forgiving; we forgive by making an intentional choice, a willful decision to let a matter drop. When we do, we make a way for our prayers to be answered.

14. PRIDE

First Peter 5:5 says that "'*God resists the proud, but gives grace to the humble*'" (NKJV). We can see from that verse that pride is certainly a hindrance to answered prayer! When we pray and ask for God's grace in a situation, pride will block it, but humility will pave the way for it. When we're proud, we don't think we need God or anyone else. We feel self-sufficient; we are self-reliant. We think we are better than other people. Pride is very serious to God. The Bible contains many Scriptures that affirm this, but one of the strongest is Proverbs 16:5, which says: "Everyone proud and arrogant in heart is disgusting, hateful, and exceedingly offensive to the Lord; be assured [I pledge it] they will not go unpunished."

Pride will keep our prayers from being answered and we must deal with our pride if we want God to hear and respond to us when we pray. We need to ask Him to show us areas in our hearts where we are proud and we need to repent. The best way to turn from a particular sin or stop an old attitude or thought pattern is to ask God's forgiveness for it and to choose to develop the opposite attitude or behavior instead. So, when overcoming the sin of pride, we need to ask God to help us develop humility and do everything we can to cultivate humility in our hearts. We need to be humble not only before God, but also in our relationships with other people.

One of the best ways to practice humility is through confession. The first sentence of James 5:16 says: "Confess to one another therefore your faults (your slips, your false steps, your offenses, your sins) and pray [also] for one another, that you may be healed and restored [to a spiritual tone of mind and heart]." If the power to be healed and restored can come through confession and prayer, then we need to know how to confess and how to pray.

Confessing our faults to someone and asking for prayer requires first of all that we find someone we truly trust and secondly that we are willing to put aside our pride and humbly share our struggles. If you find that challenging, ask God to help you grow in humility because the results are amazing if you find a friend you can trust, and you share with that person, "I'm struggling in this area and I don't want to, but I'm hurting and I need you to pray for me."

Confessing our faults to someone and asking for prayer requires first of all that we find someone we truly trust and secondly that we are willing to put aside our pride and humbly share our struggles.

→→ • ←←

Once I was really struggling with jealousy toward a friend who had received something I had asked God for, but had not received yet. I did not want to feel the way I did and I knew it was wrong, but I could not seem to break free from resenting her blessing and wishing it were mine. The jealousy was even causing me to be cold in my attitude toward her. As I read James 5:16 one day, I decided I needed to humble myself and ask someone to pray for me. I did not mind talking to God about my problem, but I certainly was not looking forward to telling anyone else (that was pride!). I went to my husband and told him I was feeling jealous of my friend. I confessed it as sin and asked him to pray for me. Sharing my feelings was embarrassing for me, but it also set me free.

I can assure you, just from these experiences and many others I have had, that when we are really struggling with something, if we will go humbly to a trusted person who really knows how to pray—someone who will not gossip or broadcast our concerns to others—and simply share our challenges with that person and ask for prayer, the results can be tremendous.

There is no need to be ashamed to tell a true, praying confidant what our difficulties are. This is one way we keep pride out of our lives and exercise humility. In fact, someone I know and respect once came to me and said, "You know, I just need to share this with somebody and I'm hoping if I just *get it out,* maybe it will break the power of Satan." This man traveled alone often, and went on to say: "I am really being tempted to think about other women when I'm away from my wife for a long period of time." He said: "I'll see a woman in the airport or something, and my mind just goes off in a wrong direction. I don't want to do that, but I cannot seem to control it."

I prayed with him and he later said: "Sharing my struggle brought a breakthrough." I would imagine that simply sharing your struggles will bring a breakthrough also. You see, Satan likes to keep things hidden. He is pleased when we try to handle situations ourselves, even when we know we cannot, because that is pride. When we ask others to help us, we are being humble. That pleases God and He releases power to help us overcome.

We all need help. We *all* struggle and your challenges probably are no worse than anyone else's. God has designed His family to need one another. Sometimes we simply cannot carry the loads of our lives alone and sometimes we are too stubborn or too proud to ask for the help we need. Remember, God will resist those who have pride in their hearts and their pride will hinder their prayers. But God hears the prayers of humble hearts and sends His grace in response.

SUMMARY

There are a number of hindrances to answered prayer and I hope learning about them will help you avoid them. I want to encourage you to do everything you can to maintain a vibrant, effective prayer life and to deal with every issue in your life that would cause your prayers to go unanswered.

Prayer Points

➔➤ Just as we need to know the keys to effective prayer, we also need to know the hindrances to answered prayer.

➔➤ God cannot answer our prayers if we do not pray.

➔➤ Lack of boldness will cause our prayers to go unanswered. Because we stand in Jesus' righteousness, we can approach God boldly and pray with confidence.

➔➤ We need to deal with sin—even unintentional sin—because it blocks the communication we can enjoy with God through prayer.

➔➤ If we want our prayers to be answered, we need to be sure what we are praying for is consistent with God's Word and His nature.

➔➤ Praying with wrong motives will not result in answered prayer. Our hearts need to be pure and our motives right.

➔➤ Doubt and unbelief are hindrances to answered prayer. We need to pray in faith and not allow the enemy to cause us to doubt.

➤ Worry keeps our prayers from being answered because it robs us of our trust in God and causes us to take our problems back.

➤ A lack of gratitude indicates that something is not right in a person's heart, and a thankful heart is necessary for answered prayer.

➤ Our words reveal what is in our hearts, and when we make negative confessions, our prayers may go unanswered.

➤ Failure to focus can hinder our prayers. When we are distracted and divided in our prayers and in our lives, we should not expect to receive anything from God.

➤ God's people are called and commissioned to care for the poor and needy. If we neglect them, God will not hear our cries or answer our prayers.

➤ Rebellion will lead to unanswered prayer. God cannot bless us if we have rebellious attitudes toward authority.

➤ Unforgiveness is probably the biggest hindrance to prayer. We simply must treat others as God treats us and extend forgiveness to everyone who offends us.

➤ Pride will cause prayers to go unanswered, but humility attracts God's grace.

13

Sure Victory in Prayer

Do you know that you have an enemy? He is invisible, but he is real, as we read in Ephesians 6:12: "For we are not wrestling with flesh and blood [contending only with physical opponents], but against the despotisms, against the powers, against [the master spirits who are] the world rulers of this present darkness, against the spirit forces of wickedness in the heavenly (supernatural) sphere."

Your enemy's name is Satan; he is a spiritual being; he commands the forces of the kingdom of darkness; and he is determined to destroy God's people. He hates God; he hates everyone who believes in God; he has a plan for your personal destruction, for the destruction of your marriage and your family, for the destruction of your health, your finances, your emotions, and every other area of your life. But there is good news: you can halt his plans—and you do that through the power of prayer. Satan is a violent enemy; he launches violent assaults against believers, but all the violence in hell is no match for the mighty power of simple, believing prayer. I like what Watchman Nee wrote on this topic: "As God hears our prayer, Satan's plan is definitely defeated. In answering our prayer,

God thwarts the evil will of Satan, and consequently, the latter is not able to ill-treat us according to this scheme. Whatever we gain in prayer is the enemy's loss."[1]

THE WEAPONS OF OUR WARFARE

Ephesians 6:13 instructs us to stand our ground "on the evil day." What is the evil day? I believe "the evil day" refers to any time in our lives when Satan attacks us. The attack could be physical, mental, emotional, or spiritual. So how do we fight back? We fight with spiritual weapons because the warfare we fight is in the spiritual realm. 2 Corinthians 10:4 says: "For the weapons of our warfare are not physical [weapons of flesh and blood], but they are mighty before God for the overthrow and destruction of strongholds." Let's look at three of the most powerful spiritual weapons we need to have in our arsenal: the Word of God, the name of Jesus, and the blood of Jesus.

Weapon #1: The Word of God

The Word of God is a powerful weapon. Andrew Murray writes that "...when God, the infinite Being, in whom everything is life and power, spirit and truth, in the very deepest meaning of the words—when God speaks forth Himself in His words, He does indeed give Himself, His love and His life, His will and His power, to those who receive these words...."[2] We find God's

> We must learn how to speak the Word to the devil if we are going to live in victory.
>
> ⤞ • ⤝

love, life, will, and power both *revealed* to us and *made available* to us through His Word; it is indeed a mighty force.

Hebrews 4:12 says, "For the word of God *is* living and powerful, and sharper than any two-edged sword, piercing even to the division of soul and spirit, and of joints and marrow, and is a discerner of the thoughts and intents of the heart" (NKJV). Just think about that: a sword with razor-sharp edges on both sides can do serious damage! When we know the Word, believe its truth, submit to its authority, and use it against the enemy, he ends up defeated! We must learn how to speak the Word to the devil if we are going to live in victory. The devil talks to us by putting wrong thoughts into our minds, and we can and should talk back to him by speaking God's Word out loud. Jeremiah 23:28 says, "...he who has My word, let him speak My word faithfully...." The Word of God is a two-edged sword and we must *wield* it, not merely *have* it (see Hebrews 4:12). We wield the sword by speaking the Word. Ephesians 6:17 specifically talks about "the sword that the Spirit wields, which is the Word of God." In my book, *The Word, the Name, the Blood*, I write about this "sword that the Spirit wields" and what that phrase practically means in our everyday lives: "I believe it means that the Holy Spirit in the believer knows exactly what Scripture to use in every situation. He knows precisely what kind of attack the believer is encountering...."[3] As we commune with Him in prayer, we are able to hear His voice whispering instructions to us. For example, if we are in a threatening situation, we might hear Him say, "Don't be afraid. Remember that My Word says to fear not."

The fourth chapter of Luke tells us that the Holy Spirit led Jesus into the wilderness for forty days. While He was there, He endured attack after attack after attack from the enemy. Every time the devil tempted Him, Jesus replied by saying, "It is written," and then by quoting a verse of Scripture.

From this chapter in Luke, we can learn that temptations come in cycles. Luke 4:13 says, "And when the devil had ended every [the complete cycle of] temptation, he [temporarily] left Him [that is, stood off from Him] until another more opportune and favorable time." We know from this verse that the devil is going to attack, attack, attack. We have to resist those attacks. We must stand firm. He will leave us alone for a little while, but we better not get sleepy and lazy. We have to be watchful because he is waiting for another opportune time and he will come back and try something else.

We often ask ourselves: *When am I ever going to get to the point where I don't have to endure these attacks from the devil?* The answer is when we get to heaven! Personally, I would be more concerned if the devil never came against me. This is because if he is not bothering me, then I am probably not bothering him! And if I am not bothering him, I am not doing what God has called me to do.

Even though the enemy will harass and attack us as long as we live, we can resist him; we can stand against him; we can push him away and cause him to retreat; we can fight back with weapons that render him powerless. If you want to really make the devil angry and send him running, use God's Word to remind him of the cross and his defeat at Calvary. Let me give you some examples:

- Colossians 2:15: "[God] disarmed the principalities and powers that were ranged against us and made a bold display and public example of them, in triumphing over them in Him and in it [the cross]."
- 1 John 4:4: "... He Who lives in you is greater (mightier) than he who is in the world."

- Isaiah 54:17: "But no weapon that is formed against you shall prosper, and every tongue that shall rise against you in judgment you shall show to be in the wrong."
- 1 John 3:8: "...The reason the Son of God was made manifest (visible) was to undo (destroy, loosen, and dissolve) the works the devil [has done]."
- Colossians 1:13: "[The Father] has delivered and drawn us to Himself out of the control and the dominion of darkness and has transferred us into the kingdom of the Son of His love."
- Hebrews 4:12: "For the Word that God speaks is alive and full of power [making it active, operative, energizing, and effective]; it is sharper than any two-edged sword."
- 2 Corinthians 2:14: "But thanks be to God, Who in Christ always leads us in triumph [as trophies of Christ's victory] and through us spreads and makes evident the fragrance of the knowledge of God everywhere."

The Word of God has power in our lives and it has power over the enemy. We need to not only know the Word; we need to believe it and to obey it. We obey it by doing what it tells us to do, by walking in God's ways and keeping His commandments. As we know, believe, and obey the Word, we are keeping our eyes and our hearts fixed on God—and He has assured us that our victory is sure if we will do that.

I encourage you to truly know the Word. Know it with your mind and know it in your heart. Love it, memorize it, and allow its truth to sink into the depths of your being. As you do, you will find yourself incorporating the Word in your prayers, speaking God's Word back to Him—and He always honors what He says.

Weapon #2: The Name of Jesus

A friend of mine, a man I taught in Bible college, was driving one day with his little three- or four-year-old son in the car with him. He did not realize that the car door on the passenger side was not closed securely, and made a sharp turn at an intersection. This happened before seat belt laws were passed, so the child was not buckled into the car. As my friend turned, the car door swung open and the little boy tumbled out of the car into the middle of oncoming traffic from every direction. The last thing my friend remembers seeing was a set of tires speeding toward his son, almost on top of the boy. Suddenly, he yelled, "Jesus!"

As soon as he could stop his car, he ran to his son and saw that the boy was perfectly fine. Understandably, the driver of the other vehicle was hysterical. My friend tried to comfort him and assured him that his son was all right. "My son is okay. Don't worry. Just thank God you were able to stop," he told the man. The man responded, "You don't understand. I never touched my brakes."

There is unbelievable power in the name of Jesus! His name is higher than any other name; it is mightier than any other name. It truly is the only name that will ultimately command obedience from all people and all principalities. Philippians 2:9–10 says that God has highly exalted Jesus Christ "and given Him the name which is above every name, that at the name of Jesus, every knee

> His name is higher than any other name; it is mightier than any other name. It truly is the only name that will ultimately command obedience from all people and all principalities.
>
> ⤞ • ⤝

should bow, of those in heaven, and of those on earth, and of those under the earth" (NKJV).

In Ephesians 1:17–21, Paul is praying for the believers in Ephesus, asking that God would give them "the spirit of wisdom and revelation in the knowledge of Him," that He would open the eyes of their spiritual understanding, that they would know the hope of His calling in their lives, and that they would know the riches of the glory of His inheritance. He also prayed that they would know "the exceeding greatness of His power toward us who believe, according to the working of His mighty power which He worked in Christ when He raised Him from the dead and seated *Him* at His right hand in the heavenly *places*, far above all principality and power and might and dominion, *and every name that is named*, not only in this age, but also in that which is to come" (NKJV, emphasis mine).

If we really understand what Paul is trying to communicate in Philippians 2 and Ephesians 1, and if we believe that Jesus has been given the name above every name, we will see that we have incredible power available to us in His name. What does it mean for His name to be above every name? It means the name of Jesus is the name above the name of cancer. It is the name above the name of poverty. It is the name above the name of drug addiction. It is the name above the name of divorce. Whatever name we can think of, the name of Jesus is above that name—and we have been given His name because He has given His life for us. We do not have to be defeated by anything that comes our way as long as we know the power that is available to us in Jesus' name.

When Jesus was talking to His disciples and preparing them to live without His physical presence on earth, He said to them: "And when that time comes, you will ask nothing of Me [you will need to ask Me no questions]. I assure you, most solemnly I tell you, that My Father will grant you whatever you ask in My Name [as presenting all that I AM]. Up to this time you have not asked a [single] thing in My Name [as presenting all that I AM]; but now ask and keep on asking and you will receive, so that your joy (gladness, delight) may be full and complete" (John 16:23–24). In these verses, Jesus was saying, essentially: *You don't have to ask Me anymore. You can now go to the Father in My name and when you speak My name, you are presenting to Him all that I am—not who you are, but Who I am!*

Every time I pray in the name of Jesus, I am saying: "Lord, I'm holding up before You the victory that Jesus won and I'm a joint heir with Him. I've got an inheritance—not because I earned it, but because He earned it and put my name on the will and signed it with His blood! And I am going to pray boldly, and my prayers will be powerful because the name of Jesus is above everything else I could ever name." The same is true for you.

So when we pray and ask for something in Jesus' name, we are really presenting all that He is to the Father and asking as though Jesus Himself is making a request of His Father. We are not going to God on our own merits; we are approaching Him on the merits of Jesus. We are holding up before the Father everything that Jesus is, not everything we are. That is why, even when we do not do everything right, we can still expect God to hear our prayers—because we pray in Jesus' name. Everything He is swallows up everything we are not, and His fullness makes up for our deficiencies.

Because the name of Jesus represents everything that He is—all of His righteousness, all of His perfection, all of His grace and love—that name is powerful. There is no power in your name or my name, but there is awesome power in the name of Jesus because of everything His name represents. As Andrew Murray writes: "The name of a king includes his honor, his power, his kingdom. His name is the symbol of his power....The name of Christ is the expression of all He has done and all He is and lives to do...."[4] He also writes: "He who gives his name to another stands aside, to let that other act for him; he who takes the name of another gives up his own as of no value. When I go in the name of another, I deny myself, I take not only his name, but himself and what he is, instead of myself and what I am."[5]

Let's think about this in practical, everyday terms. My name has not always been Joyce Meyer. I did not take Dave's last name until I married him. Nothing of his belonged to me until we entered into the legal covenant of marriage. When we married, I did not have a car, but Dave did. When I got his name, I suddenly got a car, too. I did not have much money; in fact, I was in debt. Dave did have money; so when I married him, I had money too and was able to pay off my bills. I didn't have access to anything of Dave's until I married him and took his name. When I became Mrs. Dave Meyer, everything he had became mine. While we were dating, I still had my maiden name; I still had my debt and I still had no car.

We cannot "date" Jesus and expect to enjoy the privileges that come with true commitment. By that, I mean that we cannot just spend time with Him occasionally and try to keep up a relationship only because of the blessings He offers us. We can only enjoy the privileges of a relationship with Him when we are committed. Before I married Dave, I could have told people that my last name was Meyer, but that would have been illegal. Whether we like it or not, heaven works on a legal system. God has set spiritual laws in motion and we simply cannot ignore them or get around them. God knows what kind of relationship we have with Him, whether we are "dating" or whether we have given our hearts to

Him in total commitment. When we are joined to Him in committed relationship, we can enjoy everything His name affords us.

When we are joined to Him in committed relationship, we can enjoy everything His name affords us.

→ • ←

Like so much about our lives as believers, there is no formula for using the name of Jesus and there are no rules about it—just a heart that believes in Him, trusts His power, and is submitted to His Lordship. When we employ the name of Jesus in prayer as we do battle against our enemy, our submission to God is essential. James 4:7–9 says: "So be subject to God. Resist the devil [stand firm against him], and he will flee from you. Come close to God and He will come close to you. [Recognize that you are] sinners, get your soiled hands clean; [realize that you have been disloyal] wavering individuals with divided interests, and purify your hearts [of your spiritual adultery]. [As you draw near to God] be deeply penitent...." I like the way Andrew Murray explains the spiritual principles found in these verses. He writes that we "have the spiritual power to avail ourselves of the Name of Jesus just to the extent to which [we] yield [ourselves] to live only for the interests and the work of the Master. The use of the name always supposes the surrender of our interests to Him whom we represent."[6]

In other words, we should not expect to be able to resist the enemy if we allow willful disobedience in our lives, even if we use the name of Jesus. We cannot take authority over Satan if we are living in sin. We all sin and do things wrong, but when I write about "willful disobedience," I am referring to intentional sin. This is sin that we know is offensive to God, but we still refuse to repent and give it up. The Bible says to submit to God, and if we are doing that to the best of our ability, when Satan comes against us, we need to say out of our mouths: "I resist you, Satan, in the name of Jesus!" And we need to expect the power of that name to push him back.

Anytime we stand up to the devil and come against him, we need to do it in the name of Jesus. Satan is not afraid of us, but he is afraid of the blood of Jesus; he is afraid of the Word of God; he is afraid of the cross and he's afraid of the name of Jesus. A Spirit-filled believer does have power over Satan, but only in the name of Jesus.

Whenever we use the name of Jesus, it is important to remember what the Bible says about the power of that name:

- *His name has power to save.* "And there is salvation in and through no one else, for there is no other name under heaven given among men by and in which we must be saved" (Acts 4:12).
- *When we meet with others in His name, Jesus promises His very presence.* "For wherever two or three are gathered (drawn together as My followers) in (into) My name, there I AM in the midst of them" (Matthew 18:20).
- *His name brings healing.* Peter said to a crippled man, "...In the name of Jesus Christ of Nazareth, rise up and walk" (Acts 3:6, NKJV). Peter added further illumination to this miraculous healing when he explained, "By the name of Jesus Christ of Nazareth, whom you crucified, whom God raised from the dead, by Him this man stands here before you whole" (Acts 4:10, NKJV).
- *His name sets us free.* Because of Christ's triumph on the cross, in Jesus' name, we have victory over spiritual darkness. Jesus told His followers, "And these attesting signs will accompany those who believe: in My name they will drive out demons ..." (Mark 16:17). (See also Luke 10:19–20; Colossians 2:15.)

We need to keep the power of Jesus' name in mind every time we pray and to remember that using His name is a privilege that comes from our relationship with Him. As we continue to grow in intimacy with Him through prayer, His name will become more and more precious to us and we will become more and more convinced of its awesome power.

We should reverence the name of Jesus and never use it in vain (uselessly or frivolously). Some people think nothing of taking God's name in vain one moment and then trying to pray in His name the next. Taking the Lord's name in vain is not merely connecting it to a curse word. We take His name in vain anytime we use it lightly or loosely, without honor. If we had a live wire with about 220 volts of electricity running through it, we would not throw it around carelessly; neither should we treat the Lord's name with disrespect.

In the Old Testament, God's people had so much reverential fear of the name of God that they would not even speak it. It was literally considered too holy to even pass through human lips. When Moses asked God what His name was, He replied, "I AM WHO I AM" (Exodus 3:14). God is so much and so wonderful that He cannot be accurately described. His name represents all that He is. Once again, I want to say that we should all strive to show the utmost respect for the name of Jesus (God). The more we realize what is wrapped up in that wonderful name, the more results we will see when we pray in Jesus' name.

Weapon #3: The Blood of Jesus

Just as we release the power that is in the name of Jesus by speaking that name and just as we release the power that is in God's

Word by speaking His Word, we also need to release the power that is in the blood of Jesus by including in our prayers something that declares our position under His blood, such as: "I apply the blood of Jesus to my life and I believe I'm protected as I stay under that blood." In his book *Let Us Pray,* Watchman Nee wrote: "Since we belong to God, Satan intends to frustrate, afflict, or suppress us and allow us no foothold. This is his aim, although his aim may not be achieved because we may approach the throne of grace by the precious blood of the Lord Jesus, asking for God's protection and care. As God hears our prayer, Satan's plan is definitely defeated."[7] That's what we want. We want the enemy defeated, and we can declare victory over him in prayer through the shed blood of Jesus.

> We also need to release the power that is in the blood of Jesus by including in our prayers something that declares our position under His blood.
>
> ⤜ • ⤛

Exodus 12:1–13 gives the account of the miraculous events of the first Passover and illustrates the power of the blood. In this story, an angel of death was going to pass through the land of Egypt to kill all of the firstborn sons in every household. But God instructed His people to take the blood of lambs and put the blood on the side posts of their doors and on the lintels (above the door spaces) of their homes. Then God said, when the angel of death came, he would "pass over" the blood-covered doorways, and no one inside those homes would be harmed.

Today, Jesus is our Passover Lamb. He shed His blood for us at Calvary so that we could be free from the curse of sin and death. I do not think we avail ourselves of all of the benefits of the blood of Jesus the way we should. I believe that if blood on the doorways of the homes of the ancient Hebrews kept the angel of death from visiting them and bringing devastation to their lives through the death of the firstborn sons, we also need to be diligent to apply the blood over our lives by faith and seal the doors of our lives through which Satan can gain access to us.

The Israelites had to go to quite a bit of trouble—and probably made a big mess—to get the blood of the lambs on their doorposts. They had to kill the lambs, skin them, remove the blood, and put it into containers, then get some hyssop (a plant that was used in purification ceremonies), dip it in the blood, and put the blood on their doorposts. That could not have been a neat endeavor! It had to seem unusual to them, but they did it—and they did it by faith because God told them to do so. The Israelites had to apply the blood of the lamb physically, but we can do it by faith. Jesus is the Lamb of God, and, as believers, we can apply the power of His shed blood to our lives by simply believing in it.

Many of us know that the Old Testament describes an innermost chamber in the temple called the "Holy of Holies." This was the place where God's presence dwelt, and the only way the priests could approach it was to sprinkle blood on certain items and in certain places. Basically, the blood had to go before them to cleanse everything before they could enter into the presence of God.

Similarly, we have no right to come into the presence of a holy God and pray to Him—except that the *blood of Jesus* allows us to approach Him! Many times as I begin to pray, I say, "God, I thank You for the blood and I ask You to cleanse me afresh with the blood of Jesus. As I come into Your presence, God, I thank You that I'm justified by the blood and that makes it possible for me to draw near to You." Like the Old Testament priests, we also apply the blood as we enter the presence of God, but we do it by faith.

We need to hide songs and Scriptures about the power of the blood in our hearts so that when the enemy comes against us, the truth about the power of the blood will rise up within us and make us strong and courageous. Several years ago, I felt led of the Lord to produce a music CD that only included songs about the blood. One day, a woman called the ministry and shared with us an amazing testimony. She basically said, "I was led to buy your CD on the blood, and I had it in my house, but had not yet played it. One night, I was sitting in a chair reading and all of a sudden I got the urge to play that CD. Unbeknownst to me, there was a crook outside my window, and when I got up to play the CD, he fired a shot through the window, right at the place where I had been sitting. The shot hit something in the chair, but it did not hit me! Had it not been for the fact that I had that blood CD in my house, I might be dead now."

The blood of Jesus is one of His gifts to us as believers and we do not have to wait until we experience fear or difficulty to apply it to a situation. Whenever we want or need to, we can pray a simple prayer that says: "God, I release my faith in the blood of Jesus. There is power in that blood. The devil cannot stand against the blood; and by faith, I apply the power of the blood of Jesus to my family, myself, and my life. Thank You, God, that I'm cleansed and protected by the blood of Jesus." Every time we mention the blood of Jesus, the devil trembles.

PRAYER AND WARFARE

We should consider our prayers to be highly successful if they cause Satan to lose and God to be glorified. What we should look for in prayer is the enemy's loss. What a pity that so many believers are still unaware that Satan can be immobilized through fervent, effectual prayer. Surely, if we knew the true power of prayer, we would pray more. We would see that prayer is always a privilege and never an obligation.

Satan does not just show up somewhere and put himself on display; he works through people and things. His hope is that God's people will lay blame everywhere except on him. Satan weakens believers' bodies, causing sickness and pain. He works in the physical world, bringing disaster and hardship. He creates misunderstanding among Christians and seeks to separate family members and the dearest of friends. He cuts off material supply and creates lack. He makes people feel depressed, sad, restless, and useless. He tries to render us unable to make decisions. He injects irrational fear into believers' hearts. He pushes us and drives us to work so much that we become overtired. He seeks to wear us out. Satan attacks people's minds and emotions, weakens their resistance, and tries to deceive and lead them astray. Satan's ways to attack people are endless and must be resisted. Satan must be aggressively resisted! James 4:7 says to submit yourself to God, resist the devil and he will flee.

Watchman Nee writes, "Before there is the possibility of our overcoming, we must maintain in our heart a hostile attitude towards the devil, no longer willing to subject ourselves to his oppression."[8] The Bible says in Matthew 12:29 that we cannot plunder the strong man's house unless we first bind the strong man. We can bind Satan through Spirit-led prayer. If we allow the enemy to attack and do not resist or attack in return, then we shall surely be depressed and sink very low. Satan is an enemy and must be treated as such.

My advice is to stay active against the enemy. A spiritual life must be one of usefulness. We ought to be enthusiastic and zealous for God, relentlessly attacking the devil and never allowing ourselves to sink into passivity or inactivity. Be

> We ought to be enthusiastic and zealous for God, relentlessly attacking the devil and never allowing ourselves to sink into passivity or inactivity.
>
> ➤ • ◄

aggressive in love, prayer, giving, serving, reading, praying, and everything else you do. When Satan attacks in any form or fashion, immediately go to war against Him in prayer! (See 1 Peter 5:9.)

SUMMARY

As long as we live, we will be engaged in a spiritual war and one of the primary ways we fight spiritual battles is through prayer. As we pray, it is crucial that we understand the power that is available to us in the Word of God, the name of Jesus, and the blood of Jesus. I encourage you to reread this chapter or some other book or booklet on the Word, the name, and the blood at least once per year because we need to keep the power of these weapons and basic doctrines in the forefront of our hearts and minds. We also need to continue to ask God to give us revelation about these three spiritual tools because they will help us defeat the enemy more effectively than anything else.

The more we develop a deep, rich, vibrant relationship with the Lord through prayer, the more we understand the power of the weapons He has given us. As we stay in a relationship of obedience to Him, all the power of the Word, the name, and the blood are at our disposal, and our victory is sure.

Satan is our enemy and our attitude toward him must be hostile and aggressive. We absolutely must resist him at all times. Stay active and useful and give the devil no opportunity.

Prayer Points

➤➤ Our enemy, the devil, is a spiritual being and the war he wages against us takes place in the spiritual realm. Therefore, we fight him with spiritual weapons that include the Word of God, the name of Jesus, and the blood of Jesus. All three can be incorporated into our prayer lives and will empower our prayers as nothing else will.

➤➤ The Word of God is "sharper than any two-edged sword" (Hebrews 4:12, NKJV) and it is able to utterly defeat the enemy. The Holy Spirit helps us use the sword of the Word effectively, even bringing to our remembrance or speaking to us the specific Bible verses or passages we need in certain situations.

➤➤ Jesus Himself used the Word to overcome the enemy, as we read in Luke 4.

➤➤ As long as we are doing what God has asked us to do for Him on earth, the enemy will oppose us. The Word is an effective weapon against him at all times.

➤➤ The name of Jesus is above every name on earth. It is higher than the name of anything that comes against us; it is mightier than any force that would seek to harm or destroy us; and it is louder than any voice that would seek to accuse us.

→→ We need to be in a committed relationship with God in order to enjoy the privileges of Jesus' name. When we pray in the name of Jesus, God sees everything Jesus is; He doesn't see everything we are not.

→→ Today, Jesus is our Passover Lamb. We apply His blood by faith to our lives; it protects us and seals the doorways of our lives so that the enemy cannot gain access to us.

→→ The blood of Jesus is the only means by which we can enter the presence of God—and there is mighty, overcoming power in His presence.

→→ We must aggressively resist Satan at all times, never allowing ourselves to become passive.

14

Staying Strong through Prayer

In this chapter, I want to expose one of the devil's favorite strategies—one of his most effective tactics—which is to *wear us out*. Satan seeks to wear us out, wear us down, weaken us, make us weary, and get us so tired that we quit and give up. Daniel 7:25 speaks of the devil when it says: "And he shall speak words against the Most High [God] and shall wear out the saints of the Most High." What does that mean to us today? It means that Satan will speak against God. He will tell you lies about God—lies such as, *God doesn't love **you**,* or *God is not going to come through for **you**,* or *God can't forgive **that**,* or *God's Word works for everybody **but** **you!*** Satan intentionally schemes to wear us out, but God wants us to stay strong, and one of the ways we do that is through prayer and fellowshiping with God.

I had one of those wearing-out experiences one afternoon after I left a conference session I was teaching. First, the team and I went to a nice restaurant and everything was great. But the meal was excruciatingly slow. Now "slow" does not work for me in the middle of a conference because I need to get back to my hotel and study. I also like to get a little nap! Because of several other commitments that afternoon, we were on an especially tight schedule and everything about our lunch experience seemed to take forever—which tends to happen when people are in a hurry!

After we finally had lunch, Dave and I went back to our hotel room. I had exactly two hours before I had to leave for the evening session, so I planned to spend one hour studying and one hour resting. However, our keys to our room would not work. Nobody's keys would work! The keys had worked the night before; they worked that morning, but for some reason, they did not work at that moment—when we really needed them. Then, of course, someone had to go all the way back to the front desk to get keys that would actually open the door. After we got into the room, I needed some very hot water for something, so I turned on the water to let it run in the sink for a few minutes and get hot enough. A little bit later, I heard what sounded like water spilling. I ran in there to find that the sink was clogged, so the water was running all over the sink, under all my makeup, under my combs, under my belongings, and onto the floor. Then I had to mop the floor and dry off my things.

After that fiasco, I was able to finish studying for the evening message and had forty-five minutes to rest. I stretched out on the bed and closed my eyes just in time for the hotel's fire alarm to go off. Not only did the fire alarm go off, it also played a loud message that said something like: "There is a possible emergency in the hotel. Please do not use the elevators or get into the stairwells. We are investigating this situation. Stand by for further information.

We repeat: Please do not go into the hall or get into the stairwell."
The deafening blast of the fire alarm and that annoying message
continued for thirty minutes!

When I shared that story at the conference that night, my daughter, who was staying in a different hotel, said that the very same thing
happened where she was! Do you know what? Things like that are
not accidental. I wanted a nap so badly! This is so characteristic of
Satan and the wearing-out tactics he uses. So many similar situations take place in all of our lives.

Why do these things happen to those of us who are trying so hard to serve God? Because any-time we begin to make progress against the king-dom of darkness and do something that advances

> Anytime we begin to make progress against the kingdom of darkness and do something that advances the kingdom of God, the devil does everything he can to resist us, frustrate us, and try to stop us.
>
> →➢ • ≺←

the kingdom of God, the devil does everything he can to resist
us, frustrate us, and try to stop us. When we pray Spirit-led, Spirit-
empowered prayers, the enemy knows we are waging a powerful
war against his camp. People who want to finish what they start for
God, had better be ready to stand their ground through the attacks
that will come. The enemy will oppose God's work whether it is
taking place in the natural realm or in the spiritual realm through
prayer. A person does not have to be serving as a missionary in the
Third World or preaching the gospel on television to be a formi-
dable threat to the kingdom of darkness.

The setbacks we experienced in the restaurant and hotel were obvious attempts of the enemy to harass us and wear us out. But other attacks he initiates are much subtler and harder to identify. He knows we will recognize and resist him if he shows up at our dinner table in a red suit with horns on his head and a pitchfork in his hand, but if he comes slyly, stealthily, disguised as something that is attractive or acceptable to us, we are more likely to be lured into the traps he sets for us. We must remember that God's Word says that Satan will come as an angel of light. Not everything that looks good or feels good is good.

THE SLOW, SUBTLE ENEMY

One of the tactics Satan uses to wear us out is called "gradualism," which is the means by which he very slowly, almost inconspicuously, gradually attacks us. Part of his plan is to operate so imperceptibly that we will be worn down and worn out before we realize what is happening to us. Remember that Daniel 7:25 says the devil will try to wear out the saints. The term "to wear out" means "to reduce little by little." It happens a little this minute and a little the next minute, a little today and a little more the next day. He picks at us a little bit here, a little bit there, a little bit here, a little bit there. He will tell us one little lie, then another little lie, then another and another and another until we find ourselves tangled up in a situation or a thought pattern that is totally false and deceptive. He works so carefully, so subtly, so slowly, and so intricately that we don't even realize what is happening. Before we know it, we have a massive, tangled-up problem and don't even know how we got it—and that's exactly what the devil wants.

This wearing-out tactic of the enemy is barely perceivable, but the end result is that we have nothing left—no health, no finances, no relationships, no joy, no peace, no strength, no vision, and *often* no desire to pray. That's what Satan is busily but subtly trying to accomplish in the lives of believers. He will whittle away at us until we are empty, worn-out, and ready to quit—and we won't even know how we got into such a mess!

Since Satan is the one who wears us out and leaves us in a mess, once he ensnares us, he then goes to work on our minds and causes us to think, *What's wrong with me?* Or he causes us to blame the problem on someone else. We may think of someone and say to ourselves, *If he weren't doing this to me, then I wouldn't feel this way!* Or, *Perhaps, if my boss would lighten up, my attitude would be better!* Or this: *If those children would just behave, I could get this house clean!*

How do we pray in such a way that we can gain victory over the enemy and his schemes? What do we do about this strategy to gradually deplete us and get us too tired to care about what the devil is doing? The first thing we need to do is pray that we will not be deceived by his tricks. We must ask God to open our eyes so that we quickly recognize the wearing-out tactics of Satan.

First Peter 5:8 exhorts us: "Be well balanced (temperate, sober of mind), be vigilant and cautious at all times; for that enemy of yours, the devil, roams around like a lion roaring [in fierce hunger], seeking someone to seize upon and devour." This verse tells us that the devil cannot just devour anybody he wants. He is actively and stealthily seeking someone who will *let* him get by with it. Many times we put up with the devil longer than we should. Sometimes we open a door for Satan through a lack of balance in our lives. (For example, we do not balance work with rest, so we become either "workaholics," on one extreme, or lazy, on the other.) There are several major ways Satan tries to devour us and keep us from experiencing the victory of Christ. I will highlight four here:

1. *Satan will try to wear us out physically.* One of the best favors we can do for ourselves is make sure we get good rest. We also need a healthy diet, enough exercise, and regular checkups. We need to do whatever we can to make sure we stay strong physically so that the enemy will not be able to physically wear us out. We also need to pray that God will give us wisdom and sensitivity to His Spirit so that we can hear His voice when He says things like, "You need to rest this weekend," or "You need to exercise three times a week," or "You really need to stop eating so many candy bars and start eating more fruit."

2. *Satan will try to wear down our zeal and enthusiasm.* I see too many people who are trying to serve God with no passion. They were passionate at one time; they were zealous at one time; they were enthusiastic at one time; they were excited at one time. But do you

> We need to pray that God will help us keep our passion stirred and keep our enthusiasm up to the level where He wants it to be.
>
> ➤➤ • ◄◄

know what happens? The old saying is true: "Familiarity breeds contempt." Sometimes when we become familiar with something, it loses its meaning to us and we lose our passion for it. We get used to it and it's no longer exciting. That's the devil! He steals enthusiasm a little bit at a time. We need to pray that God will help us keep our passion stirred and keep our enthusiasm up to the level where He wants it to be. He wants us to be passionate for Him, and there are several Scriptures we can apply to help us stay that way:

- Colossians 3:23: "And whatever you do, do it heartily, as to the Lord and not to men" (NKJV).
- Romans 12:11: "Never lag in zeal and in earnest endeavor; be aglow and burning with the Spirit, serving the Lord."
- 2 Timothy 1:6: Paul told Timothy, "Stir up the gift of God which is in you" (NKJV).

We are to stir ourselves up—to fan the fire of God in our hearts and not let it go out! How do we stir ourselves up? We should talk to ourselves about how blessed we are to know the Lord, how blessed we are to have Bibles, how blessed we are to have one Christian friend in our lives, how blessed we are to have something to do that is worth doing. We all have many blessings and we need to take notice of them. We should not just get so accustomed to having them that we no longer appreciate them.

3. *Satan will try to wear out our spiritual lives by stealing our prayer time and our time in the Word.* He will attempt to steal our prayer time because he does not want us talking to God or listening to Him. He will also try to keep us from getting in the Word because if we do not spend any time in the Word, we will be weak

and spiritually impotent. Another of his time-stealing strategies is to cause us to waste our time by putting people or activities in our lives that drain us. He tempts us to get involved in things that God has not asked us to get involved in, things that bear no fruit and ultimately frustrate us. Satan wants us to be busy, but God wants us to be fruitful.

4. *Satan will try to make us weary in well doing.* It is so important for us to keep steadily focused on God and His work. This will keep us from becoming disheartened when others who are not doing right seem to be prospering. Galatians 6:9 says: "And let us not lose heart and grow weary and faint in acting nobly and doing right, for in due time and at the appointed season we shall reap, if we do not loosen and relax our courage and faint."

So how can we keep from being people Satan can easily devour? The answer is in the beginning of 1 Peter 5:9 which reads: "Withstand him; be firm in faith [against his onset]." There are two things I really want us to see here: (1) being out of balance can open a door for Satan to attack us, and (2) we are supposed to resist Satan at his onset. That means the moment we perceive an attack from Satan, we need to resist him immediately!

In its entirety 1 Peter 5:9 says: "Withstand him; be firm in faith [against his onset—rooted, established, strong, immovable, and determined], knowing that the same (identical) sufferings are appointed to your brotherhood (the whole body of Christians) throughout the world." Why is it important, when we are going through hard times, to realize that other people are going through hard times, too? Because one of the things that Satan wants to do is back us into a corner and have us believe we are the only ones going through this trial. Instead of thinking, *Why me?* it helps to realize, *Hey, I'm not the only one going through stuff.* This does not mean that we should be happy that other people are suffering, but it does help to realize we are not alone in our afflictions. No matter how much we may be hurting, someone else has a worse situation. We need to avoid having pity parties and feeling sorry for ourselves. We need to resist the devil at his onset and to keep resisting.

WATCH AND PRAY

Just before Jesus went to the cross, He said to the disciples who were with Him (and having trouble staying awake!): "All of you must keep awake (give strict attention, be cautious and active) and watch and pray, that you may not come into temptation..." (Matthew 26:41). Those words "watch and pray" are crucial for us. We must pay attention to what is going on around us and pray immediately when we sense something is not right or we see a need. Our motto should be "Do not delay, pray right away!"

As I have written previously, prayer is an offensive weapon against Satan, a weapon that destroys his plans and schemes against us and those we love. We need to be especially watchful and prayerful about our relationships. God brings wonderful people into our lives—people to encourage us, people to help us fulfill God's call on our lives, people we are supposed to help, and people we can just enjoy. But the enemy can also bring into our

> We need to be especially watchful and prayerful about our relationships.
>
> ⤕ • ⤔

lives people who will be wrong for us, who will hurt us, disappoint us, betray us, drain us, and use us for their own advantage.

Watch Out for Wrong Spirits

The enemy sets up traps to wear us out and distract us from God's plan. Many of these traps come in the form of wrong spirits operating through people, and I would like to spend the rest of this chapter exposing some of them. One of the Bible's best examples of Satan's wearing-out tactics through people is found in Acts 16: 16–17, which reads: "As we were on our way to the place of prayer, we were met by a slave girl who was possessed by a spirit of divination [claiming to foretell future events and to discover hidden knowledge], and she brought her owners much gain by her fortunetelling. She kept following Paul and [the rest of] us, shouting loudly, These men are the servants of the Most High God! They announce to you the way of salvation!"

The first thing to notice about this passage is that Paul and his ministry partners were on their way to pray. The enemy does not like prayer and he will try to keep us from praying every way he can. Notice also that what the slave girl was saying was true, but it was terribly annoying because she had a wrong spirit. What she was repeating over and over was irritating, not edifying.

We need to learn to pay better attention to the discernment that God gives us inside and not to look at everything as it appears to the natural eye. At Joyce Meyer Ministries, we have hired people who had all the necessary qualifications and said all the right things, but also had something about them with which I just was not comfortable. In the beginning, I hesitated to trust my discernment at times because I did not want to turn people down for a job just because I had an unsettled feeling about them. But I have learned over the years that I need to trust my instincts. Because the Holy Spirit lives in me, I have sanctified instincts! That does not mean I get everything right all the time, but it does mean that I can trust the Holy Spirit to guide me.

When Paul had this encounter with the slave girl, for some reason he did not deal with the problem right away. The girl with the spirit of divination continued to speak. Acts 16:18 says, "And she did this for many days." When Satan decides to aggravate us, he will keep it up and keep it up and keep it up and keep it up and keep it up until he is successful—or until he is stopped. Verse 18 also says that Paul became "sorely annoyed and worn out" under that pressure. The devil had sent that girl to aggravate Paul, quite simply to wear him out. She was a tool in the enemy's hand and he used her to try to hinder, harass, and distract Paul from doing what God called him to do.

Throughout our lives, the enemy assigns people to do to us what that girl did to Paul—to aggravate us. Those people may be our neighbors, our coworkers, or our family members. They will most likely be people with whom we have regular, even frequent, contact.

This does not mean that we are to tell everyone who aggravates us to get out of our lives. At times, God Himself puts us around people who annoy us in order to teach us to walk in love even with those we consider unlovely. There is a difference between someone who aggravates my flesh and someone who aggravates my spirit. I believe one of the reasons Paul put up with the woman for so many days was that he was seeking discernment about the true source of her actions.

In Paul's case, he finally turned to the girl and said, "I charge you in the name of Jesus Christ to come out of her! And it came out that very moment" (v. 18). Please notice that he did not deal with the woman, but with the evil spirit that was working through her.

Sometimes when we pray for someone or begin to rebuke an evil force working through them, they act worse before they act better. Why is this? The answer is very simple: the devil does not give up easily. This happened to Paul after he rebuked the spirit of divination. It was not until sometime later that he experienced great victory. The people who owned this slave girl became angry after Paul rebuked the evil spirit because they realized she had lost her ability to make money for them through divination. They went to the local authorities and told them that Paul and his colleagues were "encouraging unlawful customs" (see Acts 16:21). The next thing Paul knew, they were beaten and thrown in jail!

Paul seemingly did the right thing, but his situation got worse. We all have times when we feel like Shadrach, Meshach, and Abednego, who made a right choice by going into the fiery furnace rather than to worship anyone other than God. They did what was right and yet the furnace was turned up seven times hotter. However, in the end, they came out unharmed, received a promotion, and God's kingdom grew as a result of others watching God deliver them (see Daniel 3:10–30).

Acts 16:25 says that while Paul and Silas were in jail, they were "praying and singing hymns of praise to God, and the [other] prisoners were listening to them." Envision the scene: there were Paul and his comrades, handcuffed and shackled, maybe even in stocks—and they were singing praises to God. Acts 16:26 reports what happened next: "Suddenly there was a great earthquake, so that the very foundations of the prison were shaken; and at once all the doors were opened and everyone's shackles were unfastened." Then the jailer, who was sleeping on the job, woke up and

was so startled and amazed
that the prisoners had not
escaped that he wanted to
know what he needed to do
to be saved. As a result, he
was born again and every-
one in his household heard
the Gospel.

> If we will remain steadfast and
> not give up, God will always
> work something good out
> of every bad thing the devil
> tries to do.
>
> —>— • —<—

If we will remain steadfast and not give up, God will always
work something good out of every bad thing the devil tries to
do. If we resist Satan and keep trusting God and remain steadfast
when the devil is trying to wear us out, God will turn the enemy's
schemes against him. God will bless us, and He will get glory
for Himself. Paul and his friends were irritated, annoyed, worn-
out—and nothing was going as planned. But they kept a good attitude and strengthened themselves by praising and worshiping the
Lord. They prayed and their situation got worse, so *they kept praying.* Then God turned that thing around and Satan was defeated.
Satan made arrangements for them to be stuck in jail, so God
made arrangements for the jailer to get saved. That's an example
that all things work together for good to those who love God and
are called according to His purpose and keep praying (see Romans
8:26–28).

Watch Out for Felix

There is another way the enemy tries to wear us out, and it is
through what I call the "Felix trap." Acts 24 tells us that Felix
was the governor of the region where Paul was ministering. Felix
seemed to be interested in what Paul was saying; he appeared to

want to learn from Paul. But below the surface, Felix was greedy and was hoping to get money from Paul (see verse 26).

There are pretenders, who like Felix, come into our lives and say they want help, but never seem to make any progress. I have seen this pattern more times than I can count! The enemy sends such people into our lives to drain us of everything we have and to wear us out, and they have no intention of changing. They want to talk about their afflictions, but they do not want to get over them. They want to rehearse their problems, but they do not want to get well. Like Felix, they have wrong motives. After they wear one person out, they will start all over again with somebody else.

We have to grow in our discernment about people because Satan plays on our love for God and on our desire to help people and to be used by God. Many times we feel guilty if we say to someone, "Do you know what? You really don't want help; you're just using me. So just do whatever you're going to do, and if you ever get to the point where you really want to be helped, then come back." But we think: *I can't do that. That wouldn't be good. That wouldn't be merciful.* Jesus would have done it! Do you know what He said to the crippled man who was lying by the pool of Bethesda? "Do you want to become well? [Are you really in earnest about getting well?]" (John 5:6). The man responded, "Sir, I have nobody when the water is moving to put me into the pool; but while I am trying to come [into it] myself, somebody else steps down ahead of me" (v. 7). Jesus did not hang around feeling pity for that man. After He asked if he was really serious about getting well, He said: "Get up! Pick up your bed (sleeping pad) and walk!" (v. 8). Jesus was basically saying, *Come on, I'll help you, but do a little something for yourself too. Pick up your sleeping pad; don't just drain Me dry while you do nothing but complain.*

Let me encourage you to pray and ask God to help you sharpen your discernment so that you will not innocently allow yourself to get entangled in other people's messes without really helping them because they don't really want help. When that happens, Satan is using them to drain you and wear you out! By saying this, I am not implying that we should forsake patience. We need to be patient and long-suffering toward people. But if we read the entire story of Felix, we see that Felix kept talking to Paul, day after day, week after week, with the same issue, and after two years he was unchanged. Read this account in Acts 24:26–27: "At the same time he hoped to get money from Paul, for which reason he continued to send for him and was in his company and conversed with him often. But when two years had gone by, Felix was succeeded in office by Porcius Festus; and wishing to gain favor with the Jews, Felix left Paul still a prisoner in chains."

After continuing to send for Paul and taking much of his time, Felix just went off and left Paul in jail. All the energy Paul invested did not do one bit of good because Felix did not really want any help to start with.

Watch out for the "Felixes" in your life. Be discerning and pour yourself out to those God truly sends you to help. Pray that God will help you recognize and understand why certain people cross your path and how you are to handle those relationships. Ask Him to increase your spiritual sensitivity so that when the enemy sends someone to drain you dry, you do not make a significant investment in that person's life and merely waste your time. As you pray, ask God to give you what I call "divine connections." These are people sent by God who will either help you in some way or people you will be able to help. They are people who can either add to your life or benefit from your friendship. God has called us to help people, but He has not called us to waste our time. Pray that you might be a good steward of your resources, including your time.

Watch Out for Delilah

There are also "Delilahs" who are sent to come against us, so we need to pray for the ability to recognize them. Judges 16:16–17 tells us that Delilah continually pressed Sampson to reveal the secret of his great strength so she could have him defeated. It says he was "vexed to death" by her pressure. Sampson finally gave in to her vexations, told her his secret, and was overtaken by his enemy as a result.

Let's just say that the devil sends some woman to tempt a married man who has a wonderful family. Infidelity rarely begins with two people saying, "Hey! Let's have an affair!" No, it happens gradually. It may begin in the workplace with a few compliments, then more compliments. Soon the woman begins to hang onto the man's every word, and she hangs around him more than is professionally necessary. Then this man will begin to notice that she is a little younger than his wife. Maybe his wife has had several children for him and the lady at work has not had any children yet, so her body is in better shape and she is not tired most of the time. Soon the two of them are having coffee together during break time. Then she asks him for a ride home when her car is in the shop. Then she wants to thank him for the ride, so she invites him into her house for a delicious piece of homemade pie…and, well, you can imagine how the situation could unfold.

> The minute an inappropriate thought comes to us, we have to say, "No! I'm not going there!"
> ⤐ • ⤏

This kind of situation takes place more than we would like to think. It is not gender specific—it also happens the other way around when a man tempts a woman—but whatever the case, it usually starts so subtly and becomes very destructive, which thrills the devil. That is why we have to resist the devil at his onset. The minute an inappropriate thought comes to us, we have to say, "No! I'm not going there!" The "Delilahs" in our lives come in attractive, seductive, desirable packages and they seem so innocent, even good. For this reason, we need to be in continual communication with God through prayer, constantly checking in with Him to find out what He would have us do in specific situations and with specific people.

Watch Out for Peter

The enemy will not only send people to annoy you and drain you and people to tempt or seduce you, he will also send people to directly oppose what God wants to do in you and through you. That even happened to Jesus, when the enemy used Peter, one of His closest friends. In Matthew 16, Jesus had just told Peter and the rest of His disciples that He was going to be killed and then be raised the third day. Peter, not yet understanding that the full plan of salvation would require Jesus to die on the cross, said: "God forbid, Lord! This must never happen to You!" Jesus didn't waste any time. He turned away and said to Peter, "Get behind me, Satan! You are in My way [an offense and a hindrance and a snare to Me]" (Matthew 16:22–23). Jesus corrected Peter right on the spot so that God's plan of salvation would be fulfilled and Satan's plans defeated.

As difficult as this can be, the enemy will do his best to use people we love—and people who love us—to keep us from doing God's will. They do not mean to hurt us, they simply do not understand.

When we hear God speak or sense a call from Him, we need to remember that the people in our lives have not always heard or felt what we have. It may not make sense to them, so they try to influence us not to do it. Satan loves to strike us where it hurts the most. He is not going to come against us just through strangers or through people who do not mean anything to us. He is going to come against us with something that hurts. Why? Because he does not want us to make progress. He is afraid of us! He knows that if we are willing to completely obey God, we become dangerous to the kingdom of darkness!

As we deal with the "Peters," the "Delilahs," and the "Felixes" in our lives, we need to remember that people are not actually opposing us. In reality, our opposition comes from the realm of darkness that wars against us—the realm over which Satan is ruler. The Bible reveals, "For we do not wrestle against flesh and blood, but against principalities, against powers, against the rulers of the darkness of this age, against spiritual *hosts* of wickedness in the heavenly *places*" (Ephesians 6:12, NKJV). People are not our enemies—Satan is. We must learn to love people while we resist the evil one who attempts to work through them. Pray and ask God for spiritual keenness so you can always be discerning in these matters. The simple power of prayer can save us all kinds of time and trouble if we will ask God to give us wisdom and discernment in our relationships!

> The simple power of prayer can save us all kinds of time and trouble if we will ask God to give us wisdom and discernment in our relationships!
>
> ⇥ • ⇤

SUMMARY

One of Satan's most often used and most successful tactics against God's people is to wear us out—to cause us to get tired and weary as we fight the good fight of faith. God wants us to stay strong, and one way we accomplish that is through a vibrant prayer life. When you sense a need, "don't delay, pray right away!" We need to pray that God will keep us alert and on the lookout for the wearing-out schemes of the enemy and that He will give us strategies to overcome every devilish plot against us.

The enemy will try to wear us out by keeping us so busy and stressed that we become physically exhausted; he will steal our zeal; he will try to keep us from praying and he will cause us to get tired of doing good. He will also send people into our lives who operate from wrong spirits so that he can drain us, deceive us, or otherwise knock us off God's plan for our lives. As we stay in communion with God through prayer, we will be able to receive His wisdom and hear His voice, and this will enable us to gain victory over the enemy.

Prayer Points

➤ We have a slow, subtle enemy who gradually wears us down and wears us out so that we will not have the strength or the desire to accomplish what God has called us to do.

➤ We need to pray that we will quickly recognize Satan's various wearing-out tactics against us.

➤➤ Some of the ways Satan seeks to wear us out include: wearing us out physically, stealing our passion and enthusiasm, robbing us of time to spend in prayer and in the Word, and causing us to grow weary in well doing.

➤➤ According to 1 Peter 5:9, we must resist the enemy at his onset and make sure we remember that we are not alone in our sufferings.

➤➤ We must be watchful and prayerful concerning our relationships and pray that God will increase our discernment so that we can avoid people with wrong spirits.

➤➤ We need to watch out for "Felixes," "Delilahs," and "Peters," who may be the enemy's tools to drain us, tempt us, or oppose God's plan for our lives.

In Closing . . .

I trust your prayer life has been strengthened and your communion with God has been deepened as a result of this book. I hope you have come to realize how simple prayer really is and to experience the power of simple, believing prayer in your everyday life. I trust that you are developing and enjoying a rich lifestyle of prayer and that you are more confident now than ever that your prayers do make a difference.

I want to encourage you to continue asking God to teach you how to pray, knowing that there is always a new level of spiritual maturity to be gained and that the effectiveness of your prayers can always increase. I am praying for you, believing that God has great things for your life and that you will continue to grow in your relationship with Him. God loves you and wants to commune with you in ways that are intimate and exciting—and that only happens as you pray.

I sincerely thank God for allowing me to write this book. My own prayer life has been greatly enriched during this project. I have followed my own advice to "don't delay, pray right away." I have seen some amazing results, and I know you will, too. Remember, whatever you need, prayer opens the door for God to work!

→ Notes

INTRODUCTION

1. Watchman Nee, *Let Us Pray* (New York: Christian Fellowship Publishers, Inc., 1977), p. 1.

CHAPTER 1

1. "Study Shows Only 16% of Protestant Ministers are Very Satisfied with Their Personal Prayer Lives" (2005), http://www.ellisonresearch.com.
2. Andrew Murray, *With Christ in the School of Prayer* (Greenville, SC: Ambassador Books, 2002), pp. 18, 19.
3. Charles Spurgeon, *The Power in Prayer* (New Kensington, PA: Whitaker House, 1996), p. 20.

CHAPTER 2

1. Murray, p. 16.
2. Jeanne Guyon, *Experiencing the Depths of Jesus Christ* (Beaumont, TX: The SeedSowers, 1975), p. 64.
3. Spurgeon, p. 21.
4. E. M. Bounds, *Essentials of Prayer* (New Kensington, PA: Whitaker House, 1994), p. 21.
5. Spurgeon, p. 62.

CHAPTER 4

1. "Couple Prayer" (2005), http://www.accord.ie.
2. "Columbine Victim: Faith Saved My Life," *Rocky Mountain News* (Thursday, January 27, 2000).
3. Sandra S. "God Can and Does Perform Miracles Every Day!" *Enjoying Everyday Life* (June 9, 2005).
4. Murray, p. 188.

CHAPTER 5

1. Bounds, p. 30.
2. Bounds, p. 40.

CHAPTER 6

1. Bounds, p. 83.

CHAPTER 7

1. Spurgeon, p. 136.
2. Murray, pp. 65, 66.

CHAPTER 8

1. Nee, p. 75.
2. Murray, p. 108.
3. Ibid

CHAPTER 9

1. Murray, p. 163.
2. Murray, p. 184.

CHAPTER 12

1. Bounds, p. 102.

CHAPTER 13

1. Nee, p. 45.
2. Murray, p.159.
3. Joyce Meyer, *The Word, the Name, the Blood*, Warner Books edition (New York: Warner Faith, Time Warner Book Group, 2003), p. 88.
4. Murray, pp. 172, 173.
5. Murray, p. 173.
6. Murray, p. 174.
7. Nee, p. 45.
8. Nee, p. 57.

About the Author

JOYCE MEYER, one of the world's leading practical Bible teachers, has been teaching the Word of God since 1976 and has been in full-time ministry since 1980. A #1 *New York Times* bestselling author, she has written nearly ninety inspirational books, including *Power Thoughts, 100 Ways to Simplify Your Life*, the entire Battlefield of the Mind family of books, her first venture into fiction with *The Penny*, and many others. She has also released thousands of audio teachings, as well as a complete video library. Joyce's *Enjoying Everyday Life* radio and television programs are broadcast around the world, and she travels extensively conducting conferences. Joyce and her husband, Dave, are the parents of four grown children and make their home in St. Louis, Missouri.

TO CONTACT THE AUTHOR, PLEASE WRITE:

Joyce Meyer Ministries
P.O. Box 655
Fenton, MO 63026
USA
(636) 349-0303
www.joycemeyer.org

Joyce Meyer Ministries—Canada
P.O. Box 7700
Vancouver, BC V6B 4E2
Canada
(800) 868-1002

Joyce Meyer Ministries—Australia
Locked Bag 77
Mansfield Delivery Centre
Queensland 4122
Australia
(07) 3349 1200

Joyce Meyer Ministries—England
P.O. Box 1549
Windsor SL4 1GT
United Kingdom
01753 831102

Joyce Meyer Ministries—South Africa
P.O. Box 5
Cape Town 8000
South Africa
(27) 21-701-1056

Other Books by Joyce Meyer

Joyce Meyer Spanish Titles

Come la Galleta... Compra los Zapatos
(Eat the Cookie...Buy the Shoes)
El Campo de Batalla de la Mente
(Battlefield of the Mind)
La Revolución de Amor (The Love Revolution)
Las Siete Cosas Que Te Roban el Gazo
(Seven Things That Steal Your Joy)
Pensamientos de Poder (Power Thoughts)

* Study guide available for this title

Books by Dave Meyer

Life Lines